UNDERSTANDING HISTORY
THROUGH THE
AMERICAN EXPERIENCE

Understanding History through the American Experience

CHARLES R. POINSATTE
and
BERNARD NORLING

UNIVERSITY OF NOTRE DAME PRESS
NOTRE DAME   LONDON

Library of Congress Cataloging in Publication Data

Norling, Bernard, 1924—
  Understanding history through the American experience.

  Bibliography: p.
  1. History—Philosophy. 2. United States—History—
Philosophy. 3. Historical research. I. Poinsatte,
Charles R., joint author. II. Title
D16.8.N664   901   76-637
ISBN 0-268-01910-X
ISBN 0-268-01911-8 pbk.

Manufactured in the United States of America

Contents

Foreword

This book is an outgrowth of an earlier one, *Towards A Better Understanding Of History,* by Bernard Norling (1960). That book was written to explain to college freshmen why it was worth their time to study history at all, how best to study and think about the subject, and how to do elementary historical research. It developed that the book was used in a surprising variety of ways at levels ranging from high school to graduate school and was even translated into Japanese.

The earlier book was seldom used in American history survey courses, however, even though the directions and injunctions in it were as applicable to the study of our own national history as to any other branch of the subject. Why? Perhaps because the great majority of examples and illustrations in *Towards A Better Understanding Of History* were drawn from the ancient, medieval, and modern history of Europe, and only a few were drawn from the Western Hemisphere.

The purpose of *Understanding History through the American Experience* is to provide the same sort of introduction to the history of the United States as the earlier volume attempted to do for European and world history. Hence it is a collaborative effort. Coauthor Charles Poinsatte has taught a wide variety of history courses for many years, but most of his research, writing, and teaching has been in the field of U.S. history.

Anyone familiar with *Towards A Better Understanding of History* will find the structure of the present volume quite similar. In some sections the wording is similar too. The reason is obvious: we have the same objectives in mind in *Understanding History through the American Experience* and much the same advice to offer. We are merely directing it at a new audience. Yet *Understanding History through the American Experience* is essentially a new book, updated considerably since 1960, with the bulk of its examples now drawn from the history of the United States. Occasionally an example from European history has been retained because there was no noteworthy American counterpart or because the original example seemed particularly apt. But the book, overall, is focused on the history of our own country from Columbus to the present.

Instructions for the preparation of term papers are elaborate and precise because they are directed to the particular freshman courses we teach. Formal requirements at other institutions will not, of course, be identical with these, but we hope chapter 11 will be a satisfactory guide for beginners' history research papers anywhere.

We are grateful to Mrs. Catherine Box for typing much of the manuscript.

Every time we fail to learn from the past,
we pay more dearly in the future.

1: Why Study History at All?

Every Man a Historian—History sometimes seems to be the world's most unappreciated subject. Who has not heard the old lament, "Why do I have to study history? Who cares what happened centuries ago? I'm not interested in the dead past." The trouble is that the person who feels this way has never tried to think seriously about history. Consequently, he does not understand its value or relevance to the present.

Whether he knows it or not, every person is to some degree a historian because history is the study of the past, and everyone has some sense of the past, even if only the recent past. The human mind habitually moves in familiar tracks. People constantly think of the past and try to justify or discredit present modes by reference to the past. Get a group of people together and let them talk about anything. Before many minutes have passed one begins to hear, "Now when I was a boy we did it this way . . . "; or "They tried this when Roosevelt was president. It didn't work then and it won't work now." Without being aware of it the speakers are really acting as amateur historians. What they are saying is, in effect, that experience is the usual guide to sensible action. Now history is accumulated experience. It is invoked constantly and unconsciously by every person every day. Every farmer, sailor, doctor, lawyer, engineer, teacher, judge, or politician habitually calls on his memory or on written records of past events and experiences that are relevant to his work. Persons in all these professions make mistakes, of course, but they would surely make more, and far worse ones, if they assumed that every problem they faced was unique and had no counterpart in anything that had gone before.

We are all historical-minded, too, in that our thoughts and feelings are bound to past generations. Consciousness of a common past and common traditions is the most basic thing that knits together the members of any group, be they members of a family, a church, a nation, or some other group. Who is so dead in soul that he is not thrilled by reading of heroic episodes in his nation's past? Who is not moved by accounts of the martyrdom of someone of his own religious faith? How would a whole profession, the genealogists, make a living if it did not delight people to discover that they are descended from William Penn, John Adams, or someone who landed at Plymouth Rock?

Each city, county, or district cherishes its own past in the same way an individual does. If this past is to be preserved it has to be written down. The habit of keeping records and thereby conserving the accumulated knowledge and experience of many generations is one of the obvious marks distinguishing man from the rest of the animal kingdom. Consequently, there are national, state, and local historical societies and museums; written histories of virtually every state, city, district, institution, church, and ethnic group; and records of every intellectual, political, economic, or social movement in the land. One cannot drive far in any direction without encountering markers bearing the information that here is the oldest Presbyterian church north of the Missouri River, there the site of a battle in some Indian war, or there the place where West Virginia's state constitution was written.

Understanding the Present—It is a truism that one cannot understand the present unless he knows "what made it what it is." Anyone who respects the truth will want to acquired fairly extensive, accurate information about the past in order that he may judge from real knowledge rather than ignorance or prejudice. This is particularly true of a college or university student since he or she is pursuing higher education in order to become intellectually mature: clear in thought and fair in judgment. Consider an example. Jones is known to have strong opinions on a certain subject. A shrewd observer will not simply assume that Jones has come to his conclusions by a process of pure reason alone. He will want to know what sort of a person Jones is, what his past life has been like, and what his ideas are on other subjects: in a word, "how he got this way."

The study of history is the application of this commonsense principle to a broader field. Every institution, idea, or practice of the present has been formed by the past and will influence the future. If one cannot understand a *person* without some knowledge of his antecedents and background, how can one expect to understand modern political, social, or religious institutions (whose span of existence is not one lifetime but many centuries) without studying their past history?

Evidence accumulates steadily that the world's natural resources are limited, that we are approaching some of those limits, that our wastefulness and propensity to pollute our environment may ultimately prove not merely shameful but suicidal. Moreover, there is no guarantee that the years ahead will chronicle the triumph of human liberty rather than that of some remorseless despotism. Yet scores of millions of thoughtless people still talk and act as if the late twentieth-century Western world of democracy, refrigerators, automobiles, electric power, and television represents mankind's natural, normal mode of life. They accept all of it without question and seldom think about times past when none of these things existed or even about much of the present day world in which they still do not exist.

Our comfortable, externally splendid civilization, which is almost flippantly taken for granted, is really an amalgam of innumerable ideas, forces, movements, inventions, and practices lying hundreds, even thousands, of years in the past. A few of these elements are Greek thought, Roman law, Christianity, Judaic and Islamic traditions, Renaissance art, sixteenth- and seventeenth- century scientific conceptions, eighteenth-century rationalism, American and French revolutionary principles, the Industrial Revolution, and the political habits of the English-speaking people. Twentieth-century society in the West is not one of these forces or the sum total of all of them—it is the result of an unstable fusion of all of them, for they are not all completely reconcilable among themselves. The proportionate influence of each varies from one country to another and from one generation to another. A European history course deals with each part of this mosaic in turn. An American history course considers successive portions of the whole complex and subtle subject in still another dimension: after it has been filtered through the specifically American environment and American historical experience. At the end the diligent and thoughtful student should see the complete picture.

Much of what is said and done in the world is impossible to understand without some knowledge of history. How often one hears prominent clergymen, politicians, and other public figures assert that we are all heirs of the Christian tradition and our civilization has been molded by Christian ideals which we should defend. If this be true, surely a reasonable person will wish to learn something about these ideals and this tradition. At once difficulties arise. The first is that there is not one Christian church but many different ones; and these are in striking disagreement about many of the ideals. Frequently these churches become involved in conflicts with civil governments which are supposed to be guided by the same Christian traditions as the churches themselves. From one quarter comes a declaration that the true Christian spirit is to suffer blows meekly and turn the other cheek; therefore, Christian countries ought to stop building such things as nuclear bombs and destroy those they already possess. From another comes the reply that the very existence of Christian civilization depends upon maintaining a supply of these and other frightful weapons without which the Christian countries would soon be conquered by the Communist states and Christianity systematically proscribed thereafter. Periodically, some prestigious person informs us that Christian theology has been rendered obsolete by scientific discoveries, but that it is desirable to retain the Christian ethical code. Other voices reply at once that this is the height of absurdity, comparable to trying to chop down the trunk of a tree while keeping the limbs aloft. Finally, there are many prominent and able people in the "Christian" part of the world who show, by their daily actions, that this "Christian tradition" means nothing to them.

A thoughtful student will find this state of affairs confusing. If he is ever going to have any accurate knowledge of what this "Christian tradition" is, let alone whether it is worth cherishing and defending, he is going to have to study the history of Christianity. After commencing this pursuit he soon discovers that the life and words of Christ are just the beginning. One must also learn something of the history and traditions of the ancient Jews, something about the condition of the Roman Empire in Christ's time and after, something about the development of Christian doctrine and inquisitions. Before long our student is immersed in a sea of popes, councils, heresies, conflicts between popes and kings, missionary efforts, disputes about the dividing line between the things of this world and the things of the next, schisms, reform efforts, saints, scoundrels, institutions, Protestant revolts, religious wars, quarrels between ecclesiastics and scientists, and the rise of such modern ideologies as communism and nazism that have sought to destroy Christianity entirely. He discovers that through the centuries Christianity has fought some of its opponents implacably; that in other cases there has been a good deal of compromise, or even general acceptance, of what was once regarded as unacceptable; that there has been wide variation between the Catholic and Protestant branches of Christianity in these respects; and that there has even been at least as great variation between the different Protestant denominations themselves.

At the end of his endeavors our student may well find himself more puzzled about some things than he was at the beginning. If so, this is not surprising, for the acquisition of knowledge raises more questions than it ever settles. But whatever his state of mind, he will now have a much better idea of what is meant when reference is made to Christian traditions or ideals. Moreover, he will know why these phrases have come to mean different things to different persons and groups.

The foregoing discussion concerned a broad, general area of history. Let us now consider a more restricted case: the contemporary Middle East and the problems it poses for America. To the observer who knows no history, the Middle East must appear to be a vast, outdoor lunatic asylum run by rival committees of inmates. News from there seems to be a monotonous chronicle of revolutionary plotting, street riots, assassinations, terrorist bombings, the hijacking of airplanes, competition in inflammatory sloganeering, grotesque demagoguery, Russo-American rivalry, and an absurd vendetta between several Arab states and Israel.

Some of the issues involved are centuries old, but if one would study at least the recent history of this part of the earth, he would come to better understand what lies behind this seeming missionary idiocy. In the First World War Turkey fought on the German side Consequently, British agents tried to provoke the Arabs in the Ottoman Empire to revolt against their Turkish masters. In the course of these endeavors vague promises of large sections of the Middle East were made to two different and antagonistic groups of Arabs. In the meantime the British government in London made a secret agreement with France to divide the whole area into two spheres of influence, one English and one French. Then in 1917 Palestine was promised to the Jews as a national home. There has never been any possible way to reconcile all these pledges and the corresponding claims that arose from them. To the Arabs the matter has always seemed simple: the English deceived them.

Since 1918 Arab nationalism has developed rapidly. With it came resentment of the efforts of the British, eventually backed by the Americans, to settle European Jewish refugees in Palestine. To the humanitarian plea that the horrible decimation, persecution, and suffering inflicted on the Jews in Nazi Germany and elsewhere proves the dire need of the Jewish people for an independent state of their own, the Arabs reply, "We have never persecuted Jews. If you Western peoples are sufficiently savage that you must persecute a fellow Western people, your own Jews, that is your problem, not ours. How can you possibly maintain that there is no room for ten to fifteen million Jews in all the vast reaches of America, Russia, Canada, Australia, Brazil, and Argentina, not to speak of England, France, Italy, Scandinavia, and a score of other nations? You merely took advantage of our weakness to solve *your* 'Jewish problem' by settling *your* Jews on lands that have been ours for over a thousand years." Finally, the Arabs know from the wars of 1948, 1956, 1967, and 1973 that the new state of Israel is much more powerful than they are militarily and technologically. They have already experienced territorial losses in these wars, and they fear additional Israeli expansion at their expense.

The United States got stuck in the Middle East morass because of the exigencies of American domestic politics and the imperatives of the Cold War. Jews do not number greatly in the total population of the United States, but they are concentrated in a few states, notably New York, Pennsylvania, California, Illinois, and Florida. These states cast a heavy electoral vote in presidential elections. Jews are also generous contributors to campaign funds, and they have great influence in the communications industry. Until recently the Arabs had no comparable influence in the United States numerically, financially, or intellectually.

Even now (1975) while the great wealth they have suddenly acquired from quadrupling the price of their oil has given them an equivalent to Jewish economic strength, the Arabs still lack the numerical and intellectual influence in America enjoyed by Jews. Given these considerations, it is hardly surprising that the state of Israel received American recognition during the presidential campaign of 1948 and has enjoyed consistent American support ever since. In addition, there has been widespread and genuine American sympathy for the Jews as victims of Nazi persecution. Finally, as the Korean and Vietnam wars have shown, Americans are slow to abandon allies.

The Cold War has been another complicating factor. The Near East contains the world's richest known oil reserves. Russia does not need Arab oil at all, and the United States can, with some sacrifice, manage without it. Western Europe and Japan, however, need it desperately. Thus Russia, always looking for an opportunity to weaken American strength and to sow discord among non-Communist nations, could score heavily in the Cold War if she could prevent the Japanese and Europeans from getting Arab oil. She might even destroy NATO.

The Arabs themselves face several dilemmas. Both past experience and nationalists fervor lead them to dislike and mistrust the West, yet their oil is useless if they cannot sell at least some of it, and Western countries are their best customers. In the past they have lacked the trained personnel necessary to operate the oil fields. Hence they have had to depend upon multinational corporations to explore, drill, refine, and distribute their own natural resources. Finally, the national interests of individual Arab states differ considerably, there is much rivalry among Arab leaders, and most of the states contain masses of extremely poor and semiliterate but volatile people who are easily swayed by emotional nationalist appeals. Demagogues have arisen whose power is based on their popularity with these throngs. Some of these "strong men" have tried or are now trying to gain as much as they can for themselves and their people by "playing off" Russia and the United States against each other, without ultimately succumbing, so they hope, to the stifling embrace of either giant. Because of the great wealth and strategic location of the Middle East, neither the USSR nor America is willing to see it dominated by the other. Each tries to extend its own influence in the area and blunt the designs of the other.

It is all this past history, compounded by present passions, power rivalries, and political conniving, that has made the Middle East a seething caldron. Yet without some knowledge of these matters, how could anyone hope to understand what he reads in the newspapers about the Middle East, let alone prescribe any remedies for its maladies?

Avoid the Mistakes of the Past—The great German Chancellor Otto von Bismark (1815-98) once remarked that anyone can learn from his own experience, but that it is the mark of an intelligent person that he can learn from the experience of others. One of the greatest values of history is that it enables us to learn not from personal experience alone but from the experience of the past. To portray the mistakes of other ages is equivalent to putting a lighthouse on a rocky shore. To this the objection is always raised that humanity never sees the light—that people learn nothing from history. The complaint is pointless. The lessons are there to be learned, for the past teaches certain things quite definitely. It teaches, to take an example from twentieth-century American history, that continuous discrimination breeds resentment, bitterness, protest, and, if redress is not forthcoming, revolt. Think of all the problems brought into sharp focus by the civil rights revolution of the 1960s: the deep concern with which these problems were approached by blacks and whites alike; the anger and fears that were aroused; the innumerable rash and violent words that were uttered. How helpful it would have been to our nation had all of us simply *known more* about the period of Reconstruction following the Civil War and had we paid more attention to the success and failures of that era.

History teaches that the steady accumulation and exercise of power gradually but inexorably corrupts those who wield that power. That such was the case with foreign dictators like Hitler and Stalin is common knowledge. It is harder for Americans to admit that in our own country disquieting tendencies towards executive arbitrariness have become increasingly evident with the steady growth of presidential power since at least 1933, a process which (let us hope) reached its apex in the Watergate scandals of 1973-74.

Our Founding Fathers would not have found such a development surprising. They foresaw the danger and tried to forestall it by careful separation of powers in government. To say that people do not learn lessons like these is tantamount to saying that they are too stupid or heedless to learn them, for the lessons themselves are clear. If the future of humanity is to be bright, people simply will have to learn more about the mistakes of the past and be more resolute to avoid repeating them. It is one of the grimmest facts of our age that the weapons devised by modern science and industry have made the penalties for "mistakes" incomparably heavier than in the past.

History Is Necessary for Intelligent Citizenship—The preceding considerations have particular application for citizens in a democracy. Perhaps under absolute monarchy or dictatorship it is enough if the leaders are wise, but as Thomas Jefferson knew and insisted, a viable democracy requires that the ordinary person be sufficiently informed, sensible, and public-spirited to govern himself and his fellows responsibly. This means, in practice, that he must support reasonable, realistic policies; that he must be able to distinguish the theoretically desirable from the practically possible; that he must be able to see through phony "solutions" to knotty problems; and that he must be intelligent enough to avoid being duped by political tricksters and scoundrels.

Where does one acquire such acumen? Unless he spends his life in the practice of statecraft, he will have to get it from reading about past statecraft: history. Significantly, historians used to present their books for the education of princes and kings. They hoped that their royal readers would thereby learn what statesmanship was, what problems men and governments had repeatedly faced in the past, what solutions to those problems had been attempted, and what had been the results of those efforts. In a democratic society every citizen should seek such knowledge. The twentieth century is torn by fierce ideological struggles. Their outcome will determine the character of civilization for generations or centuries to come. It is by no means certain that democracy will triumph in these titanic conflicts, but its supporters can markedly improve its chances if they study the origins, nature, and ideals of their own society and of its foes.

Consider two important questions which ought to be the concern of every American: inflation and dictatorship. The manner in which inflation is ultimately dealt with will mean much to every living citizen of the United States. Now who is better equipped to think and act sensibly about this question: the person who has read extensively in ancient and modern history and who is thus familiar with the causes, course, and results of currency inflation in the late Roman Empire; the terrible inflations undergone by Germany, Austria, and Hungary in the 1920s; the disastrous decline of the "Continental" dollar during the American Revolution and Confederation period; the refusal of the Jackson administration to control either currency or credit and the subsequent panic of 1837; or the person who knows nothing of these matters because he is "modern-minded" and "interested in the future" rather than in "ancient history"?

Think of dictatorship. Not all dictatorships are the same, not all dictators abuse their power or their subjects, and in any case the likelihood of a dictator overturning American democracy appears happily remote. Dictators have arisen frequently in democratic societies in the past; once in power, there is always a strong possibility that they will misuse their power. Hence the matter has relevance for every citizen who prizes democracy.

Aspiring dictators have a number of common features. In nearly all cases men or factions seeking absolute rule try to oversimplify a pressing problem and present it in vivid, emotional terms. They appeal to popular prejudices, flatter their intended subjects, blame most current troubles on some unpopular person or group, and promise a quick, painless solution to all difficulties if only everyone will have faith in them! Anyone who knows much history is familiar with this pattern, for he has read of it many times. Thus he is more apt to recognize some incipient totalitarian movement for what it is than is the "modern-minded" man who judges everything in terms of present appearances. In the much quoted words of the philosopher Santayana, "Those who cannot remember the past are condemned to repeat it."[1]

The value of history in a democratic society is not confined to helping thwart its enemies or providing guidance for the solution of its domestic problems. A spirit of moderation and compromise has to pervade the political life of a nation if democracy is to thrive. The study of history certainly ought to induce moderation in expectations. All nations and peoples of whom history has record have known trials, troubles, suffering, tyranny, and injustice. We ought not to lapse into despondency but to bear up bravely if we, too, suffer some of these misfortunes. Moreover, we ought to be realistic enough to realize that it is unlikely that we will escape all such tribulations. In short, history should teach us to be more mature.

History also lends perspective and helps people to avoid ignorant or shortsighted judgments. "Issues" like the hotly contended tariff question of the 1880s, elections like the Hayes-Tilden contest of 1876, and diplomatic disputes like that over the Maine-New Brunswick boundary in the 1830s once seemed of overwhelming importance. Now, after the passage of years, it is clear that they were of little consequence. Thus, to know history ought to make one less apt to be emotionally stampeded about some "crisis" in his own time. It has been well said that

> The ... essential service of history is to restore to man, absorbed in his little concerns of the moment, a sense of due proportion, of the vastness of time, of the slowness of progress, of the transitoriness of so much that is eternal in its own conceit.[2]

Appreciation of Other Peoples and Cultures—Consider how much bitterness and intolerance, how much absurdity in opinion and judgment,

---

1. John Bartlett, *Familiar Quotations,* 14th ed., p. 867.
2. Albert Guerard, *France: A Modern History* (Ann Arbor, Mich.: University of Michigan Press, 1952) p. 15.

is due to simple ignorance. How easily we all label other peoples as queer, stupid, or irrational because they do not think and act as we do. And most damning—how much of this could be moderated if we only took the trouble to learn more about others and how they got to be the way they are. History can be a great aid here. It enables us to appreciate other times, peoples, and cultures, other types of minds, ideals, and governments. It enriches our own civilization by making us more aware that the men who trod this planet before us developed an infinite diversity of ideas, customs, and institutions.

How often one hears it said that a certain foreign people have no political sense, that they spend all their time bringing down governments, quarreling over trifles, and threatening civil war. If we read the history of such a people, however, we are likely to discover that in the past they have been so often conquered by foreign enemies, duped by domestic tyrants, and exploited by both that they have come to regard government itself as an enemy. We may still think their attitude absurd, but at least we now know why it exists and why it has come to be almost instinctive to them.

Think of how much discord within our own society has resulted from lack of understanding and appreciation of minority groups and cultures. Oftentimes the misunderstanding has been worsened by some clash of interest or purpose. The fundamental reason for the steady hostility between whites and Indians throughout American history has been that they wanted the same lands for mutually incompatible purposes. White settlers wanted to clear the land of forest, animals, and Indians alike so they could farm. The Indians wanted to retain the wilderness because they had always lived by hunting and fishing, supplemented by meagre and primitive agriculture. There was never a real solution to this problem other than the eventual triumph of one side over the other. Nonetheless, relations between whites and Indians were worsened notably because neither people understood the psychology of the other or respected the other's culture.

By the nineteenth century most whites viewed Indians as lazy, dirty semisavages who had nothing important to offer anyone. A few traders still secured furs from Indians in unsettled parts of the country, and a few other white entrepreneurs sold goods to tribes receiving allotments from the government. But to most white Americans, Indians were a mere nuisance to be pushed aside so the land could be settled by civilized people. On their part, the Indians could never understand the Puritan "work ethic" that drove white men to steady toil and made their hunger for land insatiable. To them, whiles seemed only a horde of cruel and treacherous breakers-of-treaties who missed no opportunity to take Indian lands and to drive Indians closer to eventual extinction.

The same mixture of clashing economic interest and mere ignorant hostility has characterized the various nativist movements that have flourished intermittently in our country. The most famous was the Know-Nothing movement of the mid-nineteenth century. The Know-Nothings were native-born Protestants who had a particularly intense dislike for Irish and German immigrants. One reason was clearly economic: the immigrants were rivals for jobs as unskilled and semiskilled laborers. Beyond this, however, the Catholic Irish were disdained as superstitious, semiliterate peasants whose very presence was an affront to a free democratic society. In the opinion of the Know-Nothings, the Irish were subservient to an autocratic and un-American church and gave their allegiance to a foreign potentate (the pope). They were as easily manipulated in politics by corrupt, big-city political bosses as in religion by their priests. The nativists also disliked German immigrants. It was bad enough that the Germans were "odd" and clannish, and that many of them were, like the Irish, Catholics. Worse, in such heavily German cities as Cincinnati and Saint Louis, they were shameless blasphemers who spent the Lord's Day in beer gardens rather than in church.

By the early 1900s many native Americans of quite varied religious and social convictions were disdaining a new wave of immigrants: "pushy" Russian Jews and unlettered southern Italians who were Catholics like the detested Irish and Germans of former days and doubtless all members of the Mafia in the bargain. The last prejudice has not died away entirely. It is even possible that it has recently (early 1970s) been strengthened. Just as the epic movie *Birth of a Nation* (1915) presented a distasteful view of Negroes during the Reconstruction era and thereby strengthened white antipathy toward Negroes for another generation, so the Academy Award winning, *Godfather* and its sequel, *Godfather II,* may perpetuate a similarly unfavorable and unjust view of millions of inoffensive Americans of Italian descent.

The same pattern is evident in the history of the Ku Klux Klan in the twentieth century. Of all American large cities in the 1920s, Indianapolis had the highest percentage of native-born people. Many of them were lower-middle-class persons who saw their neighborhoods being "destroyed" or "threatened" by an influx of blacks and immigrants—groups which were also believed to support "boss" government and thus to undermine democracy. It was hardly a coincidence that Indiana was an important center of the nationwide revival of the Klan in that decade.

To understand any seemingly peculiar or disturbing condition, past or present, there is no substitute for learning its history.

History for Pleasure and Inspiration—Not the least of reasons for studying history is that it is great literature. Now, to be sure, few people find history immediately entertaining. That is not surprising for it requires concentration, thought, and the acquisition of some fundamental knowledge. Once this foundation is acquired, history is simultaneously as engrossing, entertaining, and instructive as anything one can read. It is the broadest of all subjects, for it deals with every aspect of man's existence. The heights to which man's spirit has ascended, the depths to which it has fallen, the most grandiose conceptions of the human mind, the most magnificent individual and collective feats of courage, the cosmic follies to which mankind has been addicted—all these form the warp and woof of history. It is the tapesty of human existence, and it is a far richer and more varied one than could be woven by the most imaginative novelist. Think of Washington's ragged, freezing, starving army at Valley Forge; of Pickett's mad charge directly at the center of the Union line at Gettysburg, an assault at once glorious and ghastly, in which 75 percent of those who charged were killed or wounded; of the explorer Columbus and his men sailing into an unknown ocean aboard three tiny ships in search of the fabled coast of Asia untold thousands of miles away; of the conquistadores Pizarro and Cortez leading pitiful corporals' guards through fire, slaughter, and fabulous adventure to the conquest of rich and mighty empires; of the half-mad abolitionist fanatic John Brown, who balked at nothing from cold-blooded murder in Kansas to an assault on a U.S. arsenal in pursuit of his dream of provoking mass slave uprisings, and who ended his brief career on the gallows, abominated by millions but a hero to millions more; of the Dantesque sufferings and incredible courage of those who endured and survived the Bataan Death March; of a dramatic case of retributive justice—George Armstrong Custer, last in his class at West Point, guilty of a wanton Indian massacre, blundering into an Indian ambush on the Little Big Horn in Montana, there to perish with all his men in Custer's Last Stand; of man's first landing on the moon, an achievement without counterpart in the annals of exploration, a triumph of the human spirit that will be celebrated as long as men write history, and quite possibly the herald of the Interplanetary Age; of the fearless defenders of the Alamo, hopelessly outnumbered, battling with knives and bare hands to the last man; of the persecutions, sufferings, and hardships endured by the intrepid Mormons who wandered across half a continent, founded a colony on some of the bleakest landscape in North America, and made the desert bloom.

These are but a few among the most marvelous episodes in man's sojourn on earth. Who can read of them without being moved to wonder, admiration, fear, pity, disgust, or tears? These are the deeds that reveal both the potentialities and the limitations of mankind—and our own potentialities and limitations too, for how many of us, after all, do as much as we can for either good or ill?

Other branches of learning study a part of man's existence and activities; his mind, his literature, his religious sentiments, or his governmental experiments. History studies everything that man has ever been or tried to be.

2: How to Study History

Study—The first and most fundamental requirement for success in any field, academic or otherwise, is willingness to work. No lazy person ever did well in a history course taught seriously in a reputable college. History is not intrinsically difficult. Unlike astrophysics or the higher reaches of mathematics, which can be comprehended only by superior minds, there is little in history that cannot be understood by a person of normal intelligence. History does, however, require persistent, systematic study, for it is not a matter of learning a technique but of absorbing and remembering a great array of facts and ideas spread over a considerable period of time. It usually involves a sizable quantity of assigned reading. Almost invariably, the best history students are those who read assigned materials carefully and do not let themselves "get behind."

Read Extensively—It is highly beneficial to read outside the assignments too. Of all major subjects history is the most easily self-taught. It is, after all, the story of the past, and one can read this for himself in the same way that he can read about anything else. Moreover, fortunately historians, unlike writers in many other fields, seldom employ technical language or jargon. The lectures of the instructor, classroom discussions, workbook exercises, reports, term papers, and examinations are all important aids to learning. But as a general rule, other things being roughly equal, the person who reads the most history learns the most. If the college library has open shelves, students should acquire the good habit of spending some spare time browsing. Pick up a book at random. Thumb through it. If your eye lights on a passage that looks interesting, read until you grow tired of it. If the book proves dull, put it back and try something else. Of course this sort of thing is no substitute for careful, systematic reading of daily assignments, but it is a valuable auxiliary. A person reads "assignments" to some extent out of a sense of duty (because he has been told that it is "good for him") or out of apprehension (lest he be quizzed about it). What he reads willingly, out of sheer personal interest, he is apt to remember longer. Fundamentally, learning is always up to the individual. The best teacher in the world can coax, threaten—sometimes inspire—but 80 percent of learning always has to come from the student's own efforts.

It is easy to coordinate assigned and casual reading. Suppose a day's assignment concerns the United States at the turn of the twentieth century. In the reading such names and terms as William McKinley, "Free Silver," "Progressives," Theodore Roosevelt, "muckrackers," and "Open Door policy" stand out. After the assignment is finished, read a couple of articles about these men or subjects in such popular historical periodicals as *American Heritage* or *American History Illustrated.* If nothing pertinent is in them, or if what you find looks dull, try the *Encyclopedia Americana* or the *Encyclopedia of the Social Sciences.* Huge reference works like these are mines of information about virtually anything. Perhaps your reading assignment contains the notation that Theodore Roosevelt once invited the eminent Negro educator Booker T. Washington to the White House. If your school library happens to have a back file of the *New York Times,* take a look at it, or at the *Journal of Negro History,* to see what contemporaries thought of this "daring" presidential act.

One ought not to feel obligated to do things like this for every assignment, of course, else the additional reading will come to seem merely like extra regular work. However, if casual supplemental reading of this sort is done with some consistency for several months, the student will find that he has learned a great deal more than if he had read only what was required. In all likelihood the course will have become more enjoyable too. It is a truth as old as the world that with interest and learning, one and one makes three. The more one learns about a subject the more interesting it becomes. The greater the interest, the more eagerly one studies to learn still more.

Here the skeptic may object that, while he likes to read, he prefers fiction to nonfiction. This condition is mostly a matter of habit and popular misapprehension. Many young persons get the idea fixed in their minds that reading fiction is fun but reading nonfiction is study or work, and therefore dull. This is not true. To be sure, some of the finest products of the human mind are in the form of fictional literature. Moreover, there are many historical novels that are both entertaining and informative. (John Steinbeck's *Grapes of Wrath* and Margaret Mitchell's *Gone with the Wind* are good examples.) Nevertheless, once a person forms the habit of reading nonfiction he comes to enjoy it at least as much as fiction and to appreciate that he can usually learn more from it. It is mostly a matter of training himself for a time until a good habit is formed.

Take Notes—History deals with a vast array of facts. Because the human memory is a fallible instrument and cannot contain all these facts the student must somehow condense them to convenient dimensions. The best way is to take notes. It is easy to imagine in September that memory alone will suffice, but by the end of the semester, or year, one will be amazed at how many details (and even matters of major significance) he once "knew" have now completely slipped his mind. No matter how industrious a person might be, how attentive in class, or how interested in the course, his memory is just not efficient enough to store thousands of facts in neat, accurate order and keep them there for months. Some sort of pencil-and-paper system has to remedy the deficiency. There is no substitute for a good set of notes when the time comes to review for an important examination.

A side benefit of note-taking is that the mere act of writing causes a person to remember something better than if he only reads it or hears it. After class it is good practice to type the notes taken. Some teachers guarantee at least a C to any student who does this faithfully—"guarantee" it in the sense that the practice itself will cause one to learn enough to earn a C. If one's schedule permits, it is a good idea to glance over one's notes of the preceding day before going to class. It refreshes one's memory about the context into which the coming day's material will fall.

There are as many note-taking systems as there are students. The best practice is to try several and then decide which one seems best for you. There are, however, a number of cautions that apply, whatever the system. First of all, take notes selectively and do not take too many. If a student takes pages of notes on every assignment it requires so much time that he soon feels the course to be a heavy burden, consuming time that ought to be spent on other subjects. Moreover, a stack of 300 pages of notes at the end of the semester will not prove very useful for review purposes. One might as well read the textbook again. The basic problem then, is to get a good, usable set of notes without taking too much time. The first trap to avoid is needless repetition. Either take notes in class and supplement them from assigned readings or take basic notes from the reading and add to them matters of some importance which come up in class but are not in the reading. Whichever one does ought to depend on the character of the class and the teacher. If the instructor is a systematic lecturer who regularly discusses most of the important matters in the assignment, it is probably better to take notes from his lectures and later add to them peripheral matters which he omitted. If the class period is devoted largely to discussion or to questions and answers, it is probably better to take notes on the assigned readings and supplement them with points emphasized in class. In either case it is a good practice to leave wide margins in the notes taken first so that supplementary details can be added easily along the sides. Likewise, if dates or the spelling of names are uncertain in your class notes, take a quick look at the text to get them straight.

Assignments from library books that the student does not own and to which he does not have unlimited and convenient access should always be summarized in note form. When assignments are from textbooks which the student owns and has in his possession every day, it may be better not to take notes at all but merely to underline and write in the margins. This is untidy, to be sure, and the resale value of the books may be rendered nil, but it indubitably saves time. If a student tries this and finds it satisfactory it will leave him more time for the casual library reading noted above. Remember, the object is to learn as efficiently as possible. Study techniques of any sort are of no value *in themselves.* They should always be measured against the ultimate objective.

Just as there is no "best way" to take notes, there is no invariable mathematical proportion of notes-to-original-material. In general, if a student is assigned ten to twenty-five pages of reading from the library he ought to take a page or two of notes—seldom more than two and frequently less. Usually it is not a good idea to take notes page-by-page since, until the end of the assignment is reached, it is often difficult to tell what is important and what is merely explanatory. A better practice is to read the entire assignment, think for a few minutes about its significance, and then try to summarize it in a page or two. After the summary is completed thumb back through the reading and add anything of consequence that might have been omitted.

When a class is over and all the notes for a given assignment have been completed, it is a good idea to take five or ten minutes and ask yourself, "What were the main issues in this assignment? If I had to compose an examination on this material and give it to someone else, what three or four essay questions could I ask?" Then write down the questions. They may prove useful to you when you are studying for a major examination some days or weeks later.

As for the assignments themselves, they should normally be read twice. Probably the best practice is to read the whole assignment rapidly the first time in order to get in mind its main features, and then to read it more slowly and carefully a second time. Some students, however, get good results reading carefully the first time and then rereading only those portions which are not completely understood. As with note-taking, try all the alternatives and use the one that works the best for you.

Use Common Sense—Unquestionably the worst single mistake many students make when they undertake the study of history is to abandon the common sense bestowed on them at birth. If a student reads a book, a newspaper, or a magazine article, he does so with the idea of trying to learn what the thing in question is all about. Study history the same way. Try to learn as much as possible about the *facts* of history,

the reasons for those facts, the importance of them, and the consequences that have flowed from them. This means, above all, striving to
understand the past; not merely committing to memory a lot of
miscellaneous, unconnected information. To spend time composing lists
of names and dates to be memorized is about as profitable as memoriz-
ing all the names in the Omaha telephone directory. When the course is
over, information acquired in this way will soon be forgotten. This is
not to say that a knowledge of names and dates is useless. After all,
things do not happen "in general"; they happen to specific persons at
specific times and places. If the student's knowledge of history is not
precise and accurate, then he does not know history any more than he
can be said to "know" any other matter about which all his ideas are
haphazard and hazy. The point is that there is a much easier and more
logical way to learn with precision than by brute memorization.

Suppose a day's assignment concerns the coming of the American
Revolution. How pointless to say to oneself, "Now I have to remember
what happened in 1733, 1756, 1760, 1763, and 1774; and I had better
make a list of all those names that appear several times—Grenville,
Sugar Act, Stamp Act, Townshend, Lord North, Quebec Act . . . that's
probably what we will be asked on an exam." Surely the commonsense
procedure is rather to ask oneself what longstanding grievances the
colonists had against George III and the English Parliament, what new
grievances had developed, why the English government persistently
refused to heed colonial complaints, and why the colonials, who had
never seriously considered revolt before 1763, not only did consider it
afterward but actually rose in revolt in 1774.

Think, too, of how some of these events were related to each other,
how one was frequently the cause of another. For instance, many old
colonial grievances against the British government in London were felt
with a new sharpness after 1763. Why? Because in 1763 London closed
the lands west of the Appalachians to colonial settlement and indicated
unmistakably that henceforth the British Empire was going to be ruled
more closely and uniformly from England. Moreover, the colonies were
going to be expected to help pay off the immense British national debt.
Consider a sequence of events in 1773. London imposed the Regulating
Act (Tea Act) to raise revenue from taxation and to undercut smuggling. How did the colonists respond? By staging the Boston Tea Party.
What was the British reply? To close the port of Boston. With what
result? Many people in all the colonies became more anti-British than
ever before.

If a student approaches history in this fashion, he will learn something of substance, something that will stick in his mind and enrich his
understanding for years afterward. Furthermore, he will find that in the

process of studying for *understanding,* he will remember more about the pertinent details (Grenville, Townshend, 1763 and so forth) than if he had deliberately tried to remember only those isolated facts. This is so because nobody can truly understand anything in general without some knowledge of its details, while it is quite possible to memorize details about anything without understand the larger situation at all.

Consider another example. The student may memorize the names of all the men who have been American secretaries of state since 1789. But what good is such information unless he is to appear on a quiz program? How much more useful to study the evolution of American foreign policy: its demographic and geographical bases, our traditional attitudes toward foreign countries, changes in our foreign policy objectives that resulted from changing national interests or needs, changes imposed on us by others, and differences in the "international facts of life" in the 1970s as compared to the last century. If he understands such matters as these, then he has learned something important. He will now comprehend much better our whole national past and present—and in the process learn a good deal about our more important secretaries of state.

When doing an assignment, think about the meaning of the material. Consider how differently things might have turned out had this or that factor been changed or absent. A helpful practice is to make up questions and then to try to answer them. How was it possible for the North and South in the United States to work out compromises about slavery and other sectional differences for forty years and then to prove unable to do this in 1861? Why were the Republicans the normal majority party from 1860 to 1932, only to abruptly become the normal minority party for the next generation? What conditions had changed? Did particular persons have anything notable to do with it? Why was the change so sudden? Does it seem that the change will be permanent? Why were the isolationists of the 1930s usually conservative people and the interventionists liberal? Why had they changed places by the late 1960s and early 1970s? Had "isolationism" and "interventionism" changed in meaning? Was the war that was feared in the 1930s substantially different from the conflicts of a generation later? If so, in what respects? Did the quality of our national leadership, in either instance, have anything to do with it? Are people in the mass just restless and fickle, and thus prone to change their minds about foreign affairs? Did America's domestic problems have anything to do with these ideological responses in either case?

If the student is to answer questions of this sort, he must do more than learn factual information. He must think about what he reads; think about what he has learned about similar situations encountered earlier in the course; think about what he personally has observed of the ways of humanity in his own lifetime. Lastly, he has to try to put all this together and make a judgment about it. This is not easy. Often the judgment will be wrong. Often it will be impossible for anyone to say beyond question that the judgment is or is not correct. But one thing is certain: the student who approaches history in this way will learn and understand far more than the one who merely memorizes in order to pass tomorrow's quiz.

Become History-Minded—History is not a series of unconnected episodes, all about equally important or equally useless, each embellished with a chapter title, and all then assembled in a book. It is a seamless garment, every part of which is related to all the others. It should be studied as such, with the object of understanding how civilizations change and why; how societies differ in many ways, yet usually have to face the same kinds of problems; and how innumerable ideas, events, and institutions from the past have made our present world what it is.

Any history course is centered around certain themes or developments. The student's understanding of a particular assignment will be facilitated if he fits it into some overall pattern. Consider a typical American history survey course. It will begin with the discovery of America, divide at 1865 or 1877 if it is a two-semester course, and conclude a few years before the present day. Now what main themes run through American history? An obvious one from the settling of Jamestown in 1607 to the closure of free public lands in the 1890s, is westward expansion: the ceaseless search of both native Americans and new immigrants for new land, more land, better land; the promise of at least a different, and a hoped-for better, life in some part of the continent still unclaimed.

Another major theme is immigration: its problems and rewards. From 1607 until the 1920s millions of white, black, and yellow people flocked to our shores, filling the vacant lands, providing cheap, abundant labor in our factories, laying down the railroads that bound the nation together, and producing marked cultural diversity. All these immigrants had a hard struggle. The earliest white indentured servants had first to secure their personal freedom; the blacks to break the chains of actual slavery. Immigrants from continental Europe or the Orient had to learn a new language and adapt to a new culture. Nearly all were poor initially. Little by little, one group or "minority" after another battled social, religious, or racial prejudice, struggled, with varying degrees of success to climb out of the slums, and gained successively greater degrees of national acceptance and material prosperity. This process is obviously far from complete even in our own day.

Much prejudice, discrimination and inequality of opportunity remains. Some groups, especially Blacks, Chicanos, and Indians, are still incompletely absorbed into the mainstream of American life. Much ethnic consciousness remains; indeed, in many ways it grows greater rather than diminishes. Thus U.S. society is sometimes likened to a tossed salad: all one dish but with its component parts still readily distinguishable. Yet the older view of America as a "melting pot" has much validity too. Whatever our differences among ourselves, to foreigners we are all distinctively Americans. Our habits and expectations, our modes of speech and dress, seem to them basically homogenous. Consider the most obviously "different" Americans: the blacks. Is it not more in keeping with the real world to regard a black person who lives in the United States as an American Negro rather than a transplanted African?

A main theme that pervades most of the century since the Civil War has been the growth of the welfare state. With only occasional interruptions or temporary reversals, the U.S. government has tended, with every passing generation, to make more laws about more things, to regulate more closely the activities of private individuals and businesses, to spend more money in more ways, and to assume a greater responsibility for the economic welfare of all its citizens.

In foreign affairs perhaps the broadest general trend has been the increasing interest taken by our country in the rest of the world. Our Founding Fathers hoped to keep us free of foreign entanglements altogether. In the 1820s President Monroe and Secretary of State John Quincy Adams were proclaiming that Europeans should keep out of the Western Hemisphere, even though our nation had no coherent national plans for hemispheric expansion. By the 1840s, however, we were fighting the Mexicans in order to expand into the Southwest, and talking a good deal about our "Manifest Destiny." In the last half of the nineteenth century that "destiny" did not appear to exceed a growing interest in Latin America. Around 1900 it was clearly extending to the Far East. By 1917 we had intervened in a major European war. In World War II we fought two major wars in two widely separated parts of the world at the same time. Since 1945 we have become closely concerned with events in every part of the globe.

Another significant development in the past century has been that the United States has changed from a largely agricultural nation to the world's foremost industrial power. This metamorphosis necessarily involved basic alterations in the manner of life of much of the population. It packed millions of people into cities. Immediately, depressions and subsequent unemployment presented incomparably more serious problems than was the case when most people were small farmers who could, in the last analysis, grow enough food to live no

matter what economic conditions might be in general. Thus industrialization soon meant the organization of labor unions, and strife between
these bodies and the owners of industry. This was followed quickly by
demands that the government curb the great corporations and guarantee a greater measure of economic security to all its citizens. When the
student reads of the Embargo Act, the Ostend Manifesto, the Sherman
Act, the Pullman strike, the McKinley Tariff, the Social Security
system, the Marshall Plan, the Civil Rights Act of 1964, or the food
stamp program, he ought at once to ask himself what is its connection
with one or more of these major tendencies in American history.

Nothing better facilitates the process of becoming history-minded
than to put one's mind back into the past and look from that time
forward. This requires some imagination and practice, but it improves
one's understanding of the past immeasurably. The deeds of men long
since dead often seem stupid and futile. This is not surprising, for who
is not wiser afterward than he was at the time he had to make some
decision? But one must always think of the circumstances in which men
act. Who can foresee the future or calculate all the consequences of his
actions? Every person alive now has to think and plan and act on the
basis of what he or she knows *now*, and the way things appear *now*; not
on the basis of what *will be known* 500 years from now. So it has
always been. Merely to praise or denounce the beliefs and deeds of past
persons or societies is fruitless. If the student wants to understand what
long-dead individuals thought and why they acted as they did, he has to
try to put himself in their shoes and to see their problems *as they saw
them.*

Suppose a day's assignment deals with the New England Puritans in
colonial times. Puritanism is currently out of fashion in our society, and
students often find the Puritans repellent as human types. What a sorry
lot of bigots and sourpusses they must have been with their stocks,
whipping posts, four-hour Sunday sermons, and prohibition of amuse-
ments that nearly all of us now regard as innocent or indifferent. How
really un-American they were at heart, driving out Roger Williams and
Anne Hutchinson because their religious opinions were unpopular. And
how sunk in ignorance, cruelty, and superstition! What can be said for
narrow-minded fanatics who would execute witches, excuse the
extermination of Indians because "they were damned anyway," and
attempt to justify beating a Quaker ninety-nine times with a tarred
whip because he had "already beaten the Gospel black and blue?"

Instead of reading about Puritans with such thoughts in mind the
student should try to imagine himself living in seventeenth-century New
England. Why had the Puritans come there in the first place? Because
they wanted to undertake an experiment in religious toleration? No.

Because they wanted to practice their religion alone, in peace, *as it suited them*. Was this attitude unusual? Not at all. All over sixteenth- and early seventeenth-century Europe, people took religion with a seriousness and determination that can scarcely be imagined by twentieth-century semipagans who retain mostly a sentimental attachment to what they imagine to be "the social gospel."

Like so many other Christians of that era, the Puritans genuinely believed that the next life was incomparably more important than this one and that faith in correct theological doctrines was essential for one's eternal salvation. They accorded Roger Williams and Anne Hutchinson the same treatment those two theological mavericks would have received almost anywhere else in the Western world at the same time. As for witches, in that age witches were executed all over Europe, in small countries and large, by Catholics and by Protestants. If this seems savage and gruesome, think of our own age when literacy rates are far higher and the world's knowledge incomparably more extensive than three centuries ago. Yet the Nazis tortured and murdered six million Jews; Lenin and Stalin tortured, enslaved, and murdered several times that many of *their own people*; the Turks killed half the Armenian population in the Ottoman Empire in 1915; the West Pakistanis starved or murdered several million of their own countrymen in the war that gained independence for Bangladesh; one tribe starved to death hundreds of thousands of people of another tribe in the Nigerian civil war, and so on. We are not more humane than the Puritans. We merely think so little of religion that we no longer persecute each other for it. We prefer, instead, to maltreat and slaughter our fellows for their unwelcome social and economic opinions, their offensive national allegiances, and the intolerable color of their skins.

Finally a student should reflect a bit on the better qualities of the Puritans. They believed in hard work, honesty, uprightness, personal responsibility, punctuality, thrift, and close attention to public affairs. Did not these qualities, however unglamorous, have a good deal to do with the development of our nation, the establishment and maintenance of our form of government, and the formation of the better side of our national character? What organization—commercial, educational, religious, even athletic—can thrive without at least some people of "puritan" habits and dedication in important positions within it? What nation in the world is strong, vigorous, prosperous, and respected without having some "puritan" traits and habits? Given the persistent hostility of peoples toward other peoples unlike themselves and the everlasting rivalry among nations, what is likely to be the ultimate fate of rich states if their people abandon all those qualities we think of as "puritan"? Thoughts of this sort should go through the mind of the student at least part of the time as he reads about the New England Puritans. It is not that he should at once abandon his own world view or condemn the one prevalent in his own society. It is that he should strive to *understand* the Puritan world view of three centuries ago, the reasons why it existed, its importance in the development of both our nation and our national character, and the relative applicability or inapplicability of its main features at any time.

Deplorably common in history is the practice of issuing indiscriminate praise or sweeping condemnation of individuals long dead without giving a thought to the problems they had to face or the way those problems looked *at the time*. A case in point is that of the Renaissance Pope Clement VII, 1523–34. Historians have not been kind to Pope Clement. They have usually depicted him as a shifty, indecisive fellow; a man insufficiently aware of the seriousness and implications of the Protestant Revolt; a bungler who handled the Henry VIII-Catherine of Aragon annullment case so badly that one of the most powerful kings in Europe deserted Catholicism and took his country into the Protestant camp. Before passing off Clement VII as a mere blunderer, however, the student ought to consider the whole European religious and diplomatic situation as it appeared to the pontiff in the years 1527–31.

To begin with, King Henry VIII of England, for a variety of motives, some personal and some political, wished to have his marriage to his queen, Catherine of Aragon, annulled so he might marry Anne Boleyn. Many years before, Henry had had to apply to Rome for a papal dispensation to marry Catherine. This was necessary since she had previously been married to Henry's elder brother, then dead. (A passage in the Bible forbade marriage to a brother's widow.) The dispensation had been granted by Pope Julius II, the marriage had taken place, and Henry and Catherine had lived as man and wife for eighteen years.

The king, however, eventually tired of Catherine and wanted to wed Anne. Hence he began to search for pretexts to dissolve the marriage. His first ploy was to claim that there were technical flaws in the original dispensation. Clement VII's canon lawyers could not find any. Then the king argued that Pope Julius had no right to grant the dispensation in the first place because the Bible expressly forbade a man to marry his brother's widow. Papal theologians considered the point, but decided that Henry's understanding of the Bible was faulty. This put Pope Clement in a dilemma. Sweden had already renounced its religious allegiance to Rome. The Lutheran movement was gaining adherents rapidly in Germany. King Francis I of France was an ambitious, unscrupulous monarch who periodically showed favor to Protestants in order to extract concessions from the papacy. At times Francis I even intimated that he might turn Protestant himself. Should he do so he would take with him millions of his subjects in one of Europe's strongest and most populous nations. The Holy Roman emperor was the Hapsburg, Charles V. He and Francis I were by far the most powerful rulers in Europe. They spent much of their time making war against each other. The pope dared not alienate Francis lest the king of France turn Protestant, whereby France would be lost to Catholicism. Yet if he showed favor to Francis, this would be resented by Charles V, and the pope did not dare to antagonize him either. He did not trust Charles because the papacy had struggled for centuries to secure independence from just such overmighty Holy Roman emperors as Charles V. Finally, Clement feared for the safety of his own kingdom, the Papal States, because Italy had been the battleground of French and Hapsburg armies for the preceding generation, and papal political and military strength was far too feeble to cope with either Francis or Charles.

In these circumstances Henry VIII pressed for his annulment. What was Pope Clement to do? He already had troubles of the utmost seriousness on every side. The last thing he wanted to do was alienate still another powerful king, a man who had heretofore been the most faithful crowned friend of the papacy in Europe. Nothing would have pleased Clement more than to have granted the king of England's request. Yet, as papal experts in these matters saw it, Henry had no case in either law or theology. Moreover, Catherine, Henry's wife, opposed the annulment. And she was the aunt of the distressingly mighty Charles V!

In 1527 one of Charles V's armies mutinied near Rome and took the pope prisoner. Now the pontiff's position seemed truly hopeless. He could not give a decision in favor of Henry, both because he was convinced that Henry had no case and because he was the prisoner of Catherine's nephew, the powerful emperor. At the same time, he feared to decide definitely against Henry, for this might mean the loss of England to Catholicism. So Clement resolutely procrastinated. He held inquiries, wrote letters, appointed commissions, suggested compromises, proposed reconciliations; in short, he tried everything he could think of to stall for time and therefore avoid having to make a decision at all. He hoped that something would change: Henry would die, Catherine would die, Anne Boleyn would die, Henry would see the error of his theological opinions and withdraw his request, Henry would lose interest in Anne, Henry and Catherine would become reconciled— that something, anything, would happen to solve the problem without the necessity of making an official papal announcement.

Now this was not a heroic attitude to be sure, but it was not an unreasonable one. After all, time does solve many problems. Innumerable tangles, from which there seemed no way out at the time, have unraveled themselves with the death of an interested party, a change of mind after reflection, or a change of circumstances. But Clement had no luck. None of these things transpired. Instead, Henry gradually lost patience with papal delays, withdrew England's religious allegiance to Rome, got his annullment from one of his own clerical appointees in England, and married Anne. At the end, the pope appeared to have played a sorry role. He had hedged and delayed in a most undignified manner, and all to no avail.

It is now clear, more than four hundred years after these events, that the pope would have been wiser to have taken a strong stand at the outset for what he believed right and to have flatly denied Henry's request without regard for the consequences. He might have lost England to be sure, but then, he lost it anyway! More important, his action would have heartened many who had become disillusioned with Rome in recent years, and he would have gone down in history as a brave man who stood by principle.

But all this is being wise after the event. What the student should ask himself is, "What would I have done had I been Pope Clement VII? How would I have faced that situation? What decision would I have made, *not knowing* what the future would bring? Would I have stood out at once for what I thought to be the right of the matter or would I too have played for time and hoped for some luck?" If the student thinks of the whole question in this fashion he may still be convinced that Clement VII lacked both judgment and heroism, or he may not, but at least he will appreciate that not all problems are simple, not all decisions are easy, not all solutions are obvious.

Similar thoughts, though leading to a different conclusion, are induced by a consideration of the last years of President Woodrow Wilson. By the end of World War I Wilson had become convinced that to insure peace and justice for all mankind the postwar world must be reorganized on the basis of national self-determination, that diplomacy must henceforth be conducted openly, that disarmament must be sweeping and worldwide, and that there must be established a league of nations. The last would act as a parliament of man and would have as its principal business the settlement of international conflicts by peaceful means. Wilson believed that common people everywhere shared his fervor for this program. He viewed himself as their leader and spokesman. He was further convinced that it was the historic mission of the United States to lead the world in pursuit of these objectives.

At the Versailles Peace Conference in the spring of 1919, the president exhausted himself working for the attainment of this program. Time and again he was compelled to make concessions to the British, French, Italians, Japanese, or others—concessions which he deemed incompatible with one or another of his famous Fourteen Points.[1] Always he consoled himself with the thought that the wrongs which he could not avoid now would eventually be set right once the League of Nations had come into existence.

After defeated Germany signed the Treaty of Versailles, Wilson came back to the United States and embarked upon an extensive speaking tour to convince his countrymen of the necessity of accepting the treaty and the Covenant of the League of Nations, which constituted a part of the treaty. The effort overtaxed the president's strength and broke him, physically and mentally.

The U.S. Senate at that time contained some enthusiasts for the League of Nations and some determined opponents of both the treaty and the League. Senators belonging to neither extreme held the balance of power. They were willing to accept American entry into the League if it was accompanied by some relatively minor reservations or interpretations that would safeguard the Monroe Doctrine and a few other American interests, real or fancied. Both the British and French governments urged Wilson to accept these proposed amendments, assuring him that American membership in the League of Nations from its birth was far more important than the matters with which the amendments dealt. The president, however, while pliable enough in his approach to domestic politics, was an intransigent idealist about the League. The United States must join it without any reservations whatever. He was additionally confirmed in this resolve by personal considerations. The Senate had opposed him many times in the past. He was determined that it should not flout him this time. Moreover, the senatorial leader of opposition to the treaty and the League was Henry Cabot Lodge, a man whom the president detested and to whom he was determined never to bow.

The outcome of this combination of dogmatic idealism mingled with mere stubbornness was that the Senate, which would have readily accepted the treaty and the League with the reservations, refused to accept either without reservations. Hence the League of Nations came into existence bereft of its richest and most powerful potential member, and the United States soon lapsed into disgruntled isolationism.

Thus if it is clear that a policy of compromise and procrastination was the undoing of Pope Clement VII, it is equally clear that Woodrow

---

1. The sardonic old French Premier Georges Clemenceau once observed that "God Himself was content with Ten Commandments. Wilson must have Fourteen."

Wilson was served no better by the opposite policy of determined adherence to undiluted principle, regardless of opposition. Clearly, we Monday-morning quarterbacks, who only observe and discuss the deeds of others, ought to show some charity when passing judgment on those harried men who have actually had to *make* difficult decisions.

Sometimes people face choices as hard as those before Pope Clement VII and Woodrow Wilson because they espouse a number of principles which are compatible in ordinary times but prove hopelessly incompatible in *some particular crisis*. For example, before the Civil War William Lloyd Garrison, Wendell Phillips, and Sarah and Angelina Grimke were among the most prominent American abolitionists. All of them were also pacifists and supporters of women's rights. Garrison, in particular, was so vehemently devoted to both feminism and the abolition of slavery that he broke up the abolitionist movement by driving out of it such persons as the Tappan brothers who regarded the feminist question as far less important than the overriding issue: slavery. To the Tappans, and even to Theodore Weld, dedicated abolitionist and husband of Angelina Grimke, Garrison was making a major tactical error by clinging to feminism since many Americans who might have supported abolitionism were unready to accept an active role for women in political life. Then came the Civil War. How could one support the war if he was a pacifist, a believer in nonviolence? But how could a dedicated abolitionist refuse to support the Union cause when a northern victory was clearly the best hope for ending slavery? Reluctantly, the abolitionists put aside their pacifist and feminist preoccupations and supported the war.

A generation earlier John Quincy Adams had been trapped in a similar dilemma. Adams hated the slave trade. He was also an ardent nationalist who had detested the British practice of impressing American sailors on the high seas, ostensibly the cause of the War of 1812. So, as secretary of state, what did Adams do? He opposed employment of the hated British navy to check the slave trade, even though that navy was huge, powerful, and effective. Then he tried to save conscience and appearances by advocating use of the small, ineffectual U.S. navy for the same purpose.

How to Become History-Minded—A sense of history can be developed in a number of specific, tangible ways. One of the best is to make personal contacts with the past. Visit historical museums such as the one in Cody, Wyoming, dedicated to Buffalo Bill and filled with memorabilia from the Old West; or the fine museum in New Bedford, Massachusetts, which vividly recalls a picturesque aspect of our national past by preserving samples of virtually everything associated with whaling expeditions. Think of the origins and meaning of such national holidays as Independence Day and Columbus Day, of religious holidays and ceremonies, and of local pageants and festivals. When possible, visit such battle sites as Gettysburg (the decisive encounter of the Civil War); Ticonderoga, an outstanding example of a restored fort (taken by surprise by Ethan Allen early in the Revolution, it was from Ticonderoga that the artillery came that Washington used to drive the British out of Boston); Wounded Knee, South Dakota (the last engagement in the Indian wars—more a massacre than a battle); or such a historic site as Valley Forge, Pennsylvania, where Washington managed to keep the colonial cause alive in its darkest hour. Try to discover the origins of various foods (roasting ears, chitlins, spaghetti), implements (the Colt revolver, Bowie knife, typewriter), styles of clothing (buckskin shirts and trousers, Levis, dungarees), and ideas (the strange notion, strongly held in pioneer days, that only heavily wooded land would make good farmland). Searches of this sort are easily combined with vacations and thus turned into fun.

Even mere words often provide fascinating links with the past. Many words in English usage are of French, Celtic, Arabic, African, Spanish, Dutch, Indian, or other origin. How, when, and why did our ancestors come to appropriate such an Indian word as "skookum" (strong), the Dutch word "boss," the Spanish words "lariat," "canyon," and "arroyo," and many terms brought from West Africa by slave traders or by the Negroes themselves? Think of how much our language has expanded merely as a consequence of technological developments. Suppose you should meet Abraham Lincoln. Could you talk to him about a radio, a movie, an automobile, a television program? Could you ask him for directions to the nearest "drive-in" or "motel"? Idle speculation of this sort can increase one's sense of historical depth.

When traveling, do not just look: think of the implications of what you see. Wilderness areas remind one of what the whole country was like five centuries ago. The cliff dwellings of the Southwest indicate much of the character of pre-Columbian Indian culture. Why should they be made of adobe and have flat roofs? Old houses in New England, by contrast, are wooden and have steep roofs. What is implied by the difference? If you are driving through the prairie states, try to find either an original sod house or a replica. How much about the lives of the early settlers on the plains is indicated by that rude dwelling alone! A drive through almost any Indian reservation, many parts of the rural South, or large sections of Appalachia provides an immediate reminder of what life was like not many years ago for all Americans who did not live in cities. The restoration of Williamsburg, Virginia, to its condition in colonial times transports the visitor back into America's past. The missions of California indicate vividly that Spanish civilization in the old Southwest was quite different in spirit from what prevails in twentieth-century California. A stroll through the older sections of New Orleans reminds one at once how different were old French ideas of architectural beauty and utility from those that prevail in present-day American cities.

Sometimes the contrast between present and past is immediate and vivid within a very limited area. In northern Indiana, just a few miles from middle-sized American cities, and cheek-by-jowl with prosperous-looking twentieth-century American farms, are Amish communities that have, in many ways, changed but little from their European forerunners of three or four centuries ago. The roads are well kept up, but they are still dirt, for the people will have no others. They lead to well-built houses, but houses without electricity or window curtains. Whole families still work together in family shops of various sorts. Farming is still carried on with horses. People travel to town in buggies drawn by horses. The men wear beards but not mustaches, and nobody wears buttons on clothing. The reason? The seventeenth-century German soldiers who persecuted the Amish in Europe wore mustaches and buttons. Such is but one example of how easily we can make contacts with the past if only we think about it occasionally and take the small trouble to be more observant.

Another excellent way to develop an interest, understanding, and appreciation of history is to read serious newspapers and magazines. An appallingly large number of young people seem to think that there is no connection between what they study in school and what goes on in the world around them. How can a person possibly claim to be a "student," in pursuit of learning, when he does not read newspapers, listen to news broadcasts, or have any but the vaguest notion about what is taking place either in his own country or elsewhere in the world? Newspapers and newsmagazines, for all their deficiencies, are contemporary history. Just as knowledge of the past improves one's judgment about the present, so a knowledge of what goes on in the world now will make a history course more interesting and meaningful. Every student should listen to a news broadcast at least once a day and spend at least two hours a week reading some reputable newspaper or newsmagazine as carefully and thoughtfully as he would prepare a class assignment. Whenever some country, issue, or situation is persistently in the headlines, one should try to read a book or serious article on its background or on some similar past situation.

Moreover, do not forget that a fair amount about recent history can be learned merely by asking occasional serious questions at home. Ask your mother why Aunt Susie and Uncle Ben, who had lived all their lives on a small farm in Tennessee, moved to Detroit in 1953 where

Uncle Ben began to work on the assembly line in an automobile factory. Ask your grandfather why he lost both his job and his savings in the Great Depression of the 1930s. What did he do then? What did other people in a similar situation do? How did he feel about what had happened to him so suddenly? When did he get a new job? What did he think about President Franklin Roosevelt's efforts to overcome the depression? Ask your grandmother how rationing worked in World War II. What did she think of it? What did her neighbors think? Were the everyday lives of any of them changed much by rationing? Does she think it might have been a good idea to have introduced rationing during the Vietnam War too? Why or why not?

Examinations–About no subject is absurdity and superstition as rampant as examinations. Nine times out of ten a student who has done well in class on a day-to-day basis, and has allowed himself time to prepare for an important examination, will do well on it. Whether the test be essay, true-and-false, completion, identification, or multiple choice is immaterial. Similarly, the person who has not studied regularly, or has not allowed himself time to prepare, will almost certainly do badly. Still, nearly anyone, whatever his abilities, industry, or past record, can usually improve his performance if he heeds a few common-sense principles.

1. How to Study–When preparing for a major history examination, the first consideration is to allow sufficient time to review and think about the course. Two or three hours a day for perhaps three days before a midterm examination and the same amount of time for four or five days before a final examination ought to be minimum. This much careful, systematic study will fix in mind many details and illustrations with which examination essays can be embellished and, lacking which, those essays will seem thin to the corrector. Review in the same way you have studied for the course. Read over several times the notes taken in class and on outside readings. Go through the textbook, reading where it is underlined or where writing appears in the margins. If you are sure you know a given section quite well, skim over it rapidly. If you feel confused or frankly ignorant about a section, then read it carefully and resume skimming thereafter. In all cases, think of the meaning of the course thus far, the chief trends that have emerged, the main problems encountered, the way one condition has gradually become another, and why.

Sometimes it is useful for several students to study together and to discuss different features of the course. A word of caution is in order here, however, Stick to business and do not let the discussion degenerate into a mere "bull session." Also, make sure that there is at least one person present who does well in the course. A good or excellent student can sometimes improve his own performance by helping others, since he must clarify his own thinking about a subject in order to explain it to someone else. By contrast, several students who have difficulty with a subject and who study together are more liable to confound the confusion than to learn much from each other.

2. *Essay Questions*—Short answer questions of whatever type are either right or wrong. There is little advice one can give about them save that the student should know the material. Essay questions, however, present a few problems of tactics and technique. First and foremost, read the directions. If the instruction is to answer three out of five questions, then do *three* of them. Do not do four or five in hope of getting extra credit or in the hope that the *best* will be counted. Quite likely the grader will read only the first three anyway. Moreover, the time allotted will be what is regarded as sufficient to do three essays *well*. If the time is spent doing four or five, all will have to be skimped. Likewise, divide the time about equally among the essays. If forty-five minutes is allowed to do three essays, spend about fifteen minutes on each; not twenty minutes apiece on two of them and five minutes on the last one. Of course, if you know two of them well and the third hardly at all, it is better to do two thoroughly and try to get good grades on them than to waste ten minutes puzzling about something you do not know anyway. Remember, though, one of the first thoughts that is apt to pass through the corrector's mind is this: "The student had fifteen minutes to answer this question. How much could a person reasonably be expected to write in that time if he knew this matter well? Maybe a page, or a page-and-a-half, or two, depending in part on how large his handwriting happens to be." If the corrector then encounters a four-sentence answer, he is not likely to be impressed, even though the four sentences may be correct as far as they go.

Before starting to write anything read the question carefully and think about it for a minute or two. Be sure you understand it and that you answer the question asked—not some other one. Any teacher will testify that he has read dozens of respectable essays relating vaguely to the question asked but not really answering it. If you know a little about a particular subject it is, of course, better to write around it than to write nothing at all, for you may thus get *some* credit. But only *some* credit will seldom be enough to enable one to pass an examination—or a course.

After thinking about the question for a moment and making sure you understand it, formulate the answer in your mind. Make sure that you get the main points in that answer down on paper. Either write them down at once and then use the rest of the essay to explain them, or else make sure that you bring each one into the essay in its proper place. The essay itself should be a blend of generalizations and specific factual details: not one or the other, but both. A student who has a good mind but studies little will often remember the main ideas in a history course but will seldom recall much in the way of illustrative details. His essays, consequently, usually consist mostly of generalities, which may fit the situation in question, but fit other historical periods and episodes almost equally well.

Another student, who has marginal ability but who works hard, may have considerable difficulty understanding ideas and general concepts but be able to memorize much specific information. His essays are apt to be masses of factual detail, often largely or entirely correct, but leading nowhere in particular and showing no comprehension of the relationship of these happenings to anything else. A good essay is much easier to describe than to produce; the ideal is a combination of these two objectives.

Assume, for example, that one is asked to write an essay on this question: "Discuss the objectives and policies of Alexander Hamilton and the results of those objectives and policies." A good way to begin would be to devote two or three sentences to a description of the state of the American government in 1789 when George Washington first took office and Hamilton became our first secretary of the treasury. Then think of Hamilton's overriding beliefs: for example, that the American government should be a government of the whole nation, above the individual state governments, and that it is mere common sense for any government to try to win the support of its ablest and wealthiest citizens since their support adds immeasurably to the stability and credit of the government while their hostility can render effective government impossible. Start a paragraph with some statement to that effect. Then add that Hamilton was convinced that the surest way to bind anyone to any cause is by bonds of gold, that is, ties of self-interest. Now illustrate these points by listing Hamilton's principal deeds: (1) he paid at par all the debts of the Continental Congress outstanding from the Revolution, whether they were owed to American citizens or to foreigners; (2) he had the federal government assume all outstanding state debts as well, no matter what the circumstances in which they were contracted; (3) to regulate credit and the currency, and to entice foreign investment capital, he established the first national bank. Indicate who supported and who opposed these measures, and why, and who profited from them.

Then start a second paragraph with the observation that the rest of Hamilton's program complemented these measures. Illustrate this by reference to his establishment of a modern tariff to provide some encouragement for American industry and to raise revenue for the federal government. Add that he imposed a tax on whiskey, partly to raise money but primarily to demonstrate the power of the new government to tax and command obedience to its laws. Note that bitter opposition to the last caused the Whiskey Rebellion of 1794.

Now you are ready to sum up. Was Hamilton able to carry through most of his program? Yes. Was it successful? Largely. "Substantial" people were won to the new republic. It became firmly grounded from its earliest years, and its credit was established beyond question. The National Bank throve. The whiskey rebels were routed.

But were there any setbacks? Yes, of course. All human achievements come at a price to *someone*. Now mention that small farmers and landowners were alienated, that there was much grumbling that the tyranny of Britain had been replaced by a domestic tyranny. Add that opponents of the Hamiltonian program soon rallied behind Jefferson—a development which gave rise to the political party system in the United State. Conclude with the observation that Hamilton's whole endeavor was challenged on constitutional grounds, and that the ensuing struggle between proponents of a "broad" and a "strict" interpretation of the U.S. Constitution has never died.

Last and by no means least, write respectable English in complete sentences. It is shameful that such an admonition should be addressed to college students, but anyone who has read many of their papers knows that it is necessary. To write in a grammatical, civilized manner ought to be a matter of pride. One who has spent ten or twelve consecutive years in school should be ashamed to write in the jargon of pocketbook private detectives or Western Union telegrams. What is the purpose of studying one's native language, or taking English composition courses, if one does not attempt to use what one has learned in *all* his writing?

Even putting ideals aside and descending to the lowest "practical" level, a well-written essay will ordinarily get a better grade than one with the same factual content but filled with abbreviations, misspelled words, grammatical atrocities, advertising mumbo-jumbo, and slang. First impressions are important, no less with teachers than with others. If a corrector sees a slovenly paper, he usually concludes one of two things about its author: (1) he is unintelligent (he cannot possibly be uneducated since he has been in school since he was six years old) or (2) he is lazy and indifferent. Neither conclusion is apt to do the student much good when a mark is put on the paper. Conversely, a corrector will have a good opinion of a student who writes correctly and expresses himself clearly, even though there may be factual errors in his essay. Naturally, the first consideration in marking history papers must be the factual accuracy of the answers, but any doubts or uncertainties are normally resolved in favor of the person who writes respectably and against the one who does not. We mortals are fools enough. A prudent person will try to avoid appearing more foolish and ignorant than he really is.

To sum up: study history by putting your mind back into the period under consideration; study to understand, not memorize; do assignments promptly; take notes; read as much history of all kinds as time permits; pay attention to current events; and prepare carefully for final examinations. If one follows these precept and is gifted with normal common sense, history will cause him no worries.

3: Things Always Change:
But Always Remain the Same

No Sharp Breaks in History—If a student thumbs his way through his American history textbook he sees it nicely divided into chapters with such titles as "The Revolution of 1800," "The New Nationalism," "The Awakening of the American Mind," "Peace and Prosperity," "The Irrepressible Conflict," "Radical Reconstruction," "The Populist Revolt," "Normalcy," and "The Great Depression." As he reads on, he encounters such phrases as "The Intolerable Acts," "The Era of Good Feeling," "The Tariff of Abominations," "The New England Renaissance," "The Silver Crusade," "The 'Big Stick' Policy," and "The New Deal." It is difficult for him to avoid the impression that the course of history is a series of abrupt shifts from one markedly different age or mood to another.

The truth is far different. The breaks in history are seldom as sharp as they seem; more things always remain constant than ever change. Human nature is much the same at all times. The interests of most people at most times revolve around their families, the way they gain their livelihoods, and the problems and activities of their immediate neighborhoods. Throughout recorded history, tribes and nations have been consistently hostile to other groups and have tried to conquer them. People everywhere have regularly, though not always with the same sense of urgency, sought to find better and easier ways of doing their daily tasks. Men have always tried to add to their knowledge. The vast majority of people are always natural conservatives in the sense that they prefer the known and familiar to the unknown. People tend to have strong, constant loyalties that are broken down or altered only gradually and with great difficulty: loyalties to religion, to country, to social ideas, or to particular forms of government. Throughout American history, for example, many people have been extremely critical of the ways in which our government has operated, but exceedingly few have ever tried to change our *form* of government. In most societies, if some drastic change is proposed, more people will have something to lose by it than will have something to gain. This is especially true of the influential people, who will be in the best position to resist change effectively.

Extent of Change Easily Overrated—Even when seemingly dramatic changes do take place the extent of the change is often illusory. There is always some sort of compromise with the past. Most old ways and habits are quietly retained, though some innovations in both substance and exterior appearance are introduced. A case in point is the alleged "revolution of 1800," which elevated Thomas Jefferson to the presidency. Jefferson was a thoroughgoing democrat: hostile to slavery, opposed to privilege of either birth or wealth, confident that the ordinary man possessed both common sense and good will. He was convinced that that government is best which governs least. He was highly suspicious of the fiscal policies of Alexander Hamilton, especially Hamilton's pet creation, the National Bank. Jefferson also deplored what he regarded as excessive government expenditures during the administrations of Washington and Adams (1789-1800). The whole Federalist approach to finance, he was convinced, could lead only to increased taxation and thereby to dangerous growth in the power of the central government. For the same reasons, he feared an increase in the size of the army or the navy, particularly the latter, since the most enthusiastic support for naval increases came from Federalist New England. He viewed with suspicion the numerous "midnight judges" appointed in the last days of the Adams administration, seeing in them a bastion of aristocracy, an exclusive Federalist clique hostile to the aspirations of ordinary people. He opposed Hamilton's "loose construction" of the U.S. Constitution, which envisioned that document as containing "implied" powers that might be invoked and exercised by the president. Thus, Jefferson and his supporters believed that their victory deserved the designation "revolution," for they were convinced that they had saved the fledgling republic from degenerating into a monarchy or aristocracy like that of Great Britain, against which Americans had revolted only twenty-five years before.

remarkably similar to its predecessors. Ceremony and official manners around the White House were simplified, but this did not diminish the fact that Jefferson was, after all, quite as much a member of the Virginia planter aristocracy as George Washington had been. The men who were closest to him were James Madison, Albert Gallatin, Nathaniel Macon, and John Randolph. All of them were also either well-born planters, wealthy, intellectually distinguished, or all three.

The new regime did make some changes. It allowed the Federalists' excise tax on whiskey to lapse. It refused to renew the hated Alien and Sedition Acts. It eased the process whereby settlers could acquire western lands. Otherwise President Jefferson soon found himself doing things he had condemned in the administrations of his predecessors.

Despite all the earlier denunciations of Hamilton's "abominable" U.S. Bank, that institution was allowed to continue under its charter. After first reducing the size of the fleet, Jefferson had to turn about abruptly and strengthen it in order to fight the Barbary pirates. A few years later he employed all the power and prestige of the presidential office to push the Embargo Act through Congress in an effort to compel the embattled nations of Europe to respect the rights of American neutrals. In order to enforce the Embargo Act he secured from Congress authority to issue general search warrants that closely resembled the detested "writs of assistance" used by British crown officials before the Revolution. With presidential approval, the Jeffersonians in Congress tried to remove their opponents in the judiciary by impeaching them. Above all, the president spent $15 million in public money to purchase the Louisiana Territory from Napoleon Bonaparte. Though he still verbally repudiated the *theory* of "implied powers" in the Constitution, Jefferson had embraced the *practice* to a degree that would have warmed the heart of the most aristocratic Federalist. Altogether, the change of presidents in 1800 had effected a tepid revolution indeed.

Should we be surprised that, despite all their slogans and campaign promises, most governments, most of the time, merely continue most of the policies and programs of their predecessors? Not really. After all, no government can ever entirely control the minds and activities of all its subjects. No human agency can yet control our physical environment. In any nation some problems are constant merely because the country lies in a desert, in the tropics, in the mountains, in the far north, is subject to recurrent floods or earthquakes, or has a strong, aggressive people as an immediate neighbor. The basic mode of life of the country in question will be strongly influenced by these considerations, no matter what sort of government or economic system it has.

There is much continuity in human history because of the very nature and structure of government. Any regime has to maintain internal order, to keep up an army to defend its people, to translate its principles into laws, to develop an administration to run the country on a day-to-day basis, and to collect from its people the taxes necessary to support these activities. All governments, whether the mildest democracies or the most pitiless despotisms, have to do these things in *some* manner.

A common type in history is the revolutionary idealist, the hot-eyed zealot, the "man of principle" who is determined to sweep out some rotten, discredited system and replace it with something totally different and radiantly pure. Sometimes this "man of principle" is able to gain office or power. One of the first things he is apt to discover is that the whole condition he has been denouncing is a lot more complex than he had supposed and that it is much harder to take "decisive action" than it was to talk about it. He discovers that many things cannot be changed at all without alienating whole groups of people without whose support, or at least neutrality, he can do little save continue to make speeches. He finds that he has to rule the country through the existing civil service (since he cannot train his own overnight), and that most of its members have no particular sympathy for his program. Before long our "man of principle" finds himself making compromises of the very sort he had previously denounced when they were made by other governments. He is able to change the direction of affairs to some degree, but in most respects public business proceeds much as before.

It is not only revolutionary firebrands who get caught in such dilemmas; ordinary politicians do too. Throughout the early and middle stages of his political career Richard Nixon castigated his political opponents for the prodigality with which they spent federal money and the "softness" with which they dealt with Communist nations. As president he had actually to deal with the existing federal bureaucracy, with a Democratic Congress, with a populace alarmed about rapidly rising prices, and with a world diplomatic situation that had changed markedly. Soon the erstwhile fiscal conservative was presenting federal budgets in worse imbalance than those of his predecessors, reluctantly employing wage and price controls in which he did not believe and which ultimately failed, and adopting toward Communist China and Russia a policy of "détente" which he surely would have condemned had it been undertaken by his domestic political opponents.

Sixty years earlier Woodrow Wilson denounced President Taft's "dollar diplomacy" in Latin America only to become embroiled in punitive expeditions in both Mexico and the Caribbean soon after succeeding Taft. Similar examples could be cited by the hundreds.

But Nothing Remains Stationary—Yet change is also a constant factor in human history. No situation ever remains entirely static. As long as men have minds, imaginations, ambitions, ideals; as long as they love and hate and fear and yearn; as long, in fact, as they remain men; some of them will strive to remedy this or that ill, long to try some new idea or system, seek power for themselves or their friends or their class, or simply strike out in hatred and frustration at what they despise. If things never move rapidly enough to suit the visionary, neither do they remain sufficiently stable to suit the conservative.

In view of the foregoing considerations textbook divisions and chapter titles may seem largely formal, mechanical, and unreal. This is only partly true. A book has to be divided in *some* fashion and titles given to its various parts; otherwise one would have to conclude that things are so much the same at all times that no divisions are possible.

This is plainly ludicrous. Moreover, if all things were alike there would be no point in studying the history of any period but one's own. Even the most conventional textbook divisions mirror reality to a considerable degree.

A good case in point concerns the New Deal of the 1930s. In that harsh decade, when the world was sunk in the depths of history's worst economic depression, President Franklin Roosevelt undertook a series of flamboyant and hotly controverted efforts to restore America's lost confidence and prosperity. Years after, when Roosevelt was in his grave and the turmoil of his administration had passed into memory, we were often reminded by historians and publicists that many of the New Deal programs, after all, had been anticipated by President Herbert Hoover (1928-32) and continued by Roosevelt's successors long after 1945. We were further reminded that despite all the fear and hatred with which the Roosevelt administration had been regarded by much of the business community, the president had sought throughout to save capitalism, not destroy it. And had he not succeeded? When the Great Depression was at length past, there had been no change in our form of government, ordinary citizens were still in full possession of their ancestral liberties, no industries had been nationalized, and no bankers had been lynched. Even the stock market had recovered! Overall, was not American democracy and capitalism stronger and more thriving in the 1940s than ever before? Surely the claim that the New Deal era was a revolutionary interlude in U.S. history is overdrawn!

All this is unquestionably true, yet it is surely the smaller half of the truth, for many of the innovations of the New Deal era did shake America to its foundations and produce changes in our national life that appear to be permanent. Perhaps the most fundamental change was that the power of politics and government began for the first time to exceed the power of business. The federal government began to assume all sorts of functions and responsibilities that had hitherto lain within the province of state and local governments or had simply been left to private initiative. The Social Security system was established, a vast array of recovery and welfare legislation was enacted, public works projects, of which the Tennessee Valley Authority is perhaps the best known, were undertaken on an unprecedented scale, farmers were for the first time not merely encouraged but actually paid *not* to produce, and the federal bureaucracy was expanded enormously to oversee the myriad of new programs. Most significant of all, for the first time in our national history, deficit financing became a respectable method of dealing with the government's routine financial obligations, whether in war or peace, in good times or bad.

Of equal importance, at least at the time, was the psychological impact of the New Deal. Long before, such "activist" executives as Andrew Jackson, Abraham Lincoln, and Theodore Roosevelt had tried their best to add to the powers and prestige of the presidency, but none did so much to make it the focal center of national leadership as Franklin Roosevelt. "FDR," as the newspapers soon dubbed him, was one of the half-dozen most eloquent and persuasive public speakers who have appeared thus far in our century. He had at his disposal a new mode of communication, the radio, which enabled him regularly to address scores of millions in his famous "fireside chats."

Within a short time President Roosevelt's inspiring words and the atmosphere of urgency and bustle that prevailed in Washington convinced tens of millions of Americans that all was not lost, that the depression could be successfully combated, that there was now in the White House a providential genius who understood the problems of the ordinary citizen, who genuinely wanted to solve those problems, and who had the ability to solve them. So widespread and deep was this conviction that the nation's voting habits changed fundamentally. Millions of lifelong Republicans on farms and in cities abruptly became Democrats for the rest of their voting lives. In a single election (1932) the Democrats displaced the Republicans as the normal majority party. Everywhere political awareness was heightened and political feeling sharpened. The country became divided increasingly into Roosevelt-idolaters and Roosevelt-haters, for few felt neutral about the avalanche of New Deal laws and programs, or what they seemd to portend.

Fewer still felt neutral about the president's wife. Eleanor Roosevelt was restless, tireless, and voluble. She traveled, seemingly, everywhere. Comedians made jokes about the places so remote that "even Mrs. Roosevelt hasn't been there." She had opinions on every public question, promoted every "worthy cause," wrote newspaper columns without number, and introduced her friends to her husband, thereby securing positions in the government for many of them. Almost as well known as the president himself, she was accorded unstinting admiration or frank detestation to at least as great a degree as her husband. She did nearly as much as he did to turn the eyes of the nation toward the White House.

To conclude, it is not difficult to demonstrate that many elements in the New Deal program had been foreshadowed in the Republican administrations of Theodore Roosevelt (1901-08) and Herbert Hoover (1928-32), or in the Democratic administration of Woodrow Wilson (1912-20). These elements had been retained and often expanded by Democrats and Republicans alike since 1945. Still, their total impact in the 1930s was so massive, abrupt, and psychologically jarring that it is not unrealistic to mark off the New Deal years as a distinctive era in American history.

Awareness of Change—We tend to be more aware of change than the ancients were because the tempo of the modern world is far more rapid than at any time in the past and is constantly accelerating. The main reasons for this are: (1) literacy is now virtually universal in the Western world, thereby making it possible to circulate new information and ideas much more widely and rapidly than ever before; and (2) the scientific and industrial advances of recent generations have given us an unprecedented power to influence our environment. Consider how much the day-to-day lives and thoughts of scores of millions of ordinary people would be changed if there were no superhighways, airplanes, frozen foods, air conditioners, radios, or television sets. Yet none of these existed before 1900. It is little wonder that unintelligent or merely thoughtless people so often believe that things change so swiftly now that there is nothing to be gained by studying the past.

Still, paradoxically, it is quite possible for people to live in an age of rapid, fundamental change and to remain unaware of it; or, even if they are aware of it in the abstract, to go about their daily affairs as if life was as serene and predictable as in the most peaceful of times. It is possible, even probable, that historians of the future will think of the year 1945 A.D. as they think of 410 A.D. They will regard the atomic bombs that exploded near Alamagordo, New Mexico, and over Hiroshima and Nagasaki, Japan, much as they have long viewed the fall of Rome to the Visigoths—as clear portents of a new historical epoch. What change, after all, could be more revolutionary than the advent of the atomic-nuclear missile age? Notoriously, it has, in a few years, dramatically altered world power relationships. More ominously, nuclear weapons and ICBMs have raised the spectre of not merely national governments, but (conceivably) groups of malign scientists, even mere revolutionary cliques, or even gangsters, gaining control of a few superweapons and, by pushing buttons, beginning a general nuclear war of unimaginable destructiveness.

It has even raised a unique theological problem: the possibility of our world being extinguished either by the deliberate design of men or, still more incredibly, by sheer accident. Of course there have always been philosophers who have maintained that existence is meaningless. Nonetheless, most of our planet's great historic religions—Hinduism, Christianity, Judaism, Islam, and others—have always taught that some sort of deity has plans for mankind and will someday bring history to an end in an appropriate manner. Builders of imposing systems of secular metaphysics have been equally convinced that history has patterns—that is "going somewhere." The eighteenth-century philosopher Condorcet believed that the adoption of a rational approach to all life's problems could produce a society that would be inherently progressive and would improve indefinitely by its very nature. Adam Smith, the father of laissez-faire, was convinced of the operation of an invisible hand that insured that if everyone was allowed to pursue his own interest as he saw fit, the best interests of the whole society would be furthered indefinitely. Karl Marx saw history as a movement, through class struggles, toward the ultimate goal of justice for all in a classless society, a condition with no discernible end. The Darwinists envisioned history as a process of incessant evolutionary improvement without a necessary conclusion. The very idea that humanity might suddenly become extinct through human folly or sheer carelessness does not appear to have crossed the mind of anyone before, perhaps, 1945!

But do people in our generation regard this totally unprecedented state of affairs with what would seem to be appropriate seriousness? Some scientists do, of course. They regularly issue solemn warnings about the dangers that engulf us. "Horror stuff" of the popular journalistic type still gets into the newspapers. More and more, however, such writings tend to appear on page 18, between the daily horoscope and advertisements for upset stomach remedies. There have been many wars since 1945, but all have been waged with traditional weapons. The only thing nuclear about any of them has been occasional veiled threats. Now, ordinary people cannot be kept in a state of high psychological tension for long periods about anything. We have simply become used to the atomic age, have come to take it for granted, have concluded that whatever its dangers there is nothing we can do about them. We have, in effect, shrugged our shoulders and returned to our traditional interests: family, jobs, recreation, physical comforts, the neighborhood, and the state of the economy. If the atomic age poses an unprecedented problem for professional theologians, well, let *them* worry about it. There is no indication that common people anywhere in the world have grown more religious since the shadow of the bomb has fallen over us. Western politicians reflect this popular apathy to such a degree that no effective civil defense program against nuclear warfare has ever been undertaken. Indeed, outside professional scientific and military circles atomic and nuclear power is discussed mostly in terms of its potential as an energy source for ordinary civilian uses.

So, even though the advent of the atomic age is almost certainly one of the great turning points in all history, quite as fundamentally as was the fall of the Roman Empire, most people seem to have only the most perfunctory awareness that they are living in such momentous times.

Historical Parallels–The way things always change yet remain similar in many essentials can be readily illustrated by any of history's innumerable parallels. Let us consider just one: the dawn of the great age of the exploration of the earth, at the end of the fifteenth century, and the dawn of space exploration in the mid-twentieth century. Portugal and, especially, Spain led the world in the first case: Russia and, especially, the United States in the second. Both outbursts of exploration were made possible by breakthroughs in technology. The invention of the compass and astrolabe, the development of more accurate maps and charts, and, above all, the building of the caravel, an improved sailing ship, had made possible more daring voyages into unknown oceans well before 1500. All these developments were the work of the Portuguese, Venetians, Genoese, Majorcans, Arabs, and Chinese–not the Spaniards. Yet America was discovered because Queen Isabella of Spain financed the fabled voyage of still another foreigner, the Genoese Columbus. Four-and-a-half centuries later it was the theoretical achievements of European scientists and the practical talents of German rocket experts that contributed heavily not only to the Russian space program but to the eventual landing of Americans on the moon.

In 1492 and after, the Spanish government invested much money in exploration even though the country had just completed a long and costly war to conquer the Moorish stronghold of Granada. The United States lavished tens of billions of dollars on space exploration in the 1960s and early 1970s while fighting a long, unpopular, and extremely expensive war in Southeast Asia. For many years after 1492 the Spanish public paid little attention to overseas exploration because it was a generation before any appreciable amount of gold was discovered. Most Americans derived a certain pride from our nation being the first to put men on the moon, and our early space explorations were sufficiently novel that they aroused much interest and comment. But within a decade it had all become so commonplace that the television networks at last no longer bothered to cover Pacific "splash-downs" of astronauts returning from space missions. Much sooner than that, grumbling was widespread that space exploration was of no practical utility, that nothing had resulted from it save the acquisition of some "moon rocks," and that the billions devoted to it should have been spent on education or social welfare. (Had the persons who took this view been alive in 1492 doubtless they would have complained that Queen Isabella wasted tax money on that good-for-nothing adventurer Columbus when it ought to have been spent on slum clearance in Seville.) Of course the discovery of America was one of the most momentous events in the whole history of mankind. Ironically, England and France, whose interest in exploration was desultory and late beside that of Spain, eventually profited at least as much or more from the opening of the New World. If the past is any guide, surely the beginning of space exploration will ultimately expand the intellectual horizons of humanity and affect every aspect of earthly life as much as did the discovery of America. Here too, in the long run other nations and other peoples will surely be affected quite as much as the American and Russian pioneers.

Thus, even though external circumstances surrounding the great explorations of 1490–1520 and 1958–74 differed enormously, many humans reactions to them clearly had changed little, if at all.

Roots in the Past—Even though most Americans are so used to change that we hardly notice the dawn of a new age, only a little reflection is needed to remind us that our ties with the distant past are still numerous and strong. Our governmental institutions and political beliefs are derived directly from a series of events, documents, and conceptions of the late eighteenth century. More remotely, they are derived from the English constitutional tradition, which is at least 700 years old. We are still professedly a Christian nation and thereby formally committed to a set of beliefs and a code of private and public conduct two thousand years old. In literature, the fine arts, science, and intellectual pursuits generally, we continue to study and admire the works of Darwin, Kant, Goethe, Newton, Shakespeare, Michelangelo, da Vinci, Thomas Aquinas, Cicero, Aristotle, Plato, Socrates—a galaxy of luminaries extending backward in time at least to the ancient Greeks.

One of the most striking examples of the complex interweaving of change and continuity in human affairs is to be found not in U.S. history but in the history of America's relentless antagonist in the ongoing Cold War, Soviet Russia. Post-1917 Russia differs sharply from Old Russia in many ways. The whole society is now officially dedicated to Marxism, and everything its rulers choose to do is justified by some reference to Marxist principles. Soviet Russia employs government propaganda, concentration camps, police surveillance, systematic brutality, and state direction of every economic and social activity on a scale without parallel in recorded history. Under Communism Russia has become a literate nation and the world's second-ranking industrial power. The regime is officially committed to the eventual abolition of private ownership everywhere, a development supposedly predestined by the operation of the inexorable laws of history. By means of Communist parties in other countries it maintains throughout the world a vast army of loyal agents vigilant to promote Russian interests at the expense of their own countries and working ceaselessly to Communize the entire world. All this seems new. Much of it genuinely is new.

Yet, the more one learns of Russian history, the more evidences of her past he can see in contemporary Russia. For generations the czars sought to expand to the east in Siberia and toward Manchuria, Afghanistan, and Persia (Iran). In the West they strove to take territories from the Swedes and the Turks, to control Poland, to gain a "window to the West" on the Baltic, and to secure Constantinople (Istanbul) or an outlet on the Adriatic Sea. Communist Russian designs are similar. Attempts to dominate Azerbaijan in northern Iran were barely forestalled by the United States and other powers in 1946. Elsewhere, the USSR has been more successful. Not only Poland but the rest of eastern Europe as well is now controlled by Soviet Russia. Naval bases were taken from Finland. Russian loans and "aid" have been granted to Afghanistan. North Korea and Vietnam have been Communized. China has become Communist—though it is hardly friendly to its ideological compatriots in Moscow. Russian influence has grown steadily in the Arab Middle East.

Czarist Russia knew the secret police, the collectivist principle in the management of village lands, and domestic tyranny of every sort, though these phenomena were less well developed and systematic in times past. Industrialization had begun on a significant scale in old Russia, and the government of Nicholas II tackled the illiteracy problem in earnest after 1900. Czarist Russia, at least as long ago as the sixteenth century, thought of Western civilization as weak and decadent beside her own. The Communists are of the same opinion, if not for the same reasons. In his reckless determination to modernize and westernize his country, in his pitiless brutality and scorn for all humanitarian impulses, even in the savagery of his personal life, the Communist dictator Stalin reminds one immediately of Czar Peter the Great (1694–1725). So many and so obvious are the similarities between old and new Russia that contemporary Russia has been defined variously as "an oriental despotism grown suddenly vigorous," and as "an efficient tyranny in contrast to the inefficient tyranny of the Czars." In fact, scholars have long disagreed about which represents the real threat to the rest of the world: the international Communist gospel backed by Russian power or Russian imperialism covered with Marxist varnish. In either case, one is reminded of the French proverb, "The more things change, the more they stay the same."

Slowness of Change—Most often than not, when change does take place it comes slowly and gradually. Often the necessity for change is perceived too late, acknowledged only grudgingly, or simply ignored altogether. All three reactions are illustrated by long-standing American attitudes toward our military defenses. The American colonies were so persistently unwilling to raise an adequate militia for self-defense, or to cooperate with one another for the same purpose, that the British government in the 1760s lost patience and decided to write off colonial militiamen entirely. Instead, they determined to station an army of ten thousand British regulars in America and require the colonials to pay one-third of the cost of their upkeep. The colonists deemed this not only unnecessary but dangerous. The issue heated so many tempers that it became one of the major factors contributing to the American Revolution. Despite the fact that the colonists could not have won that war without the regulars of the Continental army, eventually backed by French regulars, certain battles like Bunker Hill confirmed the colonials in their conviction that a small popular militia was not only the proper defense force for a free people but an adequate one as well.

This comfortable conclusion dovetailed nicely with the general belief of eighteenth-century intellectuals that standing armies should be abolished because they were tools of absolutism, instruments of despotism and privilege. Nineteenth-century liberals all over the Western world were of the same opinion. Peculiarly American conditions strengthened the conviction still further. President Thomas Jefferson was hostile to the maintenance of any sizable military establishment. Our geographical isolation and the absence of strong neighbors appeared to render such a force unnecessary. Of the millions of immigrants who flocked to our shores after 1815, many had fled Europe to escape military service.

These general American convictions, rooted in our unique geographical circumstances and historic past, virtually insured that until very recent times our nation would languish in a state of chronic military unpreparedness. With the exception of the battle of New Orleans, which took place after the war had officially ended, the performance of our militia in the War of 1812 can only be characterized as wretched.

A generation later we did little better in the Mexican War. We won mostly because our adversary was even more inept than we were. Neither North nor South was prepared, even in an elementary way, for the Civil War of 1861–65. The Confederacy for a year, and the Union for two years, tried to raise and maintain armies by calling up units of state militia, assigning quotas of "volunteers" to the states, and offering enlistment bounties. When the necessity for conscription was faced at last, efforts to implement it met with draft riots in the North and less dramatic but no less real resistance in the South. For the Spanish-American War thirty-three years later, the navy was about half-ready. This was due to Captain Alfred T. Mahan's well-publicized doctrines on the necessity of maintaining strength at sea and to the energy with which Undersecretary of the Navy Theodore Roosevelt pursued his official duties. Nothing else was ready at all. By the time the near-farcical land operations had culminated in an American "victory," nearly thirteen times as many U.S. soldiers had died of disease as had succumbed to wounds.

Sixteen years later World War I broke out in Europe. Though it is likely that a German victory eventually would have been damaging to American political and commercial interests all over the world, we did not seem immediately threatened. Consequently, we spent nearly three years giving free advice to all combatants while making only the most leisurely effort to prepare for the day when we might be compelled to intervene. Once in the conflict in 1917, our armed forces largely ignored the main tactical lesson of the war. Doubly damning, it had also been the main tactical lesson of our own Civil War, half a century earlier. That lesson was that to attack an enemy who possesses modern weapons, in a prepared position, is suicidal. Fortunately for us, by the time American troops arrived in Europe en masse the war was nearly over. Thus, we were spared the horrendous casualties that bled the British and French peoples white.

Such a history of more than a century of persistent unpreparedness, and nonchalant unconcern about it, would have destroyed any European nation half a dozen times over. Only our geographical isolation saved us, for it always guaranteed us plenty of time to prepare for war. Thus archaic habits remained unbroken. In the 1930s we fell into an isolationist funk which contributed in no small way to the successful aggressions of the world's fascist dictatorships. In 1934 the Japanese declared that after December 31, 1936, they would no longer observe the provision of the Washington-naval agreements of 1921–22, which had limited their naval strength to 60 percent of that of America. Suiting deed to word, they began to build up their fleet. Did we at once increase our own naval strength accordingly? No. We did not even improve our defenses in the Philippines! When World War II broke out in Europe in 1939, we began what was by now our time-honored course: desultory preparation for a problematical war against somebody, someday. A year later a conscription law was enacted. Only in August 1941, less than four months before Pearl Harbor, did the U.S. House of Representatives, by *one vote*, authorize the president to retain in service those who had previously been drafted for a year.

One would suppose that the cataclysm of World War II would have changed our national psychology, but it did not. Within a few months after the war was over the American army was virtually disbanded. Had it not been for our brief monopoly of the atomic bomb there would have been nothing to prevent the USSR from seizing far more of east-central Europe than she actually sequestered in 1946–48. Eyes began to open in significant numbers only after such shocks as the

Berlin Blockade of 1948 and the Korean War of the early 1950s. Soon after, Russian acquisition of atomic and nuclear bombs and ICBMs presented us with the prospect of having only minutes rather than years to prepare for war. This ominous development did spur us into hastily rebuilding a huge and expensive military establishment, but it still left many of our national feelings unaffected. The Vietnam War was widely resented and denounced. Complaints have been incessant that the money spent on that conflict should have been spent on various domestic programs. The unwillingness of men to serve in the armed forces was so widespread that our nation in 1973–74 for the first time in our history undertook an effort to maintain a permanent, sizable army composed entirely of volunteers. It all indicates the tenacity with which people cling to customary notions, habits, and hopes, even though the political, military, and technological facts of international life have undergone not one but several major revolutions in the last two centuries.

It has always been the same with many of humanity's most fundamental problems. The chief political and social conundrums that have vexed mankind appear no nearer final solution now than they were in the age of the ancient Greeks. How to combine efficiency in government with liberty for the individual? How to grant liberty to the individual without allowing him to infringe the liberty of others? How to give able men an incentive to invent, improve, and produce without allowing them to exploit their fellow men in the process? How to prevent destructive wars when nations hate, fear, and distrust one another? No matter what changes take place in modes of existence these problems are changeless, eternal.

Theories about Historical Change—Many attempts have been made to trace patterns in history or to discern the nature and direction of historical change. Many ancient speculators, and the pessimistic sixteenth-century Florentine political analyst, Machiavelli, thought that history moved in cycles, each cycle substantially repeating the course of previous ones. A slight variation of this is the common view that the life of a civilization or nation closely resembles that of a man. Applied to the United States, the theory would go something like this: in our national youth (down to about 1890) our ancestors worked hard, saved their money, served God, wrested lands from neighbors, Indians, and the wilderness, and established the foundations of our national greatness. This was followed by our zenith, corresponding to an adult's middle life (perhaps 1890–1950). In these years our industries expanded, our wealth grew, our culture flourished, our government was basically sound, and we retained healthy, progressive public attitudes. Now our period of old age or decline has set in. Many of our "intellectual leaders" scoff at the principles, practices, and ideals that made us great. We waste our substance in ruinous domestic conflicts. Vice, crime, and irresponsibility flourish to an unprecedented degree. Much of our intellectual and cultural life has become tinged with madness. Our governments have grown slack, corrupt, and hopelessly spendthrift. As our decay proceeds, hardy, vigorous neobarbarians from without wait to give us the coup de grace.[1]

Whether this gloomy scenario is historically sound or merely ludicrous is impossible to say since we live in the midst of the events. One could contend, with equal plausibility, that far from becoming decadent our country is still growing more mature culturally, more humane socially, and more just in its treatment of its citizens—not to speak of our continued growth in national wealth. Indeed, the rest of the world increasingly copies American technology and organizational methods to such a degree that a few generations hence historians may be saying that the United States was the twentieth-century forerunner of a computerized society that subsequently became global. But all this is besides the point. The point is that the whole original hypothesis is an example of a cyclical theory of historical change that has been applied to many nations, peoples, and even whole civilizations in the past.

Some have likened the course of history to the swinging of a pendulum, always striking out toward extremes and by that very effort constantly being brought back toward a center or compromise between the extremes. Many superficial examples can be cited to illustrate this conception. An obvious one concerns American governments. From the Civil War to about 1900, these were markedly conservative regardless of the party in power. The administrations of Theodore Roosevelt, Taft, and especially Wilson (1901–20), by contrast, represented a swing of the pendulum in the direction of social legislation and the assumption by the government of greater responsibility for the welfare of its citizens. In the 1920s, under Harding, Coolidge, and Hoover, the pendulum swung back to the right again. Under the New Deal of the 1930s it swung far to the left once more as Wilsonian trends were carried much further. After the Second World War it swung again to the right.

A more sophisticated version of this theory was the "dialectic" developed by the nineteenth-century German philosopher Hegel. Hegel held that historical development takes place because any given situation

---

1. Some would even deny us fleeting greatness. A Frenchman, André Siegfried, once made the jaundiced remark that "Americans are the only people who ever passed from barbarism to decadence without having been civilized."

or set of ideas, which has been called a "thesis," tends to produce its opposite or "antithesis." These two struggle, neither overcomes the other entirely, and the resultant fusion of the two produces a new thing, a "synthesis." This "synthesis" becomes, in effect, a new "thesis" which now engenders *its* "antithesis." From their conflict comes a new "synthesis." This new "synthesis" (really another new "thesis") engenders a new "antihesis," and so on. This scheme (much simplified here) is of interest chiefly because this "dialectic" was appropriated by Karl Marx and made one of the philosophical bases for modern Communism.

Perhaps the most popular theory of historical change, at least among armchair philosophers in Western countries, is the idea of "progress": the belief that human history is the record of man's steady advancement in knowledge, wisdom, control over his environment, improvement in his institutions, and elevation of his ideals and conduct. This view was popular all over the Western world about the turn of the twentieth century. Nowhere was it more generally accepted than in the United States. It then seemed clear that the spread of education, democratic institutions, and scientific knowledge was building a finer world.

However, the depressions, wars, dictators, concentration camps, irrational political movements, racial strife, and mass murders of the twentieth century, accompanied by smog, pollution, ravaging of the land, plunder of irreplacable natural resources, destruction of animal and sea life, proliferation of sprawling suburbs about decaying central cities, and the reckless habit of sacrificing the future to the present have destroyed much of the past confidence of our ancestors. It is now quite clear that while knowledge may increase steadily, wisdom (the good use of knowledge) does not necessarily do so. There is also no gainsaying that in the past "progress" has often been reversed. Whole highly developed cultures, Assyrian, ancient Egyptian, Minoan, and Mayan, to name a few, have vanished entirely and been replaced by obviously inferior civilizations.

Nobody can claim that he understands all history so thoroughly that he can discern perfectly the "pattern" that it follows if, indeed, it has any pattern at all. It is precisely the weakness of every grand philosophy of history that the "philosophy" or explanation is the first thing conceived. Only afterward does its author select from the myriad of facts about the past whatever fits his theory. Whatever does not fit is ignored. A student's thought about the whole matter may be clarified, however, and without doing serious damage to the truth, if he likens the change and continuity in history to a river. The river begins as a tiny rivulet high in the mountains but grows steadily larger from water fed into it by springs and tributary streams, the equivalent of new forces and ideas in history. The river is replete with currents, eddies, rapids, falls, pools, dams, obstructions, backwaters, and bayous, which are the counterparts of the wars, revolutions, constitutions, legislation, dynastic shifts, inventions. and social, economic, and religious changes of history. The river assumes many different aspects—now rushing and dangerous, now calm, sometimes narrow, sometimes broad and placid— but nowhere does it stop completely, nowhere does it abruptly change character, nowhere does it cease to be water. Thus follows the course of history too.

4: What Can We Really Know about History?

At some time or other virtually every teacher of history has had the following experience: he is discussing the reliability of the historical source materials relating to some controverted question. As he finishes, a hand shoots up and a student asks, "But which ones are reliable and which ones aren't?" Sometimes the discussion concerns varying interpretations of some historical event. At the conclusion the student asks, "Which one, now, is correct?" The attitude of the student here is neither surprising nor unreasonable for the human mind always seeks certitude. What the student must come to realize, however, is that certitude of the mathematical sort is not possible in history. There are many questions relating to past history that can never be answered; many disputes that can never be settled. Rarely, if ever, is a historical source so completely reliable that it may be taken at face value. Rarely is a source so untrustworthy that nothing can be learned from it.

History is our memory of the past. The whole past can never be recalled and put into print because it consists of the almost infinite number of things that each person who has ever lived has said, thought, and done. An infinite number of volumes would be required to record it. Historians select a few of these thoughts, words, and deeds that seem to have general significance, and these become history as we ordinarily think of it. Because people's ideas of what is significant change from time to time and because new knowledge frequently becomes available, history is constantly being rewritten.

Here a distinction must be drawn. What actually happened in the past is done—settled—and no amount of research or reinterpretation can ever change it. The battle of Gettysburg was fought in a certain manner in a certain place on three certain days in 1863. Historians may write about it until the end of time but not the minutest detail of what *actually happened* will ever be changed on that account. But that is not the real problem. The crux of the matter is that since we cannot relive the past what we know about it is largely what we learn from others. It is what people in the past knew and thought, and especially what they wrote, about their own times.

History No Science—History is not a science. Natural scientists (except biologists) deal with natural forces, inanimate objects, chemical substances, and the intellectual concepts related to them. All but the intellectual concepts have characteristics that are known and invariable. If a chemist wishes to confirm a conclusion derived from a certain experiment he can always repeat the experiment—repeat it a hundred times if he chooses. The historian, by contrast, cannot have the battle of Gettysburg fought over and over again so he can study it from every possible angle before writing his account of it. The best he can do is examine the battlefield in person, then reread the written materials available and think about them again.

History is not like the biological sciences either. A biologist can observe animals, insects, and plants, put them to tests, and dissect them, but the historian cannot resurrect Roger Williams or James Monroe and do the same with them. He can only deal with written records about them. Moreover, the biological sciences seek information about one individual in order to generalize about a species; while history always studies the unique, the one situation for itself, since no other will ever be exactly like it. The substance of history is the deeds of men in time. But time never ceases to move, men never cease to act, and, because men are free agents, they are prone to do the most unlikely and unpredictable things. Thus history is not a science in the same sense as mathematics or biology. It is, rather, a kaleidoscope.

If history was a science we could predict the future in detail. Now prediction is possible in a limited sense because the sameness of human nature causes the same general sort of situations to recur periodically. For instance, the past experience of mankind indicates that the persistence of oppression and tyranny will eventually produce revolt, or that mutual dislike and constant rivalry between two peoples will sooner or later bring war. But this is plainly quite different from predicting what particular individuals or nations will do at certain future times. If one is determined to foretell the course of human affairs in detail he should consult astrologers, not historians.

The Raw Materials of History—A consideration of the materials from which history is derived and the manner in which they must be used will indicate the impossibility of attaining absolute certitude about the past. History is written largely from documents: private and official records, newspapers, diaries, letters, memoirs, annals, and other accounts penned by men recently or long since dead. In recent years some historians have developed a new field of study: oral history. They interview people still living and record their words on paper or tapes. A good example of a book based on such sources is T. Harry Williams' biography of the Louisiana demagogue Huey Long, who was gunned down by an assassin in 1935. The author got most of his information about the "Kingfish" from talking to people who had known Long.

Some public figures, even presidents, have furthered the cause of oral history by recording their private conversations for future use by historians. Whether they will continue to do so in years to come is questionable. It was the appallingly frank comments of Richard Nixon and his close associates, which the president recorded on the famous Watergate tapes of the early 1970s, that provided conclusive evidence of extensive wrongdoing in high places and forced Nixon's resignation from the presidency in 1974.

Too Much Material—For the historian working in quite recent or contemporary history one of the major problems is the existence of an embarrassing superfluity of material. Books, newspapers, and magazines dealing with every conceivable subject are published in staggering numbers. Every governmental bureau and department, every local public agency, every business and labor organization, every society devoted to whatever cause, keeps records—usually in gigantic quantities. Practically every modern public figure in any field leaves behind him a vast correspondence, and usually his memoirs as well. Some of this material is valuable; much is not. Some is readily accessible; much is widely scattered. The historian who regards this Mt. Everest of paper scarcely knows where to begin his researches or when to end them and start writing.

Too Little Material—With most ancient and medieval history the problem is exactly the reverse. Much *was* written in times past but the great bulk of it has failed to survive the ravages of water, wind, fire, rats, mice, invasion, conquest, and time. Thus the historian of the ancient or early medieval world has little raw material on which to base his work. He is forced to build part of his history from archaeological findings and part from old traditions, myths, and stories handed down orally from one generation to another. Anyone knows from experience how tales of the latter sort are likely to be changed or embroidered in the repeated retelling. Yet a good deal of early Norse history, to cite an example, is based on such tales and traditions written down centuries after the events they describe.

Often history is "filled out" by adding a great many inferences to a small core of facts. The inferences may be valid—and usually are—but they are not the same things as documentary evidence. For instance, quite extensive accounts have been written of the lives of the early Germanic peoples. Virtually all the facts on which these are based come from two sources: the Roman historian Tacitus and, to a much lesser degree, from Julius Caesar's *Gallic Wars*, more than a century earlier. Normally a historian will accept and put into his own history only what is confirmed by two or three independent sources, but in this case one must either accept or reject Tactitus, feebly seconded by Caesar, for that is all that survives. Hence any account of the early Germans is Tacitus and Caesar, plus the inferences that a given writer draws from them.

Certain details of our own early national history will never be known as fully as we would wish because many records of the first years of our federal government were destroyed when the British burned all the public buildings in Washington during the War of 1812.

Sometimes considerable information exists about some historical phenomenon but it illuminates only certain aspects of the matter. For instance, we know a good deal about the beliefs, habits, and activities of American Indian tribes in colonial times but the information has come almost entirely from explorers, fur traders, missionaries and European colonists who dealt with Indians. Extremely little has come from the Indians themselves. If we possessed comparable written records produced by sixteenth-, seventeenth-, and eighteenth-century Indians, who can doubt that the treatment of Indian affairs in twentieth-century history books would be considerably different?

The same is true of Negro slaves before the Civil War. We know a lot about their lives but the great bulk of it was written either by their masters or by abolitionists, hardly unbiased sources. The slaves wrote little because most of them were illiterate.

Now there are ways of redressing such imbalances somewhat, but all are fraught with dangers of their own. Let us consider one, slavery. In the 1930s the U.S. government sponsored an oral history project in which ex-slaves who were still living were questioned by historians and their answers recorded. This provided a new perspective, to be sure, though anyone alive in 1935 who still remembered what slavery was like could not have been less than eighty years old—likely closer to ninety. The childhood memories of eighty-five-year-old illiterates hardly comprise the world's most trustworthy historical source.

More recently (1974) an attempt was made to apply quantitative techniques to the study of antebellum slavery. The book *Time on the Cross* by Robert Fogle and Stanley Engerman was an instant sensation because its conclusions called into question not merely the quality of the authors' scholarship but the very worth of efforts to study history by the use of slide rules, statistical tables, and computers. In the past these techniques have unquestionably been valuable in certain fields of history, particularly the study of trade, business, and city life, subjects about which statistical data ordinarily abound.

A famous quantitative study of raw census statistics by Oscar Handlin revealed that Boston's Irish immigrants of the 1840s and 1850s enjoyed even fewer economic opportunities than free blacks in northern urban society. The work went far to explain the seeming paradox of the Irish being pro-Union during the Civil War but hostile to abolitionism—presumably from fear of intensified competition with freed Negroes for menial jobs. In the case of *Time on the Cross*, the critics asserted that its authors employed insufficient and unrepresentative data, and then failed to analyze it competently. We need not pass judgment here on the validity of these criticisms for they have little to do with the most fundamental objection that can be raised to the quantitative approach to history: that it necessarily leaves out the *most important things*. What, after all, was the most obvious, glaring, distinctive characteristic of the slave system? That the slaves were healthy? Unhealthy? Well fed? Badly fed? Industrious? Lazy? Productive? Slovenly and indifferent? No. It was an intangible thing: the fact that they were slaves, unfree, chattels, incomplete human beings. Computers and tables of statistics cannot tell us anything about the fears, hopes, plans, longings, expectations, the *psychology*, of the slaves, for computers cannot analyze imponderables.

Perhaps the most promising approach to the problem of developing a more accurate and comprehensive knowledge of what American slavery was like would be to study the journals and diaries of the Southern doctors who treated the slaves medically. Such writings exist in great number though most have never been published or have appeared only in obscure journals that are seldom read. The doctors were southerners, to be sure, but they were not direct beneficiaries of the slave system in the same sense as the planters. Neither did they have the same mind set as the northern abolitionists. Moreover, their medical training provided an added dimension to their observation of the Negroes. Thus methodical research in their writings would seem to be a logical next step for historians interested in U.S. slavery.

Are Surviving Materials Typical?—As the foregoing discussion indicates, a vexatious problem for historians is judging whether or not such materials as have survived are truly representative. Of course much of the raw material of history is always unrepresentative merely because important and prominent people have always attracted far more attention than the humble masses. But that is not the real problem. Let us make an extreme, but not unreasonable, assumption about the *real* problem: that two hundred ancient writers might have written about a contemporary king but through the caprice of fate only the writings of his five harshest critics have survived. Some obvious prejudice can be detected, of course, and the historian can often check suspect accounts against other writings, archaeological evidence, and his own common sense. Still, who can doubt that in the case cited later generations would have a lower opinion of the king than the (unknown) facts warranted?

This example is not fanciful. A case quite similar to it concerns the

Roman Emperor Tiberius, 14–37 A.D. Nearly all ancient writers whose works have survived agree that Tiberius was a monster in human form. They ascribe to him a character that seems close to unbelievable. They depict him at the age of eighty indulging in a variety of vices that seem even physically impossible. What is the reader to think? Is he to conclude that all the ancient writers who were contemporaries of Tiberius were obviously ignorant or prejudiced and that we ought to dilute their judgments, preferring those of historians who seldom stir from libraries and who write eighteen or nineteen hundred years after the events? Is he to say, contrarily, that the ancients must be believed, no matter how incredible their accounts, because they knew of Tiberius at first hand while modern writers cannot; and that, anway, there is no proof that modern writers are necessarily more impartial and judicious than their ancient counterparts? To be sure they are trained to be, but are they always? Plainly, there is plenty of uncertainty about the whole matter.

Consider the problem in another way. Let us assume, gloomily, that in the near future World War III breaks out between the Communist and free worlds and that it is waged with nuclear and bacteriological weapons. After a short time the only humans left on earth are the inhabitants of the Fiji Islands. A few centuries hence some of them drift on a raft to the shores of what was once the United States. One of them is a scholarly sort. He decides to try to reconstruct the history of the twentieth century before the Third World War began. By the merest chance the only printed materials that have survived the holocaust are the files of the Communist newspaper, *Daily Worker*. If our Fiji scholar is a shrewd man he will make allowances for what are obviously strongly opinionated accounts of world events but, even so, will his "history" of the twentieth century be likely to depict accurately the period we have lived through and know from experience? In the descriptions of factual happenings, perhaps, but hardly in the explanations advanced for the conduct of individuals, the policies of nations, or the general drift of world events. Suppose our Fiji historian decides to write a history of the New Deal in the United States and the only materials he can find are the files of the *Chicago Tribune* and the newspaper columns of Westbrook Pegler, two sources bitterly hostile to the Franklin Roosevelt adminstration. Who would call the result "objective"? Yet things like this must have happened many times in the past. That certain ancient writings have been preserved and others lost or destroyed is largely accidental.

Frequently, too, the destruction of source materials is deliberate. Governments, political parties, business organizations, and private persons sometimes destroy all or parts of their records. Secret service agencies, from the nature of their business, do not keep records of all their activities. Many letters or other documents reflecting discredit upon a public figure have been deliberately destroyed. For example, before the papers of Franklin Roosevelt and Lyndon Johnson were sent to their respective presidential libraries they were systematically "weeded." Why? To eliminate some entirely trivial stuff, no doubt. To avoid needlessly embarrassing certain foreign governments or statesmen, most likely. Perhaps to avoid harm to national security or the public interest by publicizing matters best left in obscurity. But it is also a safe bet that certain materials were discarded merely because their publication would have harmed the reputation of either of the two presidents. Needless to say, when only materials that show a person or an institution in a creditable light are permitted to survive the possibility of an accurate assessment becomes remote.

Richard Nixon's celebrated Watergate tapes raise several knotty questions. The reputation of the whole Nixon administration would have been much higher and the president himself almost certainly would not have been forced to resign his office if only he had destroyed the famous tapes, for without them the numerous accusations against him and his associates could not have been proven unequivocally. From this it can be argued, as most of the communications industry does argue habitually in this and other cases, that all the tapes should be publicized fully in order to protect the "public's right to know." At the same time, common decency and civilized usage used to prevent public dissemination of essentially private information about the private words and activities of public men. But of course information that is properly private and that to which the public has a right are often mixed together and are extremely difficult to separate. Sometimes, too, public men will insist upon the right to privacy when they really want to conceal something that ought to be public knowledge. What, then, should we think of a president's plea that his records must be kept secret because their revelation would be damaging to the national interest? Sometimes the plea is justified. There are plenty of things, especially in our age of the Cold War and nuclear weapons, that ought never to be publicized. But of course presidents can misuse this claim, and some indubitably have done so. Anxiety has been expressed that the Watergate tapes might be destroyed and thus we would never learn much that we might like to know about our rulers. Would this serve the national interest in the long run? Partisans of the Nixon administration, of course, have no doubts. Neither do the administration's enemies. Those who try to be detached find the question perplexing.

Deficiencies of Witnesses—The use of source materials is attended by many other difficulties related to this central one. Frequently we have little or no knowledge of the mental state of those who witnessed events or of those who compiled contemporary accounts of them. If the persons concerned were faulty in observation, or if they suffered from hallucinations, prejudices, or obsessions, these factors must have colored their testimony. Many people who composed the sources on which much history is based were incompetent, unscrupulous, partisan, careless, or simply not in a position to know much about what they wrote. Often such deficiencies can be detected from the tone or content of the writings themselves, but many times it is impossible to do more than guess about the reliability of a given account.

Forgeries—The historian's task has been complicated considerably by the deplorable zeal with which many men have forged documents. Literally thousands of letters and other documents attributed to famous persons like Luther, Erasmus, Marie Antoinette, Washington, Lincoln, Franklin, Jefferson, and Napoleon have been forged because they could be sold, because somebody was anxious to enhance or destroy a reputation, or just to improve a story that seemed drab. Innumerable colorful anecdotes about celebrities have been invented to serve the last purpose.

Unquestionably the most famous forgery in American history, if, indeed, it *is* a forgery, is the Kensington Stone, allegedly discovered in central Minnesota in 1898. The inscription on the stone describes a Norse expedition to that state in 1362. If genuine, it would strongly imply regular, even systematic, contact between Norse settlements in Greenland and the North American mainland throughout the late Middle Ages. Disputes about the authenticity of the stone have been endless. They revolve about such matters as whether or not its inscription is typical of fourteenth-century runic carvings, the age of the tree among whose roots the stone was allegedly discovered, whence came the party who supposedly left the stone behind, whether or not they could have got to Minnesota from their point of departure in the two weeks specified on the stone, what possible motive any Viking explorer of 1362 could have had to laboriously carve such a message, or, contrarily, what could possibly have motivated any one of a tiny handful of modern men with sufficient knowledge of medieval Norse runic writing to undertake a forgery. There are, of course, elaborate techniques that can be employed in an effort to detect forgeries but success cannot always be guaranteed. Most scholars who have studied the case in detail think the Kensington Stone spurious, but their verdict is not beyond question.

Sometimes source materials are altered in ways well short of forgery. Many an editor has softened or sharpened the wording of a passage, or deleted parts of a narrative, without notifying his readers. When Jared

Sparks edited the papers of George Washington, he improved the grammar and eliminated a few vulgarities in order to make our first president appear to better advantage. Innumerable writers have copied from others, passing on errors in the originals and adding new ones of their own. In modern times much that is purportedly written by public figures is actually produced by "ghost writers." To determine exactly what belongs to the mind and pen of each party is a nice problem.

Bias—Much history has been distorted by the prejudices of both the compilers of source material and professional historians. A comparison of present day Communist and non-Communist accounts of world affairs provides a good illustration. Knowledgeable people in the free world take it for granted that Communists never write what we regard as an objective account of anything political. Indeed they cannot for, in the first place, they put themselves in an intellectual strait jacket by their acceptance of Marxist dogma and, in the second, they must always defend and apologize for Communist dictatorships. Thus their writings are always a mixture of facts and propaganda, worth reading mostly to see what images Communist governments wish to project at the moment. Communist historians and publicists reply that theirs must necessarily be the only accurate, objective accounts. Since non-Marxists do not understand the laws of historical development (as revealed by Karl Marx and refined by Lenin, Stalin, and other disciples), non-Communist writings on any period, past or present, cannot be anything but superficial and full of errors.

Plots—Serious difficulties arise whenever a historian has reason to believe that a plot was a significant factor in a given situation. Plots are innumerable. Every coup d'etat that overthrows a government is the result of a plot. For every such scheme that succeeds there are usually several that fail and some that are abandoned by the plotters because they lose their nerve or circumstances change. These we sometimes learn about afterward when it becomes safe to make the revelations. Often we never learn of them because plotters are not in the habit of leaving filing cabinets full of records for historians to peruse at their leisure.

It is for reasons like this that our knowledge of unrest and plotting among slaves in the Old South will always remain incomplete and one-sided. That such unrest existed is certain. That it was widespread is likely. That it gave rise to considerable plotting that never went beyond talk is also likely. Yet actual slave uprisings were few and the plans of the rebels are poorly understood. The reasons are obvious. Most of the slaves were illiterate. Most slave rebels were killed either in the rebellions or soon after. All the records were kept by the slave owners, and it was they who controlled the public press and all the organs of local and state government. Perhaps most important, it seemed to them simply unbelievable, incredible, that black slaves, little better than animals, could be genuinely motivated to revolt because they loved personal liberty in the same sense as educated white men. To slaveowners, such leaders of slave uprisings as Nat Turner and Denmark Vesey were wild-eyes barbarians, madmen, malignant criminals. (The European nobility had viewed rebellious peasants and serfs in exactly the same way during a hundred rural uprisings spread over ten centuries.)

The extent to which U.S. political history has been affected by plots, real or imaginary, will never be known beyond question. There have always been people, some of them both sober and knowledgeable, who have believed that persons high in the U.S. government, quite possibly even members of the cabinet, were involved in the assassination of Abraham Lincoln. Great numbers of people of all sorts seem half-convinced that Lee Harvey Oswald was only the "trigger man" of a conspiratorial group that sought the death of President John Kennedy. In each instance certain considerations seem less than adequately explained by the "official" version of events, but in neither case is there any convincing evidence that the "official" version is wrong. Many Americans have long believed that President Franklin Roosevelt and others highly placed in Washington plotted in 1941 to lure the Japanese into an attack on Pearl Harbor in order to shock America into entering World War II. Again, not all official explanations to the contrary have been entirely convincing but, all things considered, it seems likely that mere wholesale incompetence of a sort all too common among governments was the reason the Japanese achieved complete surprise and did so much damage to the U.S. Pacific Fleet on December 7, 1941.[1]

---

1. Perhaps the student can better appreciate how much personal impressions, unspoken assumptions, and "gut feelings" shape the assessment of an episode like Pearl Harbor if he will consider the following. The two authors of this book are approximately the same age. We went to the same graduate school and have known each other for twenty-five years (in 1974). Both of us have taught history regularly for more than twenty years. Our views on most public questions are similar. We are about equally knowledgeable about the background of the attack on Pearl Harbor. Yet we have never agreed in our interpretation of that event. One of us is convinced that no plot existed; that the "warnings" of an impending Japanese attack, intercepted by U.S. military intelligence, seemed clear only *after* the event and could not have been clear before it because they were mixed with myriads of other information that admitted of many other interpretations; and that, in any event, if the president wanted to start a war with Japan it would have served his purpose quite as well to have led the Japanese into an ambush. The

Sometimes indications of a plot are stronger than in the foregoing examples. On February 15, 1898 the U.S. battleship *Maine* blew up in Havana harbor and provided the pretext for the outbreak of the Spanish-American War. American divers investigated *inside* the hull of the sunken ship. They reported that the explosion must have come from the outside. Spanish divers, who could examine only the *outside* of the hull, said the blast had come from the inside. Since the Spanish government was currently trying hard to keep on good terms with the United States the conclusion of the Spanish divers seems plausible, though of course it is possible that Cuban revolutionaries might have set off an explosion outside the ship in hope of bringing about American intervention in Cuban-Spanish differences. It is also possible that nobody deliberately did anything: that a vagrant mine happend to strike the *Maine* by accident. Whatever the case, the aftermath was interesting. In 1911 U.S. naval experts examined the *Maine* again. Their report was highly technical, but offered no judgment about how the ship came to blown up. Soon after, the *Maine* was towed out to a deep part of the Atlantic and sunk—this time for good!

If, and it is a big "if," plots figured importantly in any or all of the foregoing instances the plotters did not leave us records of their designs and activities. What is the historian to do in such cases? If he takes the narrow view—"no records, no history"—he will consciously tell less than the whole truth. If he decides to deal with the real or imagined plots in his narrative he must resort to speculation in the absence of tangible documentary evidence.

Innate Deficiencies in Various Kinds of Materials—Many types of historical raw materials and written history have weaknesses that are peculiar to their nature and that the historian must consider when using them.

---

immense destruction wrought by the Japanese indicates that their attack genuinely caught U.S. forces by surprise.

The other of us believes that the president and his advisers thought war with Japan both inevitable and imminent. They wished it to begin with some act of obvious Japanese agression in order to end isolationist opposton to war in the United States, and to unify the country. They devoted much thought to how to induce the Japanese to launch such an attack and successfully maneuvered them into the desired act of aggression. They miscalculated mostly by grievously underestimating the size of the Japanese force that would be involved and the amount of damage it would do.

When the lineaments of a puzzle are themselves not entirely clear, when crucial pieces are missing, or when the puzzle must be put together in the dark, what varied pictures emerge!

1. Biography—One such type of history is biography. Many people love biography and develop an interest in history largely as a result of reading biographies of famous persons. This is in no way surprising or disreputable. It is people, after all, who make history, and it is not possible to understand the past without understanding the psychology of the chief persons who have shaped it. Good biography is just as sound and just as valuable as any other type of historical writing.

Yet history is easily distorted by biographers. To begin with, why does one person write a biography of another? Usually because he has a keen interest in his subject and strong feelings about him. More often than not he will be an admirer of his subject, though many a biography has been written to expose what the author regarded as the infamy of another person. A trained and conscientious biographer will attempt to be fair and factual, but if one has sympathy for his subject it is deceptively easy to emphasize the subject's virtues and strengths, and to minimize or suppress his mistakes and weaknesses. Occasionally biographers become so infatuated with their subjects that they abandon their critical faculties altogether. Biographies written by persons of the same religious, ideological, or party affiliation as their subjects are not infrequently of this type. "Campaign biographies" of politicians are notoriously so. Sometimes a biography is "authorized"—the subject or, if he is deceased, his family, allows the biographer access to correspondence and other materials on condition that a veto is retained over statements the biographer may make in his book. In these ways many half-truths and distortions creep into history to be repeated in secondary works for decades or generations.

The same thing frequently happens when a biographer, or ordinary historian, journalist, or movie producer for that matter, sets out to "expose" or "debunk" some historical personage. From the deliberate or inadvertent slanders so inflicted the subject may recover only after many years, and then not entirely. Thaddeus Stevens was perhaps the most uncompromising hater of slavery in the U.S. Congress before and during the Civil War. At the war's end he opposed any concessions to slaveholders and insisted that the defeated Confederacy should be regarded as conquered territory rather than as several former states. He was a major influence in the formulation of the Reconstruction Acts so bitterly resented by the South. For two generations Stevens was generally vilified in print as an irresponsible extremist. In the movie "Birth of a Nation" (1915), he was depicted as a veritable ogre. Since the 1940s, however, Stevens's stock has risen, and so has that of the other Radical Republicans. In our time a strenuous effort is being made to overcome racial prejudice and all its fruits. Hence the congressmen who strove to compel white southerners to accord to Negroes voting rights and a greater measure of equality have begun to look more like statesmen than villains.

To many writers, not to speak of millions of ordinary voters, Herbert Hoover was long not only the author of the Great Depression of the 1930s but an unfeeling president who did little to aid its victims. No serious historian any longer entertains this view.

The "muckrakers" at the turn of the twentieth century, followed by platoons of historians and journalists for forty years afterward, lambasted such big city political "bosses" as Tweed, Pendergast, Hague, Curley, Kelly, Nash, and Cox as shameless corrupters of the democratic process, little better than thieves in office. Since World War II most of these old-style "bosses" have died, been overthrown, or have otherwise vanished. Are the cities they once ruled better off? Some are, but others are even more deeply mired in vice, crime, violence, dirt, and decrepitude than they used to be—and are plagued by perpetual budgetary deficits in the bargain. This condition has caused the old "bosses" to be viewed with a little more respect in recent written history. One now reads that at least the "bosses" got the streets paved and kept them a good deal safer than their successors have done; that they provided floods of European immigrants with jobs and help in adjusting to American life; and that they ruled rapidly growing cities with commendable humanity. To be sure, they exacted a price: the votes of the immigrants whom they aided. Moreover, considerable public money stuck to the hands of the "bosses" and their underlings. But even now it still sticks to the hands of a lot of their outwardly more virtuous successors!

Finally, it is easy for biography to distort history for a reason that has nothing to do with the frailities of biographers. It is in the nature of a biography to make its subject everywhere the center of things: to describe every idea, event, and development in terms of its relationship to the principal figure in the book. Real life is just not like this.

2. Memoirs—Memoirs are a valuable source of history because they are usually written by statesmen, soldiers, or other public figures who have had a good deal to do with making history. Nonetheless, they must be used with caution, for memoirists want to portray their ideas, deeds, and careers in the best possible light. Moreover, memoirs are normally written in old age, many years after the events they describe. If the author has kept a diary or careful notes throughout his life he may be able to describe quite accruately his ideas and feelings decades earlier. If he has not, if at the age of sixty, seventy, or eighty he has to rely on his memory to describe events and thoughts when he was twenty, thirty, or forty, the pitfalls are obvious. Let the reader ask himself, "How many conversations of five years ago, one year ago, one month ago, can *I* recall accurately? How exactly can *I* reconstruct my state of mind with regard to this or that matter of four or five years ago?"

3. Diplomatic Correspondence—One of the best sources for political history is diplomatic correspondence. But it is a two-edged sword. The public statements of diplomats are notoriously full of lies, half-truths, and sentiments which the diplomat or his government may wish to get into public circulation. Private dispatches, intended only for the eyes of political superiors, often tell quite a different story. Official diplomatic correspondence is easily misinterpreted too. It is full of conventional expressions which do not mean what they appear to mean. Worse, the conventions change from time to time. This is not much of a problem in our time because ideological hostility is now so fierce and undisguised—and the prospect of war has grown so appalling—that heads of state often exchange insults in their spoken and written communications without fear of provoking anything worse than a similar barrage of words from the enemy state. This was not the case in times past. In the nineteenth century a note sent from one foreign office to another might contain some such phrase as "His Majesty's government must reserve the right to deal with this matter as later circumstances indicate." The real meaning of such a seemingly innocuous statement was that the second government was being warned that the situation could lead to war.

This general state of affairs is, of course, well known to scholars who work in the field of political and diplomatic history, and suitable allowances are made, but it is still easy for those writing long after the event and perhaps not completely familiar with the conventions of an age to misinterpret.

4. Propaganda—Governments, organizations, and private individuals have always striven to present a favorable picture of themselves to the world. But the problems posed by this for the writer and reader of history were incomparably smaller before the age of general literacy, mass circulation newspapers and magazines, radio, and television. Most propaganda is not harmful or packed with lies, as is sometimes mistakenly thought though of course it may be so. It is, however, always an organized effort to influence public opinion in some way. It rarely attempts to tell the whole truth about anything. Rather, it strives to leave a certain impression in the mind of the reader or listener.

The course of modern history has been affected strongly by propaganda of various types. British and American propaganda, centered about President Woodrow Wilson's "Fourteen Points" and his proposed League of Nations, certainly hastened the Allied victory over Germany and Austria-Hungary in World War I. Less happily, it also gave rise to immoderate expectations of a finer and more peaceful world afterward—expectations that proved illusory and bedeviled international politics for a generation.

In the 1930s Adolf Hitler cleverly employed counterpropaganda, some of which emphasized the unfulfilled promises embodied in the Fourteen Points, to gain the support of most of the German people and to weaken the wills of neighboring nations to resist Nazi agression. During World War II when the United States and the USSR were allied against Nazi Germany much American propaganda played down the deep and permanent differences between American and Russian wartime objectives. We were treated to such puerilities as "the U.S.A. is a political democracy, but the USSR is an economic democracy." Stalin was depicted as a basically friendly, good-natured fellow with whom we should have little trouble after the war. Thus some existing illusions about the Russian state and Russian policies were strengthened, and new ones were created. These illusions did not begin to fade among the majority of our people until 1947. Some of them have never been entirely destroyed.

In American domestic politics the propaganda effort of the Democrats to depict the Republicans as the party of big business, depressions, and callous disregard for the "little man" enjoyed considerable success for a generation after 1932, as election results showed. A Republican propaganda effort to link the Democrats with Communism had a briefer and more limited success in the decade after World War II.

More narrowly, it is notorious that the announcements of White House press secretaries need to be taken with the proverbial grain of salt. It is not that the secretaries are liars and scoundrels (worse men than any of us), but that their function is rather more than merely to disseminate information. They are also concerned to present the ideas, plans, and purposes of their employers as favorably as possible and to explain governmental deeds in a fashion that will reflect credit on the president. (Of course businesses, labor organizations, educational groups, and innumerable wealthy or prominent private citizens employ press agents for the same purpose.)

The Historian's Function—Much historical writing needs to be read criticallv merely because past chroniclers and historians had a different view of their function than do their modern counterparts. A modern historian trained in a reputable graduate school tries to put into his work "the facts, the whole facts, and nothing but the facts"—nothing further. that is, than "the most reasonable interpretation of the facts." Like all goals, this one is never attained completely, for historians are as fallible as other men. Nonetheless, most contemporary historical writing is as accurate and impartial as can reasonably be expected.

This was not always true in times past; not because our ancestors were less honorable or possessed feebler intellects than we but because they had a different view of the historian's task. The chief concern of the writer of history then was to amuse his readers by telling a lively story or to edify them by pointing lessons in his works. Thus the Reverend Mason Locke Weems, biographer of Washington, saw nothing unfitting in inventing the story of the youthful George Washington and the cherry tree because he could thereby simultaneously emphasize the nobility of Washington's character and impress upon children the desirability of being truthful.

Similarly, such American colonial writers as John Winthrop in his *History of the Massachusetts Bay Colony* and William Bradford in his *History of the Plymouth Plantation* saw the tribulations of the early English colonists as a test imposed upon them by God and as divine punishment for their sins. The eventual triumph of the colonists over great obstacles they attributed to Providence: it was God's reward bestowed on those who had been faithful to Him. In doing this Winthrop and Bradford were not being consciously fanciful, much less dishonest. It simply did not occur to them that the proper function of a writer of history was merely to record and explain what happened. They took it for granted that it was also their business to teach, to edify, to persuade men to live better lives and to lead them to God by displaying before them evidences of divine favor and chastisement.

Much history has been written to serve national purposes. The famous Black Legend about Spain is a case in point. The Black Legend originated partly in the religious and political turmoil of sixteenth-century Europe. From this strife Spain emerged steadfastly Catholic while England became largely Protestant. The two countries became both political and religious enemies. The Black Legend also derived somewhat from the writings of the sixteenth-century Spanish missionary Las Casas who denounced in unmeasured terms the treatment his countrymen accorded to the Indians in the New World. As a result there developed in British, and later in American, historical writing a stereotype of Spaniards as uniquely cruel, ignorant, superstitious, and bigoted. Not surprisingly, such unpromising people were shiftless and unprogressive and governed both themselves and their colonies badly. Hence it could be argued by American expansionists of the nineteenth and twentieth centuries that it was not only to our national advantage to sequester such Spanish territories as Florida, Cuba, and the Philippines and such Mexican (Spanish-Indian) territories as Texas, New Mexico, and California, but that we had something close to a duty to the people languishing under such tyranny to free them and bring them the blessings of American institutions and habits. Only in the twentieth century when Herbert E. Bolton began the study of Spanish influence in California were a lot of old anti-Spanish myths broken down and American interpretations of Spanish-American colonial history substantially revised.

In our own time there are few historians who still think history ought to be a branch of literature. Unhappily, there are many who are so infatuated with one or another of the secular ideologies that currently poison our planet that their "histories" are a hopeless mixture of "facts" and special pleading for some cause. A few of these visionary dogmatists are obsessed with notions about international Jewish conspiracies. A greater number see some dread and seemingly omnipotent entity which they call "communism" behind everything from high prices to bad weather. Still others ascribe all such evils to "big business" or the "military-industrial complex." Among the many tribes of historians-as-evangelists the most prominent, influential, and currently fashionable are the new leftists. Mostly neo-Marxists, they complain that "objective" history really shores up the unworthy status quo. They seek openly to create a "usable past," that is, to employ history as a tool to effect political and social changes that they deem desirable. Given this avowed objective, it is hardly surprising that they oversimplify complex issues and read the concerns of the present back into the past. In their writings one seldom discovers anything admirable about American society or the purposes of our governments. Rarely does one read of an international dispute anywhere in the world in which American influence was not exercised in some malign fashion. All such person, whether new leftists or ideologues of other dispensations, are missionaries and propagandists quite as much as historians. They see history primarily as a storehouse of evidence from which to extract whatever happens to serve the needs of the particular ideology that gives meaning to their personal lives.

History is also viewed differently by people of different cultures. American Indians, for instance, have never attached great importance to precise factual accuracy in historical narration. It has always seemed to them that the major consideration when passing on tribal lore or providing information about past events was to make sure that the Indian ideal was presented convincingly, to see that the account reflected the tribal tradition, or to describe an episode with sufficient skill and embellishment that it would be long and deservedly remembered. As with the ecclesiastical writers Winthrop and Bradford, this was not conscious dishonesty at all: merely a conception of the historian's function which is quite different from our own.

Historians Create History—In a way, historians do not merely record history: they *make* it as well, for the way they write about the past influences the way their readers think about the future. Throughout the 1930s and early 1940s we were told in innumerable books that one of the principal reasons the League of Nations had not been effective was because the United States had refused to join it. The nation as a whole became so convinced of this that there was little popular opposition to our entry into the United Nations in 1945. The Senate voted overwhelmingly for our entry, the newly formed UN established its headquarters in New York, and our country has always borne, with little complaint, a large share of the financial upkeep of the UN. Since the UN has been little more effective than was the old League of Nations, American membership or lack of it could hardly have been crucial to either organization. Nonetheless, the writings of historians and publicists had markedly changed American public opinion on the subject from 1920 to 1945.

Nearly a century ago it was generally concluded that Reconstruction policy after the Civil War had been a failure. For two generations most historians accepted this without question and wrote it in their books. They added that the experience showed the impossibility of altering race relationships in the South by legal devices. Consequently, until the late 1940s and 1950s no serious attempt was made by the federal government to promote a greater measure of racial equality.

Mechanical Errors–History composed from written documents may sometimes be distorted by unavoidable human or mechanical errors. Documents relating to ancient and medieval history are extremely scarce. In many cases original documents have long since been lost or destroyed. All that is left are copies and copies of copies. Even if the originals still exist they are usually locked in rarebook rooms of museums and libraries, very likely on a different continent. Thus what the historian in these fields normally uses are copies and copies of translations. The possibilities of errors creeping in are endless. For centuries medieval monks copied entire books, but they were never able to reproduce them exactly like the originals in every minute detail. It is easy to mistake words, to skip lines, to be unable to decipher the handwriting of the original, to "guess at" what it was likely to have been, and so on. By the time this has been done several times by different persons a great many errors have usually crept in.

More serious are changes of meaning introduced by translations. Every language has shades of meaning impossible to duplicate exactly in other languages. Oftentimes even the most able and conscientious translator can only approximate the meaning of the original. In the historic past many translators gravely altered meanings in materials they handled. Suppose a given document was written originally in Hebrew. Then it was translated into Greek, the Greek translation was then rendered into Aramaic, and the Aramaic version was then translated into Latin. In each case the translation was done by a different unknown person. In the process everything but the final Latin version was lost. Who can doubt that it was probably different in many particulars from the original Hebrew?

Other Sources of Information—Not all historical knowledge comes from written records. A great deal can be reconstructed from monuments, inscriptions, ruins, coins, seals, and other artifacts. From them the historian not only secures much information about the past but he is better able to assess the meaning and worth of written records. Studies of this sort, however, are no magical remedy for the defects of documents, for these materials become meaningful only after much "interpreting" by archaeologists, anthropologists, experts on coins, and students of ancient or rare languages. Their interpretations, in turn, often change as more information becomes available.

The Historian's Bias—Lastly, perfect certitude in history is impossible to achieve because even the most carefully trained and conscientious historian is still moved by his personal feelings. Nothing indicates more clearly the dissimilarity of history and science than the fact that the historian has an *attitude* toward his subject matter while the natural scientist does not. Every historian has political, social, national, religious, and economic beliefs. He admires some human traits and human types, and he thinks others despicable. He regards some historical developments as constructive and praiseworthy, and others the reverse. These preferences are bound to color both his selection of materials (for he cannot include everything) and the use he makes of them. A mathematician, by contrast, does not admire plus signs and detest minus signs. A physicist does not feed kindly toward velocity but averse to acceleration.

A distinguished English historian, Herbert Butterfield, refers to the "magnet in men's minds" that leads them to draw out of raw historical materials just those facts and examples that fit the shape of the story as they conceived it beforehand; that confirm all their prejudices; that solidify long-accepted views; that illuminate maxims already in their minds. The same predilection is, of course, close to universal among the general public. A lifelong Republican and an admirer of Franklin D. Roosevelt each read an academic history of the New Deal. Does each put down the book with the feeling that he has gained a new appreciation of the reasonableness of the other's position? Occasionally, yes, but much more often each merely grows more deeply convinced of the iniquity of the other's views and learns a few new arguments to support his own.

Consider the book you are now reading. If it had been written by someone else it would still have been the same sort of book and its message would have been similar, but it certainly would have been different in many particulars. Other authors would have chosen different examples to make some of its points; parts of it probably would have been left out entirely; other parts would have been expanded; some things which are not in this book at all would have been added; and some matters discussed here would have been interpreted differently. So it is with all history. It has been well said that "the only completely unbiased historian is . . . the Recording Angel: and doubtless he has convictions which to Satan . . . would seem prejudices."[2]

This is not a plea for no interpretation in the writing of history. That is absurd, impossible. History has to be interpreted to have any meaning. The difference, in practice, is not between an interpretation or philosophy of history and the absence of one, but between a sensible philosophy and a ridiculous or pernicious one. The thing for the student to remember is that everybody has one of *some* kind, be it sensible or not.

What Can We Know?—By now the reader is probably disconsolate, disgusted, thoroughly confused, or all three. He may well think that history is such a hopeless jumble of uncertainties and subjective judgments that the late Henry Ford was right when he once declared, "History is bunk." He should take heart. Things are not as bad as they seem. All of the foregoing discussion is designed to demonstrate one truth: that from the nature of man and the nature of the materials with which he has to deal, the historian cannot achieve certitude of the type the mathematician possesses when he says that the area of a circle equals πr^2 or that the chemist has when he says that hydrogen and oxygen when mixed under the right conditions in the proportion of two to one will yield water. It does not mean that the historian cannot achieve the degree of certitude that all of us accept without question every day of our lives.

Skepticism has its place but it must be guided by common sense. In everyday life we all take for granted most things we read or are told by others. How else could we live? How could chemistry, medicine, physics, astronomy, or any other science ever progress if each scientist rigorously refused to accept any information reported to him by his fellows unless he could personally verify it by experiment? It is equally reasonable to believe what we read about the past provided we do not let our critical faculty go to sleep in the process. Think for a moment of Abraham Lincoln. He is commonly held to have been a

---

2. Allen Nevins, *The Gateway to History* (New York: Heath, 1937), pp. 41–42.

great American president. Is a man foolish and credulous because he believes this without having personally investigated every aspect of Lincoln's personal life and public career? Suppose everyone acted on the principle of refusing assent to any proposition not personally investigated? The world would be a bedlam. Everything would collapse while we feverishly pursued absolute certitude.

There is a vast difference between skepticism about facts and about their interpretation. What sane man doubts the existence of England, even though he has not been there personally and even though he may entertain erroneous ideas about the place? Who doubts that George Washington existed, commanded the Colonial army in the American Revolution, crossed the Delaware, and was president? Though we were not there ourselves innumerable men who were have testified to the truth of these statements and a vast array of written materials concerning them survive. Only a lunatic would disregard it.

Where skepticism is legitimate is not when one reads of Washington crossing the Delaware but when he reads that on some particular occasion Washington was thinking this, planning that, estimating the possibility of something else, or convinced of this or that. Here an assertion can be *probable* but nothing more. Many human attitudes are generally uniform and predictable merely because of the sameness of human nature. Parents generally love and protect their children. A man will usually defend his possessions with tenacity and vigor. A person of recognized integrity normally does not commit shocking crimes. A man commonly prefers members of his own tribe, race, party, or religion to others. Most men are moved to some degree by ambition, vanity, and love of power. The historian knows all this, and if he is familiar with Washington's character he may *reasonably infer* that Washington was thinking or planning this or that on the occasion. But he cannot *know beyond question,* for what person understands completely all *his own* thoughts and motives for contemplating or undertaking a certain action? How much less certain must he be about those of another person? How much less certain still about those of someone long since dead? Nobody can ever get inside the mind of another. Thus judgments about the ideas, plans, and intentions of historical figures are only inferences; accurate ones most of the time, no doubt, but never beyond question.

History is full of instances where the *deeds* of men are clear but their *motives* are not. There is no dispute about the facts of Alexander the Great's conquests but there are two theories about Alexander the man. The first is that he was a genius who set out, consciously and deliberately, to spread Greek civilization over the then (fourth century B.C.) known world. The second is that he was a madman (albeit one with military gifts), an egomaniac who thought only of conquest. According to the second view, the spread of Greek civilization was an incidental by-product of the conquests. Most of the relatively little that we know about Alexander supports the first interpretation but one can never be certain because it will never be possible to get inside the mind of Alexander and find out what he thought and planned.

A more complex case from American history is that of the "conspiracy" of Aaron Burr. Following the Louisiana Purchase of 1803 the political situation in the lower Mississippi Valley was fluid. The boundaries of the newly acquired territory were vague, and there was much dispute about them with the Spaniards who were settled in West Florida. Hostile Indians from Florida complicated matters further by regularly raiding American frontier settlements. In and around New Orleans there was much discontent with the governor, a frontier politician named Claiborne, who had been sent from Washington. Worse, the commander of the American troops in Louisiana was James Wilkinson, a general of dubious character and background who had once been in Spanish pay and who was suspected of being so again. Into this volatile situation came Aaron Burr in 1805. In the previous year Burr, then vice-president, had planned to desert the Republican party, go over to the Federalists, and with Federalist backing run for governor of New York. If elected, he was then to lead New York and New England out of the Union. Alexander Hamilton had learned of the plot, exposed it, been challenged to a duel by Burr and, tragically, had been killed in the duel.

Now, Burr, discredited in the East, went out to the Mississippi Valley and spoke freely of having come west to resume his political career in a new locale. To the British minister, he was more specific. He proposed to raise a private army of one thousand men in Ohio, and float them on flatboats down the Ohio and Mississippi rivers to New Orleans. There, with the backing of the British fleet and the aid of British money, he would persuade the Louisiana legislature to declare its independence from the United States. With British support, Burr would then become the ruler of an independent state bordering on the United States, Mexico, and the Spanish holdings in West Florida. He also outlined a similar scheme to the Spanish minister, but omitted the portions that would have required British aid. To various Americans on the frontier he hinted at plans for the creation of a separate nation, the Mississippi Valley Confederacy, to be formed from either the territories of Spain, or the United States, or both. To others he spoke expansively of American attacks on Vera Cruz or Mexico City. Still others were led to believe that he wanted to set up some sort of southwestern buffer state against the Spanish in Mexico.

Whatever his ultimate intentions, Burr took in General Wilkinson as a partner-of-sorts. Eventually, in November 1806 a small expedition set off in river boats down the Ohio. Soon after, Wilkinson, perhaps from fear of the consequences of being exposed as an accomplice in Burr's designs, denounced Burr as a traitor to his (Wilkinson's) father-in-law, President Jefferson. Burr tried to flee the country, but was caught. He was then tried for treason by none other than Chief Justice John Marshall, though Marshall was acting in his other capacity as federal district judge in Virginia. Burr was acquitted on the technicality that there were insufficient witnesses to an *overt* act of treason *in Virginia*. The openness with which Burr had spoken of his many and often contradictory projects and the low reputation of Wilkinson for either integrity or truthfulness have caused a few scholars to doubt that Burr really had any treasonable plans. In any case, the point is that while much is known about Burr's *words* and *activities* west of the Appalachians in 1805–06, nobody knows what his precise *intentions* were. It is extremely unlikely that anyone ever will know, for Burr carefully avoided putting anything in writing that would illuminate his activities in these years.

While deficiencies in source materials present obstacles to the searcher for truth, these are not insurmountable. Many writers in times past may have been uncritical by modern standards, but where it has been possible to check their credibility from other sources the great majority of them have been found to be trustworthy in essentials if not always in details. This is often the case even with myths and legends. For centuries the Homeric account of the Trojan War was thought to be mythical, but in the nineteenth century, archaeological excavations by Schliemann and others established the existence of Troy and the substantial accuracy of the tale related in Homer's *Iliad*. Ought we to be surprised? Not really for, after all, people normally tell the truth as they see it, particularly when they have no motive for not doing so. When ancient writers were biased or had some ulterior motive, this is often obvious from the tone of their writings. Anyway, what modern writer is entirely free from these faults? We do not refuse to believe things written by contemporaries merely because we happen to know that not every one of them is simultaneously deeply learned, wholly impartial, and infallibly correct in his judgments. Suppose five serious but quite different American magazines, *New Republic, National Review, Ebony, Ramparts,* and *U.S. News and World Report*, print articles on some controversial subject. The accounts and judgments will be different in many ways, perhaps drastically different in some, but anyone familiar with the magazines will expect this and make allowances for it and will not think any of the writers liars, fools, or charlatans. It is the same when reading history. A knowledge of the reputation, background, and affiliations of the historian or the author of source material is most enlightening, and the student ought to acquire it if he can. Nonetheless, whatever it might be it does not *in itself* invalidate the person's statements or judgments. If we know that the author of a history of the United State Steel Corporation was hired by the company to write the book we will read it more warily than if we lacked this information but it does not follow that everything in the book will be false or willfully distorted.

The Rewriting of History—History is constantly being rewritten. Does this prove that we do not know much about the past? No. History is rewritten for three basic reasons: (1) because new information becomes available, (2) to weed out inaccurate, misleading, biased, or false statements or conclusions, and (3) because men's intellectual interests change and new problems arise which provide new views of the past.

1. New Information—History must be rewritten frequently and its interpretation changed because new knowledge becomes available. The discovery of the Rosetta Stone by Champollion in 1799 made it possible to decipher Egyptian hieroglyphics and thereby to add vastly to our knowledge of ancient Egypt. The rewriting of that history followed. It has long been known that a well-developed and thriving civilization existed on the island of Crete before 1000 B.C. Not until 1952–53, however, was anyone able to decipher the Cretan language. Even then, only a portion of it (Linear B script) was successfully fathomed. Since Linear B is closely related to early Greek it seems beyond question that the Mycenaen (later) period of Cretan history was an age of considerable Cretan influence on early Greek development. The rest of the Cretan language (Linear A script) has not been deciphered. Scholars are unsure of its origin, doubtful that it is even related to Greek, and agreed only that it was the form of writing used during the Minoan (early) period of Cretan history. Altogether, unraveling the puzzle of Linear B while Linear A remains a mystery has given rise to the formulation of a number of interesting hypotheses and produced much scholarly disputation, but it has not added much to our hard factual knowledge of this portion of ancient history. When and if Linear A is deciphered, almost certainly much of the history of ancient Greece will have to be rewritten. The Dead Sea Scrolls discovered in Palestine since World War II have caused the writing of scores of books and articles, and some spirited controversies among scholars about problems related to the early history of Christianity.

The details, though seldom the main lines, of diplomatic history have to be altered from time to time since governments generally refuse to make diplomatic records available until many years after the events with which they are concerned. Similarly, statesmen ordinarily write their memoirs in old age, long after the important events in which they played a part. The fact that historical knowledge is incomplete does not mean, however, that it is not now reasonably sure. The governments of Russia, Great Britain, and the United States will probably not release all their records relating to World War II for some time yet, but nobody claims on this account that our knowledge of the causes, course, and results of that conflict is not substantially correct. It is merely incomplete.

Sometimes "incomplete" is apt to last forever. While we know in a general sense what went on in the deliberations of the Continental Congress during the American Revolution (1774–83), all those discussions were secret and, apparently, nobody took notes. Thus, barring such a wholly unexpected development as the discovery of such notes hidden away somewhere for two centuries, we know all we are ever going to about the Continental Congress. By contrast, James Madison kept careful notes on the debates of the Constitutional Convention of 1787. Had he not done so we would know much less about these momentous deliberations, since no official minutes were kept.

Are such conditions peculiar to history? Not at all. They exist in every field of study. The ideas and discoveries of Newton, Planck, Einstein, and others have successively shaken the basic concepts of physics far more radically than has ever been the case with the writing of history. Three physics textbooks, written in 1880, 1920, and 1960, would bear small resemblance to one another. Yet nobody says it is useless to study physics. The most fundamental idea in ancient and medieval astronomy, that the earth is the center of the universe and the other heavenly bodies revolve around it, was discarded in the sixteenth and seventeenth centuries, but this did not cause men to abandon the study of astronomy. We do not refuse to go to a doctor when sick merely because we know that in the past many medical ideas and practices were injurious or absurd. Medical knowledge even now is extremely imperfect but this does not prevent doctors from curing many ills and trying to remedy others.

In the search for knowledge complete victory will never be achieved. Yet added knowledge in any field clarifies situations that were formerly vague, corrects errors, and provides the basis for new advances. The fact that not everything is known about history or that not all historians agree about the meaning of what is known is no argument for refusing to study history or saying that one theory is as good as the next. It is an argument for studying more, and more carefully, and trying to come as close to the truth as possible.

2. Correction of Errors—Much history is rewritten to correct inaccuracies or biases in past accounts. This is a pressing necessity when dealing with highly controversial episodes in the past: revolutions, civil wars, religious upheavals, or sweeping economic and social changes. The first books on the American Civil War attempted to prove that one side or the other was completely at fault. Those published in the North alleged that the war had been caused by wicked slaveholders and traitorous secessionists who had conspired to destroy the Union. Southern authors retorted defiantly that the North had repeatedly violated the Constitution by prohibiting slavery in western territories, failing to enforce the Fugitive Slave Law, and imposing tariffs against the will of the South. It was this sustained policy, they said, capped by the words and deeds of abolitionist fanatics, that had caused the war.[3] These pseudoscholarly tirades gradually gave way to a consensus that the war had been primarily about slavery. A decade or two later it was seen as essentially a struggle between the principles of federal centralization and states' rights. This was, in turn, superseded by claims that the war had been basically an economic struggle between the industrial North and the agrarian South or that the cultural and intellectual differences between the two sections of the country had been the crucial factor. By the 1930s, influenced by the general disillusionment with all wars that developed in the aftermath of World War I, scholars were proclaiming that the Civil War had come because a generation of blunderers had allowed their emotions to overcome their reason and so had failed to effect a rational compromise of the issues that had divided the nation in the 1850s. With the rise of the civil rights movement since World War II the importance of slavery has received renewed emphasis. As a by-product, the reputation of the abolitionists has soared. Where previous generations viewed them as extravagant, irresponsible agitators, they are now seen as righteously indignant humanitarians whose historic mission was to stir the consciences of men.

The treatment of American big business by historians has shown a similar wide variation in tone. At the turn of the twentieth century there appeared an array of writers whom Theodore Roosevelt called "muckrakers." They frequently lambasted such nineteenth-century captains of industry and finance as John D. Rockefeller, Andrew Carnegie, Jim Fisk, Jay Gould, E. H. Harriman, Daniel Drew, Leland Stanford, and C. P. Huntington. These men, said the muckrakers, were "robber barons"—rapacious plunderers of natural resources, unprincipled

---

3. The difficulty involved in attempting a judicious assessment of a situation about which feeling is still intense is illustrated by the title of one of the innumerable books that have appeared on the Civil War: *An Impartial History of the Civil War from the Southern Point of View.*

exploiters of labor, deceitful masters of stock market manipulation, and a malign influence on government from county seats to Washington D.C. Grim humor abounded: for example, "The Standard Oil Company did everything to the Pennsylvania state legislature except refine it." With the onset of the Great Depression of the 1930s this critical attitude became even more intense, for big business now appeared not only heartless and menacing but incompetent as well.

After World War II, however, many historians began to see things in a different light. During that fearful struggle, when the very existence of democracy seemed at stake, it was evident that eventual Allied victory owed much to the phenomenal productivity of American industry. It was also clear that the vaunted American standard of living derived from the same source. Henceforth, accounts of the rise of American industry laid greater stress on growth and productivity, less on its social cost. More attention was paid to the abilities and achievements of industrial titans, less to their "robber-baron" features. At about the same time some major corporations began to make their records available to historians. This enabled such scholars as Allan Nevins, Edward C. Kirkland, and Hal Bridges to acquire a better understanding of the complex problems of industrial management, finance, and marketing than were possessed by such muckrakers as Ida Tarbell and Henry Demarest Lloyd. Soon those who were not dogmatically anticapitalist were acknowledging that many of the achievements of the so-called robber barons had been due more to business acumen than to cutthroat practices. They also began to draw the sort of distinctions competent historians have always drawn between worthy and unworthy members of other human classes or occupational groups. To call such characters as Jay Gould and Jim Fisk "robber barons" still seems fair enough. Not so figures like Rockefeller, Carnegie, and Harriman. Hard-boiled businessmen they were, to be sure, but their importance in history is clearly as industrial pioneers and builders, not speculators and stock-market buccaneers.

What happens in cases like these is that a truer perspective emerges as a controversial episode recedes into the past. At first everyone who has an interest to serve writes his version of it. Then detailed research is undertaken by generations of scholars increasingly removed from the happenings. All the opinionated versions are compared. The obvious errors, biases, and lies are gradually weeded out. In the meantime public tempers moderate. Then the rewriting begins. After a couple of generations—or centuries—a fairer and better balanced account emerges.

3. *Changing Interests*—Changing circumstances cause variations in intellectual interests. These, in turn, color the writing of history. It is not that the facts change but that our interest in them changes and the

vantage point from which we view them changes. New problems arise in the present which cause us to become interested in past people and episodes that have not attracted our attention heretofore. Since not *all* facts can ever be put in any one book or in any 1 million books, what *is* put in reflects what any given generation thinks is significant. Our ancestors used to think that the doings of kings and governments were the most important public events. Consequently, history used to be mostly "past politics." Eighteenth- and nineteenth-century European writers, however, broadened its scope. Voltaire wrote history primarily in terms of ideas. Montesquieu, and later Buckle, wove much information about climate and geography into their histories. Karl Marx and innumerable disciples emphasized economic factors.

Similar changes have been equally evident on our side of the Atlantic. In the nineteenth century H. H. Bancroft's histories, largely political in substance, emphasized the theme of the inevitable expansion and triumph of American democracy, a message remarkably attuned to the spirit of "Manifest Destiny" then popular in the United States. In the 1890s the last free land of any value in the United States was settled. At almost exactly the same time the works of Frederick Jackson Turner began to appear. Turner's key idea was the "frontier thesis," the contention that from colonial times to the then-present, the most important fact in our history had been the existence of an abundance of land to be had virtually for the taking. This had meant that in settled regions social discontent had never assumed crucial dimensions because dissatisfied people could simply pack up, go West, and take up a new life. Most important, Turner thought that "free land made free men": that is to say that the long existence of the frontier and the conditions of life on it had gradually transformed the American national character. On the frontier everyone started out even: that is, democratically. Titles, formal learning, culture, even to some degree material wealth, were of little practical use. Those who survived and throve where change was rapid, work was hard, movement was easy and common, and where traditions were nonexistent were the brave, hardy, resourceful, and self-reliant. Such conditions had produced people who prized personal freedom and were well qualified to look after themselves. This whole conception of our history attracted much attention again in the 1930s when the whole nation was paralyzed by the depression and contained millions of discontented people but no longer had a frontier as a "safety valve."

Early in the twentieth century Charles A. Beard drew attention to economic factors as shapers of our history, particularly during the period of the framing of the Constitution. The rapid expansion of cities and the worsening of every sort of problem connected with them has led historians since 1945 to pay more attention to their role in the evolution of our nation. Courses in urban history now appear in colleges throughout the land.

Recently, the rise of the Women's Liberation movements has directed attention to such early feminists as Fanny Wright, Elizabeth Cady Stanton, Susan B. Anthony, the Grimke sisters, and Sojourner Truth. In times past slavery as an institution received much notice in histories of the United States because it was recognized as one of the major causes of the Civil War. *Individual* Negroes and specifically Negro feelings, interests, and problems, by contrast, were scarcely mentioned. With the rapid development of "black consciousness," however, much more notice is now paid to such black figures from our past as Frederick Douglass, Nat Turner, Benjamin Banneker, Booker T. Washington, Marcus Garvey, Harriett Tubman, Denmark Vesey, and W. E. B. DuBois and to such subjects as the nature of the slave trade, early efforts at black liberation, slavery in cities, post—Civil War race riots in northern cities, and the relationship of black people to the labor movement in both the North and the South. Similarly, a national bad conscience about the internment of Japanese-American civilians during World War II has provoked considerable scholarly writing about this particular group and the wrongs done to them. A new self-consciousness has developed among American Indians in the 1960s and 1970s too. It has assumed such forms as demands for the adjustment of nineteenth-century treaties, the revival of Indian claims to old hunting and fishing rights, and even, in 1973, a "second seige" of Wounded Knee, South Dakota. Consequently, there is now more serious writing about Indian history and culture than in generations past. The Mexican-Americans (Chicanos) of the Southwest have been stirred by the same "winds of change" and are now accorded more official attention as a distinct category of humanity than heretofore. It is not that Frederick Douglass, Nat Turner, Fanny Wright, Indians, Chicanos, or the Nisei are any different, or any more or less *intrinsically* important than they ever were: it is merely that we have become more interested in them and so they seem more important to us.

Partly in emulation of the growth of black consciousness and Indian consciousness, partly in reaction against it, many second and third generation Europeans have developed a heightened interest in their homelands and the culture of their ancestors. Programs and courses in "ethnic studies" have begun to proliferate in colleges. Whereas a genera-tion ago it was a standard U.S. ideal to persuade all citizens to think of themselves as wholly "American," now it is fashionable to be a member of a "minority" of some sort and to take a certain ostentatious pride in one's racial or national lineage. History books reflect the change in the public mood by paying more attention to the pedigrees of the persons who appear in their pages.

Changes in the flavor of written history have followed changes in other aspects of our national life too. The rising crime rate in the United States and the omnipresence of urban violence in recent decades have produced an outpouring of historical literature on violence in earlier periods of American history. Widespread opposition to the Vietnam War has stimulated reexamination of opposition to earlier wars and of citizens' opposition to government generally. The passing of J. Edgar Hoover, for half a century the undisputed ruler of the FBI, was followed by the public ventilation of much information about FBI activities that had not been widely known before. The public image of the FBI was darkened appreciably as a result.

The spread of democratic ideas and institutions since 1776 has led to a widespread interest in tracing democratic practices and experiments back into the past. Predictably, some zealots have "gone overboard," in this case professing to discover the germs of modern British and American governmental practices among the Germanic tribesmen of the first centuries A.D. In the late 1920s and 1930s there was a pronounced tendency to interpret history in terms of economic changes and rivalries, a condition which derived in considerable measure from the impression made by the Communist experiment in Russia and the worldwide depression of the early 1930s.

The conviction has grown rapidly in recent decades that the Middle Ages were much more important than used to be thought and that the modern world has grown more directly out of them than out of Greek and Roman antiquity. One reason (among many) for this is that scholars have shown that American Puritanism, so fundamental in the formation of our national character, was firmly rooted, intellectually, culturally, and psychologically, in late medieval Europe, particularly in England. Consequently, the Middle Ages now get more careful and respectful treatment in textbooks than used to be the case. Any number of similar examples could be cited.

Let us sum up by considering just how history is written. Normally, a considerable number of scholars are working in any one field at any given time. Each searches for materials, weighs his findings, evaluates, considers, questions, speculates, and then writes. Each reads and criticizes what his fellows have written, pointing out any errors into which they have fallen. In the end the result is not absolute certitude about every detail but as close an approximation to the truth as men are ever apt to achieve when they must describe the deeds and intentions of other men.

The recording of history may be compared to a trial by jury. Some of the evidence leads to quite definite, certain conclusions. Some of it consists of a converging series of probabilities which amount to moral certitude. Some of it gives rise to interesting speculation and hypotheses that in the absence of proof must be (often reluctantly) ruled out. The jury weighs, considers, and comes to its conclusion. The result is generally acclaimed as just and reasonable. There the matter rests unless someone turns up new evidence or demonstrates some error in the trial.

In actuality the historian is in a better position than a judge and jury to be just, fair, and certain because there is no time pressure on him. He can study more thoroughly and deliberate longer and more calmly before making his decisions. He therefore has a better chance of being right.

5: Is History the Work of Great Men?

The student of history is perenially troubled by the problem of causation. Why do things change? What is the most important factor or factors in producing historical change? Why did the Roman Empire fall? What caused the Great Depression of the 1930s? Can the American Civil War be ascribed essentially to one issue, one man, or one event? Questions of this sort pose themselves at every turn in history. Innumerable attempts have been made to answer them. Some of the proffered answers will be discussed at length in later chapters but here it is essential to first draw a distinction between immediate and remote causation.

Remote and Immediate Causes—Most complex or important developments are precipitated by some happening that ought more properly to be called an occasion rather than a cause since it is usually trivial in comparison with the events that follow from it. The stock market crash of October 1929 "caused" the Great Depression in the sense that it set off a train of events which produced a worldwide economic decline and paralysis that lasted several years and was particularly severe in the United States. The "real" causes of the depression, however, were at once more remote and more general. Among them were: (1) undue expansion of American agriculture during World War I that continued into the 1920s, depressing farm prices and burdening millions of farmers with mortgages; (2) industrial overexpansion that piled up a surplus of manufactured goods that could not be sold either at home or abroad; (3) a high-tariff policy that engendered retaliation by other countries and thus reduced the number of potential foreign customers for American surpluses; (4) the retention by industrial owners of too large a share of profits, thereby retarding the expansion of purchasing power that would have resulted had employees been paid higher wages, (5) ruinous overextension of credit which led millions into excessive installment buying and other millions into disastrous speculation on the stock market; and (6) political and financial instability in many parts of the world. These phenomena would likely have produced an economic depression at *some* time not long after 1929. The celebrated stock market crash merely precipitated it at a *particular* time.

The immediate "cause" of the Civil War was the election to the presidency of Abraham Lincoln in 1860 and the subsequent secession from the Union of eleven southern states. These two events, however, were mainly indications that both North and South were at last "fed up"—determined to have a showdown over issues which had divided them long and sorely. A southern secessionist might have summed up his grievances and those of this fellow southerners as follows. "Slavery is essential to our economic livelihood and social system. Yet how much longer can we preserve it? Every year the northern states outstrip us in population growth. They use their superior numbers in Congress to load us with high tariffs, deny us the right to extend the slave system into western lands, and forbid us to expand into Cuba? How is it possible to deal with the North reasonably and hopefully when northern state governments and people alike wink at violations of the Fugitive Slave Law and when the murderer John Brown is openly regarded by millions as a brave idealist? What hope do we have of saving our institutions and interests by ordinary political means when we can no longer control the nomination of a Democratic presidential candidate, much less elect a president to our liking? Soon even our federal patronage will be lost. The election of Lincoln, a purely sectional candidate whose name did not even appear on the ballot in ten southern states, is the last straw. There is nothing left now but to stand and resist. If this means war, so be it: for time is with the enemy."

These two considerations, then, the reader should keep in mind as he reads the rest of this book: the *immediate* cause of an event is not the same nor, usually, nearly as important as the *basic* causes; and almost any complex or important development will be the result of several forces or causes. Some of the more important of these factors will now be considered in this and succeeding chapters.

The Individual in History—The importance of the individual person in shaping the course of history has long been the subject of heated argument. The nineteenth-century British historian Thomas Carlyle thought that men of genius were the prime movers of the world's affairs and that history was, essentially, the sum of innumerable individual biographies. The ordinary person tends to agree. He thinks of politics, government, warfare, and other human activities primarily in terms of men prominent in these fields. Less often does he think in terms of ideas or institutions. If something goes awry in the world his natural tendency is to blame some man for it—Roosevelt, Hitler, Stalin, Johnson, Nixon. As a reaction against this excessive personalization of events many historians have gone to the opposite extreme and denied the importance of the individual. Instead, they ascribe change to ideas, geography, economic conditions, or other impersonal factors. In their view, the individual person is not the master of these forces but is largely swept along by them. The truth of the matter lies between these extremes.

It is absurd to deny the importance of great men in history when the significance of the individual is a matter of common experience in everyday life. Who thinks it of no consequence what partner he has in business? What congregation is indifferent to its pastor? What owner of a baseball team thinks one manager is as good as another? What manager is unaware of the difference between the "winning ballplayer" and the nonperformer who tends to "choke up in the clutch"? What teacher gives all students the same grade on the ground that they are equally intelligent and worthy? Any organization, private or public, civilian or military, past or present, functions more efficiently when headed by an able man and staffed by capable personnel.

The importance of the individual is evident in many other ways too. Most of the great ideas, deeds, and inventions that have successively changed the human environment have been the work of exceptionally talented and/or determined individuals. Who can reasonably claim that Aristotle, Shakespeare, Newton, Isabella of Castile, Queen Elizabeth I, Beethoven, Washington, Lincoln, Frank Lloyd Wright, Einstein, Marie Curie, MacArthur, and Edison were ordinary people, mere products of their environment? The opposite is obvious: some were true geniuses; the others were persons of exceptional ambition and determination. The ideas, works, and example of all of them strongly influenced subsequent times. The course of history has always been affected markedly by the dreams, pride, and willfulness of individual rulers, soldiers, and prophets. Men have always done many things merely because they were resolved to triumph, to "be first," to impose their ways on others rather than suffer the ways of others to be imposed on them. The famous mountaineer Sir Edmund Hillary was once asked why he risked his life to scale Mount Everest. He replied, "Because it is there." This spirit has always been part of the human makeup.

America would have been discovered at *some* time had Christopher Columbus never been born. Its discovery at a *particular* time, with reverberations which revolutionized the history of three continents, was due to the determination of Columbus. Not only did he push on with his plans when all the geographical knowledge and sound nautical advice of his time indicated that a nonstop voyage westward to eastern Asia was impossible; he did so even though the Portuguese seemed on the verge of opening a better route around Africa anyway.

On the night of September 12, 1759 the British general James Wolfe was determined to find a way to bring his army up the cliffs below the Plains of Abraham, which overlooked Quebec, so that he might compel the French to do battle, come what might. Eventually he discovered a route. The next day Montcalm's French forces were defeated by Wolfe in a fierce, bloody struggle in which both commanding generals were killed. It was the only important victory Wolfe ever won, but it decided that Canada, and possibly much more of North America, would henceforth be English and not French. To stretch a point—if Wolfe had lost you might today be reading this book in French rather than English.

In innumerable cases a nation's history has been shaped strongly by the acts of its rulers. This is so obvious in the absolute monarchies of old and the totalitarian states of our own age that the mere citation of examples comes close to beating the proverbial dead horse. When all proper allowances have been made for the force of ideas and the pressure of circumstances, what would nazism have been without Adolf Hitler's matchless oratorical gifts, keen insight into the German national character, and remarkable talent for manipulating men? Nobody is more dogmatic than Marxists about the unimportance of individuals and the paramountcy of impersonal considerations (in this case economic forces) as movers in history. Yet Communist and non-Communist historians alike ascribe much of the success of the Bolshevik Revolution of November 1917 to the personal abilities of Lenin.

The principle is no less operative in democracies. In 1799—1800 President John Adams strove tenaciously to find a peaceful solution to current differences with France. He was opposed by his own secretary of state, Timothy Pickering, by several other members of his cabinet, and by powerful figures in the Federalist party, including the redoubtable Alexander Hamilton. Though Adams knew that he was sacrificing his own chances for reelection, he pressed on resolutely. He even fired Pickering. Had he done the easy, popular thing and let war with France come it is most unlikely that the United States would have been able to purchase the vast Louisiana Territory from France a few years later. How different, then, would have been the whole subsequent history of North America!

In 1832 the South Carolina legislature asserted that the federal tariff law was null and void within that state. President Andrew Jackson, himself a southerner, at once made it known by word and deed that he was prepared to take any measures necessary to enforce the tariff and to "nullify" the action of the would-be nullifiers. Within a few months a face-saving compromise on the tariff was arranged, South Carolina withdrew its Act of Nullification, and the Union was preserved.

A generation later another president, James Buchanan, reacted far differently. Sympathetic to the South, and lacking the will to face up to southern extremists, he dawdled through the late 1850s while Kansas drifted into anarchy over the slavery question. Following the election of Lincoln in November 1860 he watched hesitantly while one southern state after another seceded from the Union. By the time Lincoln took office, four months later, only Fort Sumter remained as a symbol of U.S. authority—and its garrison had not even been reinforced. By then any chance of checking secession had been lost. The Civil War followed soon after.

Humane treatment of criminals, paupers, and mental defectives, especially the latter, owed enormously to the efforts of the indefatigible Dorothea Dix (1802–87). Miss Dix was in many ways the most able and successful of a legion of nineteenth-century women who devoted their lives to social reform. Always pragmatic, interested in results rather than social theorizing, she spent years investigating prisons and asylums. Her method was to gather evidence carefully, document everything, construct an airtight case that no intelligent and detached person could gainsay, and then push it relentlessly in state legislatures. If her evidence was of a sort that people in the Victorian age regarded as unseemly for a woman to discuss in public (and this was often the case) Miss Dix got a man to present it for her. To her the important thing was not who got the personal credit but that the poor wretches who inhabited the dismal penal and mental institutions of the day got better treatment.

Oftentimes the course of great controversies, whether intellectual, political, or both, is determined less by the intrinsic merits of the cases than by the accident that most of the personal ability, even most of the merely literary ability, happens to be on one side. Now, two centuries after the American Revolution, any knowledgeable professional historian or impartial student will acknowledge that good theoretical cases can be made out for the positions taken in the years 1763–76 by both the British government and the discontented colonists. The polemical warfare of that era, however, was most uneven. The only English orators comparable to Patrick Henry were Edmund Burke, William Pitt the Elder, and Richard Brinsley Sheridan. All were either friendly to colonial aspirations or critical of their own government. Neither defenders of the government in England nor "Tories" in America produced phrasemakers, pamphleteers, or political thinkers to compare with John Dickinson, James Otis, Samuel Adams, Tom Paine, or, above all, Thomas Jefferson. The vast difference between the two sides in ability, both political and polemical, is indicated by a mere listing of some of the English statesmen who were in office in those years: King George III, a heavy mediocrity who later lost his mind; Chancellor of the Exchequer George Grenville, remembered chiefly for his extraordinary obstinacy; his successor, Charles Townshend, known to his friends as "Champagne Charlie"; Colonial Secretary Lord George Germain, once cashiered from the army for cowardice; First Lord of the Admiralty Lord Sandwich, a paragon of corruption; and Lord North, of whom Sheridan said, "The noble Lord has exceeded even the exploits of Alexander the Great, for Alexander conquered only nations while Lord North has managed to lose an entire continent." Whatever the merits of the dispute between colonies and the mother country, the quality of the disputants was decidedly unequal. It had more than a little to do with the eventual outcome of their disagreement.

An even clearer case relates to the controversy over slavery before the Civil War. No Southerner ever produced any book, pamphlet, poem, or speech that had anything comparable to the emotional appeal and lasting impact of *Uncle Tom's Cabin*. That book persuaded innumerable hitherto indifferent people that slavery was a raging abomination, intolerable in a modern civilized nation. It also had great influence overseas. In France it provided much ammunition for those who sympathized with the North. They were able, ultimately, to dissuade the government of Napoleon III from recognizing the Confederacy. Repercussions in England were similar, if less marked. The influence of the book within the United States was acknowledged by Abraham Lincoln himself, who reportedly remarked when meeting Harriet Beecher Stowe for the first time, "So you're the little woman who wrote the book that made this great war."

History is replete with instances in which imposing political systems or designs crumbled when their creators passed from the scene. The political and military skill and personal prestige of Charlemagne enabled him to rule most of western Europe for nearly half a century (767–814). Under his weak son and quarrelsome grandsons the Carolingian empire was divided, and seventy-five years after Charlemagne's death it had ceased to exist. Early in the nineteenth century the Indian chief Tecumseh realized that one of the principal reasons white settlers were able to press persistently westward and drive the varied Indian tribes before them was that the whites were united and the Indians were not. Displaying a degree of statesmanship hitherto unknown among Indians, Tecumseh strove to organize all the Indian tribes, north and south, into a great Indian confederation. The confederation would be ruled by a warriors' congress which would jointly control all the land of all the tribes. Tecumseh even arranged for an informal alliance with the British in Canada, for their fur trade was also imperilled by the westward march of American farmers. Henceforth all the Indians, united and with covert British backing, could face the land-hungry American settlers and prevent further encroachments into Indian territory. Had Tecumseh's design matured it might well have constituted a formidable barrier to American westward expansion. However, Tecumseh was killed in battle during the War of 1812. With his passing the Indian confederacy at once collapsed, never to be revived.

After World War II a series of revelations of vital security leaks caused millions of Americans to become deeply concerned about Communist infiltration into our government. Seizing advantage of peoples' understandable fears, the noisy and unscrupulous Senator Joseph McCarthy made life exceedingly uncomfortable for many well-intentioned but gullible people by exposing their past association with Communists and Communist organizations. Intoxicated by his success, McCarthy soon made so many inflammatory and unsubstantiated charges about Communists lurking in so many places that the whole, and originally legitimate, effort to root Communist influence out of government fell into general discredit. Since McCarthy's downfall and death no other U.S. politician has attempted to emulate him.

It is often alleged that certain developments are inevitable. In the long run this must frequently be true, but in the short run what happens depends largely on what key individuals do. In our own time the mass passion of nationalism seems truly irresistible. Since 1918 it has dissolved half a dozen empires. One such, the former British Empire, now formally renamed the British Commonwealth, nominally contains such nations as Canada, Australia, and India, though they are in fact as independent as France or Brazil. Most likely the United States would by now have gained a similar degree of independence had the American Revolution never been fought. If one considers, however, not these perhaps "inevitable" triumphs of nationalism but one specific case, the actual American Revolution of 1775–83, things do not look nearly so "inevitable." In fact, it is hard to see how the colonies could possibly have won that conflict without George Washington and French aid. That the French government eventually gave aid to the colonies was due chiefy to the diplomatic talents of one man, Benjamin Franklin, and the covert activities of another, Beaumarchais. Franklin proved to be an extraordinarily shrewd envoy in Paris. For several years, Beaumarchais pleaded the cause of the embattled American colonials to highly placed French officials, notably Foreign Minister Vergennes. For a time they secretly advanced him money, which he used to purchase arms and ammunition for the colonists. Eventually he succeeded in drawing the French government into open and full-fledged participation in the war.

If Just One Thing Had Been Different–Not infrequently great events are strongly affected by chance, accident, the caprice of an individual, or an unlikely sequence of entirely unpredictable happenings. The classic case of the last, in U.S. history, was the Louisiana Purchase. As noted earlier, even the possibility of annexing Louisiana would not have existed had not President John Adams defied much of his own party to make peace with France in 1800. At about the same time, Napoleon Bonaparte, then the ruler of France, pressured Spain to cede the

Louisiana Territory to France. Napoleon dreamed of recreating the great French colonial empire that had been lost to the British in 1763. He dispatched some thirty-five thousand troops under his brother-in-law, General Le Clerc, to Haiti. There Le Clerc was to establish a strong French base. The Louisiana Territory was then to be developed as a source of supplies for a revived French Caribbean empire.

Almost at once Napoleon's grand design began to come apart. In Haiti a native leader with no formal military training, Toussaint l'Ouverture, resisted the French with great skill. Yellow fever provided the coup de grace, carrying off the invaders in droves—a particularly vivid illustration of how history can be shaped by a plague.[1] A plan to send reinforcements had to be abandoned when an exceptionally early and cold winter froze the European ports of embarkation. By the spring of 1803 these setbacks had caused Napoleon to change his mind. He now decided to renew war with England, even though such a conflict would require much money and would render French overseas possessions vulnerable to the superior British fleet. While these developments were taking place Robert Livingstone, the American minister to France, had been negotiating for the purchase of West Florida and a small tract of land around New Orleans. At just the time when Napoleon made his decision to go to war with England James Monroe, President Jefferson's minister extraordinary, arrived in France with instructions to offer up to $10 million if an opportunity should develop to secure both East and West Florida and New Orleans. The French startled the Americans by abruptly offering the *entire* Louisiana Territory for $15 million—four cents an acre. Without authorization from President Jefferson, the American envoys accepted. Without authorization by either house of Congress Jefferson, hitherto a "strict constructionist" of the Constitution, backed his diplomats in what they had done. By such an unlikely chain of strategic misjudgment, medical catastrophe, capricious weather, changed minds, and sheer accident was consummated "the greatest real estate deal in history." It was, more than any other single event, responsible for the eventual development of the United States into the world's richest and mightiest nation.

In a less clear-cut case, the death of President Zachary Taylor in 1850 and his replacement by Vice-President Millard Fillmore probably postponed the Civil War for ten years. Possibly it changed the war's

---

1. About twenty-one thousand of Le Clerc's troops died of yellow fever and another seven thousand perished in combat within ten months of their arrival in Haiti. By the end of 1803 some fifty thousand French soldiers and civilians had expired from all causes. Yellow fever had killed the great majority.

outcome as well. The Compromise of 1850 carefully balanced an array of northern and southern interests and demands. It was constructed only with extreme difficulty and against a backdrop of southern threats of secession. It was then meticulously separated into five different bills, each of which required a different majority to pass through Congress. Even then, only the vigorous support of the sympathetic and conciliatory Fillmore sufficed to mollify the dissidents on both sides. Had Taylor lived longer it is extremely unlikely that he would have accepted the Compromise of 1850, for he hated the doctrine of secession quite as heartily as Andrew Jackson. Indeed, he had no patience with any kind of assertiveness on the part of states. On one occasion he had publicly threatened to lead an American army in person to prevent Texas from adding the upper Rio Grande valley to the territory open to slavery. Thus, save for Taylor's death, the Civil War might well have begun in 1850 rather than 1861. If so, the chance of an ultimate southern victory would have been considerably greater for northern advantages in population, industry, agricultural resources, and railway transport were markedly smaller in 1850 than in 1861.

Assassination—Few developments in history illustrate more dramatically the importance of individual men in shaping the course of human affairs than assassinations and their effects. This was especially evident in ages past when governments were less efficiently organized and bureaucracies were far smaller than they are now and when the industrial and scientific revolutions had not yet produced cameras, fingerprinting equipment, telephones, radios, draft cards, social security numbers, and a dozen other means of watching and controlling people. The assassination of King Henry IV in 1610 plunged the French government into fifteen years of chaos from which it emerged only when another strong man, Cardinal Richelieu, came to power. The murder of the great mercenary soldier Wallenstein in 1634 removed a potential rival of the Emperor Ferdinand II for the imperial throne. It also destroyed any chance that the Catholic side might win a general victory in the Thirty Years War (1618–48). Nobody else in Europe possessed at once the prestige, wealth, industrial and agricultural resources, organizational capacity, and military skill necessary to raise and manage armies like those commanded by Wallenstein. To eliminate the man was to erase the threat posed by his entire system.

Government is so much more complex in the twentieth century that, on a day-to-day basis, it comes close to running itself. Yet the "man at the top" still makes an enormous difference. American history has been changed strikingly many times by both assassinations and the failure of assassination attempts. Had Lincoln not been murdered in 1865 there is a good chance that Reconstruction in the South would have aroused less rancor and the ultimate reconciliation of the two sections of the United States would have come sooner. It is not that the Reconstruction programs of Lincoln and his successor, Andrew Johnson, differed in essentials, but that Lincoln possessed all sorts of political assets that Johnson lacked. He was a shrewd, patient, and conciliatory man: a politician of exceptional skill. Johnson was hot-headed and stubborn. Lincoln belonged to the same party as the Radical Republican opponents of his Reconstruction program; indeed, he was head of that party. Johnson was a War Democrat who had become vice-president mostly because of a purely political desire to "balance the ticket" in 1864. Lincoln enjoyed great prestige from having led the North to victory in the war, thereby saving the Union. Johnson was an ex-tailor from North Carolina with a reputation for drinking too much. Altogether Lincoln would have had a better chance than Andrew Johnson to persuade Radical Republicans to make a moderate settlement with the defeated Confederacy.

Before the assassination of President Garfield in 1881 the spoils system had been encrusted onto American politics for two generations. All attempts to end it had failed. The president's death at the hands of a disgruntled job seeker changed everything. The dramatic impact of the foul deed produced crucial support for the Pendleton Act, which established the civil service system for making appointments to many federal jobs.[2]

The murder of William McKinley in 1901 brought to the presidency the dynamic and widely mistrusted Theodore Roosevelt. Roosevelt had a far more "active" conception of the presidential office than did McKinley. In short order "Teddy" was "busting trusts," pushing hard for a pure food and drug act, starting the nation's first serious federal conservation program, wielding a "big stick" in the Caribbean, and delivering pugnacious pronouncements on an amazing variety of public and private questions. Thus did he arouse public opinion and set in motion programs that would influence our whole history from his time to the present. Had McKinley served out his second term little or none of this would have been done, and Roosevelt would not have had much chance, then (1904) or later, to gain his party's presidential nomination in an open convention.

If Lee Harvey Oswald had been a poor rifle shot President John Kennedy almost certainly would have been reelected in 1964. While one cannot *know* what this would have portended in either domestic or

2. For a brief estimate of the effect, often undesirable, of the Civil Service system upon the whole American political apparatus, see Chapter 7.

foreign affairs, many think that Kennedy would not have embroiled the country as deeply in the Vietnamese War as did his successors, Lyndon Johnson and Richard Nixon. Had not Robert Kennedy been murdered in 1968, it is likely that he, rather than Hubert Humphrey, would have gained the Democratic presidential nomination in that year. Since Humphrey was barely edged out in the extremely close presidential election of 1968 it is probable that the younger and more popular Kennedy would have defeated Nixon, a development with momentous implications for subsequent U.S. domestic history.

The murders of the black leaders Martin Luther King and Malcom X in the 1960s effected immediate, marked changes in various aspects of the effort to improve the lot of U.S. Negroes. Both men were exceptionally able organizers. Black conversions to Islam increased rapidly while Malcolm was alive but slackened after his death. His Organization of African Unity collapsed. Under King's successor, Rev. Ralph Abernathy, King's Southern Christian Leadership Conference declined sharply in influence. More immediately, King's assassination produced a wave of riots in several big cities that resulted in an estimated $200 million worth of damages. Many black activists became more militant and more alienated from American society, particularly after the murder of King who had long appealed to white consciences as a technique for promoting black interests. Many blacks jumped to the conclusion that the CIA or FBI must have had some role in one or both crimes.

Yet it is impossible to do more than speculate about the long-range effects of the assassinations, both because we are still close to them in time and because the ideas of both victims were changing at the time of their deaths. Malcolm X was an antiwhite crusader who had great influence among black intellectuals and white radicals. Yet shortly before his death he appears to have been moved profoundly by a trip to Mecca during which he was in close contact with white Muslims. There is reason to believe that he soon would have adopted a more conciliatory attitude toward the white community. King, by contrast, had long preached conciliation, cooperation, and nonviolence, but was clearly pondering the employment of more active and forceful efforts to promote "black power" at the time of his death. He had also begun to oppose the Vietnam War. What effect these changes would have had ultimately on his enormous influence within black America and with many prominent white people is impossible to say, but it surely would have been considerable.

Even the failures of assassins can be extremely important. Had those who tried to assassinate Adolf Hitler on July 20, 1944, succeeded (and they came within a hair's breadth of it), any subsequent rulers of Germany almost certainly would have sued immediately for an end to

World War II. Such a development would have left the Soviet Union in a much less dominant position in postwar Europe, since the most extensive Russian territorial conquests came in the winter of 1944–45. Had the would-be assassin of Franklin Roosevelt in 1933 killed the newly elected president instead of the mayor of Chicago, the history of the United States in the 1930s would have been quite different. Roosevelt's remarkable capacity to inspire confidence in the hearts of tens of millions was a crucial factor in restoring public morale during the depression.

Medical Crises–Notoriously, history does not record catastrophes that never took place. If it could, textbooks would enshrine a whole new roster of heroes and many a conventional hero would become a villain. Occasionally, though, we can be reasonably sure that a certain action prevented an incipient catastrophe. Such an instance was a successful operation on President Grover Cleveland in 1893. In 1890 the Sherman Act was passed. One of its clauses required the annual purchase of 54 million ounces of silver. Against this, treasury notes were issued. They were redeemable in gold. Not surprisingly, the silver-producing states and their congressmen were enthusiastic supporters of the measure. Unhappily for the country, gold was more valuable than silver at the official sixteen-to-one exchange rate. By 1893 this situation had produced a veritable panic. Foreign governments scrambled to exchange silver for gold, and domestic banks closed on every side. The government's gold reserves fell rapidly. Now President Cleveland was a "sound money" man who opposed the continuous and costly exchange of gold for silver and urged repeal of the silver clause in the Sherman Act. Due mostly to his influence, the clause was eventually repealed on October 30, 1893, and the crisis passed. But we are getting ahead of our story . . . In June 1893, it was discovered that Cleveland was suffering from cancer of the mouth and would require a major operation. Secrecy was successfully maintained, the president underwent two operations, and he recovered routinely and fully. However, had it become public knowledge in June–July 1893 that such an operation was impending doubt about his recovery would have been widespread and politicians would have become more deferential toward the person and ideas of the vice-president, Adlai Stevenson, known to be "silver" man. In that event the silver clause of the Sherman Act almost certainly would not have been repealed, the domestic and international "run" on the U.S. Treasury would have continued, and the consequences for the country could hardly have been anything but disastrous.

Sixty years later President Dwight Eisenhower was three times stricken with illnesses, any one of which could easily have killed him. In such a case Richard Nixon would have become president, not in 1968 but in the 1950s. How different might have been the whole subsequent political history of the United States!

What can be concluded is that not just the qualities of individual men, not even the presence or absence of great men, but the mere accidents that happen to men in crucial places, often make a great difference in the turn taken by events.

Things Do Not Happen "In General"—One must never forget that no matter what abstractions and generalizations are used in historical description it is individual human beings who think and act and to whom things happen. One reads in a textbook that on March 5, 1770, a "mob" in Boston hurled jeers, then stones and snowballs, at a detachment of British troops. The troops promptly opened fire. Five civilians were killed and several others injured. Now that "mob" was not just an abstraction. Its members were fifty or sixty flesh-and-blood human beings like ourselves. They individually picked up their missiles and threw them at the soldiers. When they were dispersed it was not "the mob" that suffered "casualties"; it was five separate, individual men and boys who stopped musket balls and lay dead on the pavement. It was no "mob" but several other individuals who got their heads cracked, limbs broken, or flesh torn, and who ran off to nurse their wounds and their grievances. So it is with war, or government, or science, or literature, or anything else. "American literature" is not the product of "Americans" in general: it is the sum of the writings of a number of individual American men and women. "Science" does not produce anything. It is individual persons working in laboratories who discover and develop all sorts of things. So with history too. Such general terms as the "Age of Jackson," the "Gilded Age," and the "Progressive Period" may be appropriately applied to certain eras or situations in history, but one must remember that the generalizations refer to the activities of innumerable individual men and women. It was *their* words and deeds which gave the age its special character, not vice versa.

Moreover, each such "age" or "era" contains individuals of talent and worth who are quite out of step with the prevailing spirit. The Abolitionist editor William Lloyd Garrison narrowly escaped lynching by a Boston mob in 1835 but was widely regarded as a hero after the Civil War. Herman Melville's pessimistic writings were so out of tune with the ebullient spirit of nineteenth-century America that his literary career seemed ended in the 1850s. The twentieth century, however, has had more and better reasons than the nineteenth to take a somber view of existence. One result has been that Melville is much more appreciated now than he was a century ago.

It is particularly important that citizens in a democracy not forget these elementary facts. Any society that prizes individual liberty and allows each person to take part in choosing his own government necessarily assumes that man is free and that his individuality is meaningful and deserving of protection. While a society organized on collectivist principles of either the old peasant-village type or the modern totalitarian type may logically deny the importance of the individual person in history, it is surely absurd to be an advocate of republican government and at the same time a disciple of some determinist theory of history which envisions men as mere puppets manipulated by vast, impersonal, irresistible forces.

Limitations on Individual Achievement—Yet if man is basically the master of his destiny, he is never entirely so. No man, however talented and ambitious, can make the world over as he chooses. He can sometimes guide a people, change some of their ideas, make some of their ideas his own, and channel their desires and ambitions to suit his own purposes. Still he can never for long force a whole people to do what is against their wills. More specifically, what any man can do is always limited in varying degrees by the physical environment, the level of literacy and political sophistication of his followers, the contemporary level of technological development, and other factors beyond his control.

In a nation like the United States no president, regardless of his ability, can do just as he pleases. He is limited by the Constitution, the Supreme Court, Congress, and the regular governmental bureaucracy. These entities all have a constitutional position, enjoy public respect, have much direct power and indirect influence, and cause the government to be run on a day-to-day basis in much the same way no matter who is president. Only in the most extraordinary circumstances could the president appeal successfully to the armed forces to allow him to override these other branches of the government. There is no doubt that the government of the United States operates more effectively when an able man like Theodore Roosevelt or Woodrow Wilson is president than it does under a Grant or a Harding. All modern governments in Western countries, however, are so complex and highly organized that they operate with moderate efficiency, at least for a time, no matter who is president or premier.

Do Times Make the Man?—Many a man has gained a place in history because he happened to live in a particular time or place that offered him a special opportunity. Wars, revolutions, and other crises produce "fluid" situations in which ability of any sort has a much better than usual chance to become evident. Undoubtedly, many of history's great soldiers and statesmen would have made little impression on their times had wars not occurred to give them a chance to shine.

By all ordinary reckoning, young Samuel Adams was a failure. There is no reason to suppose that he would ever have been anything else in normal times since the only talent Adams ever displayed at any period in his life was for the production of propaganda and the organization of revolutionary groups. Only in the years immediately before 1775 did there happen to be a situation in Britain's American colonies where these qualities had obvious utility. Hence the name of Samuel Adams, pamphleteer for independence and organizer of the first Committees of Correspondence, has been enshrined in countless U.S. history books.

The renown that eventually propelled Andrew Jackson into the presidency was gained chiefly by his victory over the British at New Orleans, January 8, 1815, in a battle that should never have been fought. Unknown to Jackson, the British and Americans had signed a peace treaty in Europe two weeks earlier. Had Jackson lived half a century later, after the invention of the wireless, he would never have had a chance to gain fame in such an accidental manner.

Had it not been for the outbreak of the Civil War Ulysses S. Grant would have been remembered by no one save relatives and a few acquaintances. A mediocrity at West Point, an alcoholic as a regular army officer, a failure at nearly everything he tried before the age of forty, Grant was able to regain a military commission only because the Civil War broke out. He soon displayed abilities no one supposed he possessed. In short order, he became the chief Northern hero of the war, and, three years later, president.

Dwight Eisenhower almost certainly would have lived and died an obscure career army officer had not World War II presented him with opportunities similar to those that had suddenly become available to Grant. Within a couple of years Eisenhower was commander of all the Western Allied armies in Europe, and by 1952 president of the United States.

The whole, essentially nonmilitary, career of Alexander Hamilton hinged on the American Revolution. Hamilton was an illegitimate son of a Scottish trader in the West Indies. Though he possessed high native intelligence, he had little formal education when he arrived in the mainland English colonies at the age of seventeen, shortly before the Revolution began. He wrote several pamphlets on behalf of the colonial cause. These caught the eye of General Nathanael Greene, who introduced young Hamilton to George Washington. Washington took a liking to Hamilton and made him his adjutant. The start was all the brilliant Hamilton needed. Within a few years he was helping to write *The Federalist Papers* and playing a prominent role in the formation of a new government. Eventually, he became secretary of the treasury. Had it not been for the opportunities afforded by the Revolution it is hardly possible that one with his background could have attained a high position in the government of an important country.

A man born out of his time gets nowhere. Barry Goldwater, the conservative Republican senator from Arizona, gained his party's presidential nomination in 1964 and was promptly buried in one of the most one-sided elections in American history. Had he lived half a century earlier and been nominated at any time before 1932 he would have had a good chance to win, for most of the presidents elected from 1860 to 1928 were conservative Republicans. What chance someone like him might have in the future is, of course, unknown and unknowable. What is clear is that Goldwater's views and program were out of step with prevailing national sentiment at a particular time: 1964.

In centuries past when most people thought of monarchy as the natural, normal form of government a political philosopher who defended the theory of the divine right of kings was regarded as a level-headed man. But the greatest genius who ever drew breath would be laughed at and regarded with wonder if he advocated this conception now. With few exceptions, particularly in the Mideast, our age simply no longer takes kings seriously. In those Western countries where they still exist their function is chiefy decorative.

Sometimes a man is born at very nearly the right time, but not at exactly the right time, so his ambitions remained unfulfilled. Such a one was Secretary of State William H. Seward. Seward was an able and ambitious man and a zealous proponent of adding to the United States as much territory as could be secured, in continental North America or the Caribbean, by purchases or annexation. He became secretary of state in Lincoln's administration during the Civil War. At that time the attention of the country was fixed wholly on this domestic conflict. After the war the public became preoccupied with Reconstruction of the South, land and monetary issues, and efforts to recover from the severe economic depression of 1873. American industry was expanding rapidly inside the United States and had no need to look abroad. It was precisely the wrong time in American history to promote a program of territorial expansion. All Seward was able to secure was Alaska, purchased for $7.2 million in 1867. Even that bargain-basement acquisition was accepted grudgingly by the public. It was widely regarded as a favor to the Russians in return for their friendly attitude toward the Union during the Civil War.

Had Seward been secretary of state during the 1840s, when enthusiasm for expansion into Mexico was high, or in the heyday of the "age of imperialism" from about 1890 to 1910, he would have enjoyed far greater success. In the latter era the United States acquired Puerto Rico, Hawaii, the Philippines, Guam (all in 1898) and the Virgin Islands (1917), and domination over Cuba and Panama, even without missionary imperialists like Seward in the State Department. What might not have been secured had he been Theodore Roosevelt's secretary of state? But Seward lived twenty years too late to promote expansion successfully in one era; thirty-five years too soon for the next imperialist era. It has been well said that "history is made rapidly when a great man and his opportunity appear simultaneously."

The Man Who Is "Made" by a Movement—What history calls a "great" man is sometimes merely a sensitive, alert man. Not infrequently an individual is raised to power and prominence because he has a keen intuition of what people want and which contemporary ideas and movements have a future. He vigorously espouses these and in due course becomes the "leader" of a movement. This is a common phenomenon in revolutions. In a revolutionary era chaos and bewilderment spread as established institutions break down or are attacked. All sorts of immoderate expectations are aroused by the slogans and shouts of the revolutionaries. A man of ability and daring who can discern what a large number of people want and then champion it vigorously stands a good chance of emerging from the turmoil in control of a nation.

The classic example is the Russian revolutions of 1917. In March of that year the regime of Czar Nicholas II collapsed and was replaced by a democratic government of the Western type, headed by Alexander Kerensky. Kerensky tried to keep Russia in World War I on the side of the Allies but the Russian people were thoroughly sick of the defeats, heavy casualties, corruption, and inefficiency that had characterized every aspect of the Russian war effort since 1914. Furthermore, the peasants were anxious to seize the lands of the aristocracy. In this situation Lenin, the prescient leader of the tiny Bolshevik movement, called for "Peace, Bread, and Land"—precisely what tens of millions of Russians wanted to hear. It mattered not at all that the Bolsheviks had no intention of delivering on any of these promises in the way the peasants understood them. The peasants were swept along by the surface meaning and seeming implications of the slogans. By November the Bolsheviks were able to overthrow Kerensky, and with surprisingly little difficulty.

American history is replete with similar, if less important, examples. It was the free silver "crusade" of the 1890s that made possible the meteoric rise to national prominence of the Boy Orator of the Platte, William Jennings Bryan, a man of modest commonplace native talents. A man of even more modest natural endowment was Warren G. Harding. In 1920, however, he typified and articulated exactly the national mood of that particular time—the desire to return to "normalcy." He was elected president in a landslide.

In the late nineteenth century, labor unions were being organized in all leading Western countries. The feeling was widespread in the United States that the time had come for the formation of similar organizations to protect and promote the interests of at least skilled craftsmen in our country. An exceptional opportunity thus existed for an organizer of intelligence and vision. Samuel Gompers proved to be such a man. He founded the American Federation of Labor in 1881 and guided it skillfully from victory to victory. By 1914 the AF of L had 2 million members and was the generally recognized representative of the "aristocracy" of American labor. A similar chance to organize unskilled workers into industry-wide "horizontal" unions existed in the 1930s. In the depths of the Great Depression the need for an organization to protect the jobs of those fortunate enough to have employment seemed especially urgent. Moreover, the famous Section 7(a) of the National Industrial Recovery Act, and the subsequent Wagner-Connery Labor Relations Act guaranteed the right of employees to organize and bargain collectively through representatives of their own choosing. This time it was John L. Lewis who seized the opportunity. He sent his organizers into such great mass-production industries as steel, automobiles, furniture, textiles, rubber, and aluminum. Within a few years he was president of the Congress of Industrial Organizations, a gigantic union of 4 million members, nearly as numerous and influential as the American Federation of Labor.

Limitations Imposed by Impersonal Factors—If genius is to be effective, a certain minimum level of general civilization is a prerequisite. No Abraham Lincoln ever appeared among the Austrial aborigines, no Henry Ford among the Iroquois, no Hemingway among the Eskimos. The ideals and temper of a people likewise limit what any man can do or become among them. It is safe to say that the pacific Amish will never produce a Genghis Khan. Had ancient Sparta survived a thousand years its society would never have known a gentle apostle of peace like Tolstoy or Gandhi. An irreverent skeptic like H. L. Mencken is inconceivable in the theocratic society of the Massachusetts Bay Colony—at least for long!

Uncontrollable Forces—Sometimes people set in motion forces which acquire a momentum of their own and largely pass out of human control, sweeping their instigators with them. Such was the case with the American annexation of the Philippines. When the year 1898 opened few Americans had ever heard of the Philippine Islands, much less cherished a desire to sequester them. Most of our people, as always, regarded the acquisition of overseas empires as something peculiarly and distastefully European, a mingling of greed and aggression incompatible with our form of government and national traditions. Available evidence indicates that both President McKinley and his advisers offhandedly shared this general American view. But changed circumstances have a way of changing opinions and policies, especially those of politicians dependent on votes. In the spring of 1898 some of the less responsible American newspapers were trying to increase their circulations by printing lurid denunciations of Spanish rule in Cuba. By April 25 they had created so much furor that vote-conscious congressmen had taken up their cries and pressured the administration into declaring war against Spain. Once the war began, there was no *political* reason why fighting should not have been confined to Cuba where the real and imaginary Spanish atrocities had taken place. American professional military men, however, like their counterparts in other countries, had been brought up on the ideas of the German military theorist, Clausewitz.

Clausewitz had taught that the main objective in war should be to destroy the power and will of the enemy to fight. This surely meant attacking enemy forces anywhere, not just in Cuba. When the war began Commodore Dewey commanded an American naval detachment which happened to be anchored in the British Crown Colony of Hong Kong. Britain promptly declared her neutrality, so Dewey had to move his ships. He cabled to Washington for orders. Since there was nothing *obvious* for him to do, the instructions he eventually got from Washington were to do what seemed natural to military men: strike at any Spanish interest in the vicinity. The nearest target was some Spanish ships in Manila harbor. They were duly attacked and destroyed. What next? Steam away? Land and occupy Manila? Try to conquer the Philippines? Dewey had no plans. Neither did anyone in Washington. Eventually Washington decided to send an army to the Philippines to reduce Spanish power there and maintain security while the United States occupied the islands. Then what? Both the McKinley adminstration and responsible segments of the press agonized. Nobody seemed really to *want* the Philippines. Great Britain declined to take them as a gift. It did not seem reasonable to return them to Spain, so recently defeated. The native population appeared clearly unsuited for self-government. President McKinley said, doubtless sincerely, that he prayed for divine guidance. Months passed. American troops arrived in the Philippines. Soon many an American politician or other public figure who had never dreamed, previously, that we should acquire an overseas empire now began to develop an imperial appetite. To stay, subdue, occupy, and annex the Philippines came increasingly to seem the *obvious* course.

Thus were America's leaders and the general public alike swept along by the momentum of unforeseen events, unplanned contingencies, and appetites that grew greater with unexpected feasting. Eventually we fought a small but bloody war to secure an island chain nobody originally dreamed of taking, one which was to embroil us in Far Eastern politics thereafter, and which was to cost us far more to administer and develop than we ever drew from it in trade.[3]

*Summary—*On the question of whether men control events or are controlled by them, Machiavelli, writing at the turn of the sixteenth century, probably came as close to the truth as anyone has ever done. He likened the course of events to a river: ordinarily controllable by building dikes and levees, but sometimes given to irresistible floods that sweep away the most careful designs of men.

A good specific example of how important one man can be in a historical epoch, and at the same time of the degree to which any man is dependent on circumstances, is the career of George Washington. It is difficult to see how the American Revolutionary War could have been won without Washington as our commander-in-chief. Though he was not a brilliant battle tactician, Washington was a man of incontestable courage, integrity, and determination. He possessed exceptional ability to inspire the men he led, and he followed the wise strategy of retreat and delay, for as long as his army remained "in being" the colonial cause was not lost. Yet these qualities alone would not have guaranteed eventual American victory. It was Franklin's diplomatic skill that secured the French financial and naval aid which almost certainly made the crucial difference between victory and defeat. It was sympathetic Germans like DeKalb and Steuben, Poles like Kosciusko and Pulaski, Frenchmen like Lafayette and Rochambeau, who provided the professional military expertise that was so glaringly absent among most of Washington's colonial subordinates. British shortcomings helped immensely too. British troops were not exactly "lions led by asses,"[4] but such officers as Gage, Howe, Burgoyne, and Clinton will never be confused with Hannibal, Napoleon, Rommel, or Patton. How different it would have been to have faced the same troops commanded by James Wolfe who, when still a young man, had fallen in his hour of victory at Quebec in 1759! The Americans had exceptional luck, too, in that British political leadership (Germain, Sandwich, George III, North, "Champagne Charlie" Townshend) was more than usually inept. How different things would have been for the colonials had the British war effort been directed by the elder Pitt, the brilliant, energetic statesman of the Seven Years War (1756–63)! Fortunately for the insurgents, Pitt, by the 1770s, suffered intermittently from insanity and was perma-

---

3. Our acquisition of the Philippines is discussed succinctly by Louis J. Halle, "Dream and Reality," in *Issues in American Diplomacy*, ed. Armin Rappaport, vol. 2 (New York: Macmillan, 1965), pp. 81–90.

4. A devastating, but sadly accurate, characterization of the French army that was swiftly overwhelmed by Prussia in 1870–71.

nently out of favor with George III. Even geography and nature aided the rebellious Americans. After 1780 the British had also to consider that half the states of Europe had become not merely hostile to them but quite possibly willing to intervene actively in the war on the colonial side. Clearly, George Washington alone did not win the Revolution.

The same mixture of crucial personal ability and mere circumstance is evident if one considers the political role of George Washington in the formation of our nation. Most major revolutions in recent centuries have ended in the rule of a military dictator of some sort. In this respect Washington was unique in history. He never regarded himself as an indispensable man; and he proved it not once, but twice. At the end of the Revolution he resigned, at once and without conditions, as commander of the victorious American army. As president, Washington served two terms and stepped down. Thus were set invaluable precedents for our future. One of the principal reasons the quarrelsome states finally adopted a federal constitution in 1787–88 was the general expectation that Washington would be the first president elected under it. If most of the people had become aware of the inadequacies of government under the Articles of Confederation, it did not follow that they were enthusiastic or even well-informed about the constitutional regime devised in Philadelphia to replace it. But if it looked like Washington had faith in the proposed new government and would be its first executive, most were willing to take a chance on it.

Still, Washington did not create the new government, nor did he shape its main contours. Though he was known to favor a stronger government, he wrote neither the Constitution nor those profound arguments in its favor, *The Federalist Papers*. The eventual launching of the new government under the Constitution owed greatly to the contributions and exertions of Franklin, Jefferson, Hamilton, John Adams, Madison, Robert Morris, and a score of less well-known men. Perhaps most important of all, it owed much to the common sense of the American people: to their willingness to accept peacefully the replacement of the inadequate but by now familiar regime of 1783 with the untried system created from the incisive debates in Philadelphia.

So, the gradual emergence and firm establishment of the American Republic during the period 1775–1800 is inconceivable without the character, abilities, and example of George Washington; but the winning of independence and subsequent formation of our nation also owed much to the abilities of other men, to the ineptitude of opponents, to the imperatives of geography, and to sheer chance. Neither the man nor the circumstances alone would have sufficed. Both were essential.

6: The Role of Ideas in History

Popular Ideas Determine the Character of Society—It has been said that ideas rule the world. Like most such generalizations, the statement is exaggerated, but it does contain a large measure of truth for ideas are the cement that holds society together. If most people did not share the same fundamental concepts about how life should be lived and how people should deal with one another, society would have no stability. Suppose half the people of a given country believe firmly that war is the noblest expression of the human spirit and the other half that war is never permissible; half that every respectable person should work for a living, and the other half that it is only more sensible to try to live by one's wits than by working; half that the fullest democracy is the only tolerable form of government, and the other half that absolute monarchy is the only acceptable form. The society in question would be torn to pieces by constant ideological battling. Community life is possible only because most people in civilized countries think theft and murder wrong, prefer to live in family units rather than in some other fashion, and do not ordinarily try forcibly to impose their own views on others.

Men always have ideas about how the world's affairs should be handled, and they always have ideals they wish to serve or see realized. Such will be the case as long as they continue to be men. Human beings have always had strong opinions about the relationship of God to man, of man to man, of God to government, of man to government, of freedom and order, of what is desirable and what is undesirable conduct, of what is bad but can be tolerated, of what is so bad that it cannot be tolerated, of how one should get along with neighboring peoples and nations, of how one social class ought to be related to another, and so on. The views on these matters that prevail at any one time and place powerfully affect the character of the society in question. A state like ancient Sparta, divided into two sharply distinct classes, rulers and ruled, and saturated with a spirit of militarism, is bound to be quite different in popular outlook than, say, modern Denmark or the Netherlands.

Historians themselves unconsciously testify to the power of ideas as movers in history when they write their books in terms of ideas. The pages of textbooks are peppered with words and phrases like capitalism, socialism, nationalism, Manifest Destiny, social Darwinism, pragmatism, collective security, and others. Historian and reader alike take it for granted that such abstract designations are an accurate and meaningful way of discussing the past. In fact history touches the domain of ideas in more places than any other study, for history deals in some fashion with everything. New ideas in any field necessarily affect it.

The Pursuit of Ideals–The course of history has been changed in innumerable ways by the pursuit of ideals—perhaps most of all by the desire to secure universal acceptance for particular ideals. An example from recent history would be the numerous proclamations of President Woodrow Wilson that the world should be reorganized on the basis of independence and democratic government for every nationality. These declarations helped the Allies win World War I. More importantly, perhaps, they also poured fuel on the fires of nationalist zeal in every corner of the globe.

No modern idea has affected history more than the passion of nationalism. In the nineteenth century it produced wars that unified Italy and Germany. It stimulated rebellions in Poland, Hungary, Belgium, and half-a-dozen Balkan states. In the United States it did much to bring about the War of 1812 and the Mexican War; and it steeled the determination of the northern states and people to go to war if necessary to prevent the secession of the South. In the twentieth century the fruits of nationalism can be seen on every side. Among them are claims that the Russians invented everything, denunciations of "Yankee imperialism," proud talk about the "African personality," and claims for the preeminent virtue of something called "the American way." It has produced milling, faceless mobs bawling "Heil Hitler," "Il Duce," "Tito," "Viva Castro," and "Ho, Ho, Ho Chi Minh"; and quieter mobs professing to be convinced that all the world's accumulated wisdom is to be discovered in the "thoughts of Chairman Mao." There is not an important part of the globe in which the ideal of nationalism has not produced "patriotic" political parties, agitation for independence, "wars of liberation," governmental repression, and attempts to "reeducate" national "minority" groups in order to make them 100 percent patriots. It has been truly said that nationalism is the religion of the twentieth century.

Likewise, no one in our century needs to be reminded how strongly every part of the world has been affected by another ideal: the Communist dream of destroying capitalism and communizing the earth. Pursuit of this objective has already entailed history's most sweeping governmental, economic, and social changes in half of Europe and Asia. It has produced small and medium wars and skirmishes, military preparations of unparalleled dimensions in both the Communist and non-Communist parts of the world, and a permanent state of international tension as severe as any in recorded history.

Perhaps the predominant ideal that runs through all American history is the notion that we are a people with a mission, that we have been selected by God or by destiny to show the rest of the world a way to live and aspire that is simultaneously nobler, more practical, and more enriching than anything humanity has ever known. John Winthrop, the leader of the Massachusetts Bay Colony, was probably the first American to reduce the sentiment to memorable phraseology. Preaching a sermon to his Puritan flock aboard the *Arabella*, which had not yet even landed in the New World (1630), Winthrop declared, "Wee shall be as a citty upon a Hill. The eies of all people are upon us." A century and a half later Thomas Paine proclaimed that "the cause of America is in good measure the cause of all mankind." The men who drew up and signed the Declaration of Independence in 1776 agreed. They did not think they were merely establishing a new nation. As Thomas Jefferson put it, "A just and solid republican government maintained here will be a standing monument and example for the aim and imitation of the people of other countries." Years later, as president, Jefferson was still exulting that "we can no longer say there is nothing new under the sun. For this whole chapter in the history of man is new."

It is easy to pass off the early nineteenth-century advocates of Manifest Destiny as mere land grabbers with a talent for unctuous phraseology. Land grabbers they were, but they also believed that Providence had destined American democracy to spread from ocean to ocean, and that the world must be improved as a result of it. Lincoln's ringing proclamation in the Gettyburg Address that "government of the people, by the people, and for the people, shall not perish from the earth" echoed the same idealistic and universalist aspirations as the Declaration of Independence and Jefferson's perorations.

At the turn of the twentieth century, when we were momentarily undecided about whether to annex the Philippines, prominent American statesmen like Senator Albert Beveridge were quick to emphasize that annexation would further the work of Providence in the Far East. William Howard Taft, later to be president, echoed the sentiment when he referred to the Filipinos as "our little brown brothers." As noted earlier, we were not content to enter World War I to prevent Germany from dominating Europe. We were at once assured by President Wilson, and we largely believed just as did Wilson himself, that we were struggling to "make the world safe for democracy," end war altogether, secure independence for all the "subjugated" peoples of Europe, and assure freedom of the seas for everyone ever after.

Several months before we became embroiled in World War II President Franklin Roosevelt and English Prime Minister Winston Churchill issued the famous Atlantic Charter in which they proclaimed the right of all peoples to the form of government they preferred, equal access to all the world's raw materials, and many lesser blessings, all capped by a guarantee to everyone everywhere of "freedom from fear and want." Of course there was never the slightest possibility that the Atlantic Charter could be implemented, but it exemplified perfectly the crusading spirit in which our country customarily embarked on wars before 1950.

In his inaugural address (1961) President John Kennedy adjured America's young people to "ask not what your country can do for you but what you can do for your country." Attempting to suit word to deed, he soon organized the Peace Corps to tap the idealism of American youth and channel it into projects that would be beneficial to poor, ignorant, sick, or exploited people in less fortunate parts of the world. Looking back, it is easy to see that all these admirable sentiments were never completely reconcilable among themselves. Worse, in practice, most of them got mixed up with many base and mercenary considerations. Nonetheless, all of them taken together illustrate the persistence and strength of our national conviction that it is our historic destiny to set an example for the rest of mankind. We have been equally convinced that, abroad, all well-intentioned people know this to be true and long in their hearts to imitate our institutions, savor our "freedom," and enjoy our "standard of living."

The character of a society is also formed quite as much by the unspoken assumptions that most of its people make on a day-to-day basis as it is by the grander and more encompassing ideas which are publicly proclaimed to be an integral part of the national heritage. The popular American belief that ours is uniquely a land of opportunity was reflected in the nineteenth-century immigration policy that barred nobody. Though that policy has long since been severely narrowed, the belief is still strong that the United States remains the land of opportunity. Chronic welfare recipients and "hippie types" who deliberately reject American ideals are widely regarded as persons who have failed to make proper use of their opportunities.

At the same time the American belief that everyone deserves an equal chance remains strong. Even though our society (like all others) has many inequalities, any of our people can attract widespread sympathy and support if they can show, with some plausibility, that they are victims of discrimination or get less than an equal chance at the "good things of life." Indians, for instance, came from an alien culture and so were psychologically unprepared for the white world. The relatively few of them who, in the past, became well educated really did not fit either in the white world or on the reservations from which they had come. Blacks, even after emancipation, notoriously had poorer schools than whites, particularly in the South, and so were badly equipped to compete with white youngsters in mixed schools when blacks began to move into northern cities in large numbers. The whole United States has not rushed immediately to redress these imbalances, needless to say, but they have been widely acknowledged, and serious efforts have been made to overcome them. It all indicates that faith is still widespread and strong among us and that most other Americans are reasonably well intentioned at heart. If they fail to prosper, it is probably due not so much to individual deficiencies as to the malfunctioning of schools, the inadequacies of programs, or the absence of proper legislation—all matters that can be set right by the proper kind of action. This attitude has stimulated reform movements of every imaginable type throughout our history. As the perceptive French aristocrat Alexis de Tocqueville observed as long ago as 1840, following his celebrated travels in America, "Aristocratic nations are naturally too apt to narrow the scope of human perfectibility; democratic nations to expand it beyond reason."[1]

The United States is a rich country, and most of us are the recent or remote descendants of peasants. Consequently, it is hardly surprising that we have striven to attain a high living standard. Though ours is already lavish by general world norms, most people have long expected it to continue to rise indefinitely. To insure that one's children work less and live "better" than oneself has been a traditional and widespread aspiration. Our social critics and crusaders have shown great concern that the goal should be attained by all, not merely a select few. Politicians discovered long ago that, whatever might be their private beliefs or what they intended to do if they gained office, it was necessary to show at least verbal respect for these "standard" American attitudes if they expected to be elected.

Finally, people have a certain image of themselves and their compatriots that is clearly reflected in their national conduct and prejudices. Americans have always liked to think of themselves as an honest and generous people. We are quick to send help of every sort to victims of

---

1. *Democracy in America*, ed. and trans., Henry Reeve, revised by Francis Bowen, further corrected by Phillips Bradley, vol. 2 (New York: Alfred Knopf, 1953), p. 34.

natural disasters in foreign lands. We are equally quick to feel, and express, disappointment when other nations do not repay war debts or do not show gratitude for U.S. aid during and after wars.

Even preferences in entertainment indicate a people's image of themselves. Cooped up in huge cities, vexed by omnipresent traffic jams, chained to routine employment, beset by complex everyday problems, forced to make decisions in situations that are opaque, we show our nostalgia for a (seemingly) simpler, more open, and more honest age by patronizing an endless array of cowboy-and-Indian movies and television programs in which heroes, villains, problems, and decisions are sharp, clear, and simple. The heroes are strong, sometimes silent, and either athletic or romantic—just what we would like to be ourselves. Most of them would have starred on the varsity team and won the hand of the prettiest cheerleader. Athletic contests of a dozen different kinds are more popular with most of the population than are opera, concerts, art exhibits, or garden shows. The athletes who are most admired are not so much the most shrewd, the most calculating, or those who save themselves and last the longest. They are, instead, the "biggest" in every way: those who go "all out," who hit home runs, who throw touchdown passes, who score the most points, who hit the longest drives, and who get paid the most. It is all a reflection, albeit often distorted, of our view of our country and ourselves: big, free and easy, openhanded, where opportunity exists for all, and where the greatest rewards go, justifiably, to those who see things clearly, shoot straight, and give it all they have.

One Man's Ideals—History has often been changed remarkably not merely by the ideas of whole societies or large groups but by the dreams and convictions of individual persons. Such cases as Christ and Mohammed are obvious. In recent times history has been heavily influenced by the writings of many men of much less than universal fame. Four examples, chosen at random, will illustrate the point.

In the 1890s there appeared a series of books by the American naval captain Alfred T. Mahan. They stressed the vital role of sea power in war and the attainment of national greatness. These works profoundly influenced many persons in military, naval, and governmental circles in several major nations. The extensive naval building programs undertaken around 1900 by most of the great powers, especially by Germany, were due in considerable measure to Mahan's books. The ensuing naval rivalry was one of the contributing factors to the First World War.

The thesis of the American historian Frederick Jackson Turner that the whole course of U.S. history has been vitally influenced by the constant presence of the frontier has been questioned on the ground of its intrinsic validity, but there is no doubt whatever that it has markedly affected the way most Americans think about themselves and their history.

The ideas of the philosopher-educator John Dewey have had an enormous influence on twentieth-century American education and jurisprudence. Dewey held that education should not aim primarily at transmitting the accumulated knowledge and wisdom of the past but at developing socially useful attitudes. This was to be achieved by relating education to students' natural interests, having children learn by experience rather than through formal instruction, and stressing occupational and vocational education. Dewey's critics grumbled that his ideas produced a generation who could not spell and did not want to do anything but be entertained. But this does not diminish the fact that his ideas had a strong and lasting impact on American education. Philosophically, Dewey rejected the contention, derived from both Christianity and the conceptions of Isaac Newton, that natural laws exist which flow from an unchanging order in the universe. Such a belief, he thought, tended to reinforce dogmatism of all sorts. He held that ideas should be viewed as instruments to change society. No idea is "true" because of its moral grandeur or its logic and consistency. An idea is "true" *for a particular time and place* if it contributes to the needs of society in that circumstance. It would not necessarily be "true" for some other time or in a different situation. These views strongly affected the manner in which the famous Supreme Court Justice Oliver Wendell Holmes and other "legal realists" interpreted the law and its application. Holmes' views, it might be added, were abominated by other jurists like Roscoe Pound, who held that any legal system must be based on a fundamental or natural law which is, or is assumed to be, unchanging.

The injunctions of Rev. Martin Luther King to blacks to espouse nonviolence and passive resistance, to appeal to the consciences of opponents by demonstrating to them that they were betraying their own finest principles, and to look forward to the day of which he said, "I have a dream . . . ," simultaneously inspired most of the American black community to protest against injustices and to strive peacefully for their rectification.[2]

Changes in Basic Attitudes—Oftentimes important historical changes are impossible without a prior or accompanying general change of mind or a new approach to a question. The momentous scientific advances of the sixteenth and seventeenth centuries—the theory of a sun-centered universe and the discovery of the laws of gravitation—were due quite as

---

2. As noted earlier, there is evidence that King's own ideas were changing in the last year of his life. See Chapter 5.

much to a changed basic approach to knowledge as to new inventions or the acquisition of new information. Natural scientists came gradually to think about the universe less in qualitative and philosophical terms and more in quantitative, mathematical terms. This proclivity, in turn, produced an awareness of the need for more accurate instruments to weigh, measure, and observe, and the need for more advanced mathematical techniques to deal with the facts so acquired. The invention of such devices as the telescope, slide rule, microscope, barometer, and more accurate clocks; and the development of such new branches of mathematics as logarithms, analytic geometry, and calculus, soon followed.[3] It is an excellent example of a phenomenon common in history: when a need comes to be generally felt, strenuous efforts are undertaken to satisfy it. Surprisingly often, they prove successful.

In our own age a reverse tendency is easily detected. The disinterested pursuit of scientific knowledge has produced things of inestimable worth, obviously, but it has also produced mass-destructive weapons and an array of industrial products and processes, which, if not controlled, pollute the environment. Equally ominous, all too many governments have displayed a suspicious eagerness to use the products of science to fingerprint us and to amass voluminous national, even international, "files" about us. Many think this bodes little good for the cause of individual freedom. Many people, too, are coming to fear that the world is growing impersonal, technicized. The individual is no longer treated as a person but as a collection of coded numbers and symbols—social security number, draft card number, blood type letter, credit card number, insurance policy number, fingerprint type, I.Q. test achievement number, psychological type designation—all presided over somewhere by Big Brother and his computer.

There is much complaining that the myriad separate human and governmental activities no longer make any overall sense. They lack inner coherence. They do not tell us where we are going or, even more important, where we *ought to be going*. It is alleged that what we need to do is return to a more qualitative and philosophical approach to life instead of merely pursuing any and all kinds of knowledge without regard for where this process may take us. Some thoughtful people believe the principal appeal of the totalitarian ideologies of our century is that they at least *claim* to have answers to all questions, that they interpret life *as a whole*, that they profess to be able to make sense of all the seemingly random activities of humanity. Where all this will lead, if indeed anywhere, we do not know, since we live in a time when all

---

3. This point is discussed in detail in Herbert Butterfield's fine introductory work, *The Origins of Modern Science*.

these misgivings are being voiced but have not yet appreciably altered *popular* faith in and admiration for science and all its works. All that can be said for certain is that our age *may* be on the verge of a fundamental change in basic attitudes toward learning and science comparable to the easily observed intellectual revolution of 300 to 400 years ago.

In our own country, ever since the founding of the earliest colonies, a majority of the people wanted to settle the land rapidly. Thomas Jefferson's belief that the ideal republic should have a majority of small, independent farmers unquestionably muted whatever doubts he had about the constitutionality of the Louisiana Purchase. That momentous territorial acquisition guaranteed an ample supply of land for American settlers for the next two generations. There ensued a struggle between settlers seeking farms of their own and a much smaller group who wanted to use federal land as a "national domain." The former settlers won victory after victory, culminating in the Homestead Act of 1862, which finally gave land free to anyone who would settle on it and till it. Although concern for land conservation was aroused by 1900, and much was done in the early decades of the twentieth century to preserve animals, forests, and scenic or historic sites, it was not until mid-century that real *mass* opposition to unlimited private "development" of the land took shape.

The modern welfare state could never have arrived without a fundamental change in popular ideas about the nature and causes of poverty. In the nineteenth century the prevailing view was that poverty was akin to sin: that it was due to sickness, stupidity, immorality, intemperance, or laziness—usually some combination of the last three. Whatever its cause, it was held to be the responsibility of the persons concerned. If individuals or churches wished to give alms to the poor, that was their business, but there was no obligation to do so. Since the end of the nineteenth century, however, many people have gradually changed their minds about poverty. Now, rightly or wrongly, they commonly ascribe it to social forces beyond the control of the individual and hold that the state is responsible for its relief. A clear indication of the change of mind may be gained from a comparison of the actions taken by Presidents Cleveland and Franklin Roosevelt, both Democrats, in the depressions of 1893 and 1933 respectively. In the first case, Cleveland saw it as the duty of the federal government to balance the budget, put its own affairs in order, and let private businesses and individuals get out of the slump in any way they could. Roosevelt combatted the depression of the 1930s by a program of extensive public works, governmental aid to industry, and massive federal spending. In each case a majority of the public approved the action taken.

Many people in the United States still hold to the former view of poverty and believe that governmental interference in individual and private business affairs should be sharply reduced, but they are nowhere near a majority. Politicians who maintain these views no longer possess widespread national appeal. The Republican party in the United States has come in practice to accept extensive governmental initiative in shaping national social and economic policy just as the Tory party in England has come to accept tacitly most of the social welfare legislation enacted by the Labour government of 1945–51. In each case there have been many wry faces, but the more conservative parties have given way because the programs of their opponents have been approved by most of the voters—and they must approve too if they expect to win elections.

Treatment of the newly freed Negroes after the Civil War illustrates the same development. So strong was the spirit of individualism in the 1860s and so well-rooted the conviction that the less government the better that about all that was done, tangibly, for the freed slaves was to set up the Freedman's Bureau. That body carried out sorely needed relief work among both Negroes and whites, scrutinized labor arrangements made between whites and blacks in the South, and helped some freedmen acquire land; but it did nothing further, and it passed out of existence in a few years. In our own times, in similar circumstances, the federal government would probably give all the freed slaves farms of their own on easy terms. Then it would establish a wide array of federal training programs to aid these suddenly independent farmers. Finally, within a few years, it would abolish the payments originally due for the lands.

If the reader objects that these last speculations are unduly fanciful let him reflect that in recent decades various branches of the government have loaned or given great sums of public money to such diverse parties as farmers, small businessmen, the railroads, maritime shippers, and the Lockheed Aircraft Corporation in order either to aid them in competitive situations or to save them from bankruptcy. Furthermore, our government has financed low-cost housing for persons of low income, Federal Housing Adminstration loans, free education for millions of war veterans, food stamps and rent subsidies for the needy, and job training for those lacking salable skills. Who can reasonably doubt that newly freed slaves would be treated with similar generosity?

Ideals versus Realities—Often ideas gain currency less from their instrinsic merit than from the fact that they are seen as alternatives to imperfect present concepts and conditions. Whatever exists, especially if it has existed a long time, shows its defects to the world. Whatever is proposed as a replacement displays chiefly its theoretical virtues and advantages. Only when the replacement is put into practice do *its* defects become apparent. In the late eighteenth and early nineteenth centuries laissez-faire ideas enjoyed great vogue among the educated because people tended to contrast the speculative virtues of laissez-faire with the obvious defects of mercantilism.[4] After about 1880 an increasing number of intellectuals grew highly critical of the harsher features of "free-enterprise" capitalism and advocated greater state control of economic processes. After a couple of generations of steady drift toward the welfare state, with its numerous neomercantilist regulations, there are increasing signs, even on the political Left, of dissatisfaction with the erosion of individual liberty that has resulted.

For seventy-five years before 1917, Marxian socialists enjoyed the tremendous progaganda advantage of being able to contrast the theoretical glories of a Communist society with the glaring defects of the capitalist world. Undoubtedly many people became converts to Marxism thereby, and others became willing to adopt a wait-and-see attitude toward it. Since 1917 this advantage no longer exists. Russia has now been a Marxist state for two generations; China and several Eastern European countries since shortly after World War II. Now the comparison has to be between capitalist practice and Communist practice, not the theory of one and the practice of the other. Not surprisingly, communism makes fewer intellectual converts than it used to.

Ideas as Fads—There are what can only be called fashions in ideas too, quite as much as in ladies' apparel. In the eighteenth century, if one wished to command intellectual respect he endeavored to demonstrate, above all, that his ideas were reasonable and logical. Human nature was held to be everywhere the same. Law, politics, and government were thought of as exact sciences. It was assumed that something near perfection could be achieved in each by "reasoning" about them. Early in the nineteenth century there developed a marked reaction against this cast of mind. So far did the pendulum swing[5] that the period is still called the age of romanticism. Now one with intellectual pretensions affected an exaggerated sentimentality, emphasized the beauty of everything "natural," considered problems related to government from the standpoint of past traditions rather than pure "reason," and regarded the diversity of human nationalities, types, and habits as delightful and wholesome instead of merely evidence that some people were less civilized and enlightened than others.

---

4. Mercantilism involved much government regulation of economic activity. Advocates of laissez-faire believed in complete free enterprise.

5. See Chapter 3.

Similar shifts of opinion have taken place in the United States. In the 1930s, for example, it was intellectually fashionable in certain circles to refer scathingly to the "failure of capitalism" in the midst of a paralyzing depression. Some then expressed sympathy, by contrast, for the "great experiment" being undertaken in Russia and professed confidence that the more disagreeable features of communism would soon disappear. In World War II it became popular to speak favorably of our Russian allies in virtually every respect. Shortly after the war, however, Russia clearly became a threat to American security and interests. Moreover, past Communist infiltration into some of our government departments and defense industries was widely publicized. Soon anyone who expressed even the mildest approval of communism was regarded as an ignoramus at best and a traitor at worst. Then in 1973 came the détente with the Soviet Union and a dramatic improvement in American relations with Communist China. Once more it became fashionable to refer with respect to at least *some* features of these societies: in particular to express admiration for the Chinese people, even if one remained silent about their government. What will be intellectually popular on this subject by 1990 God only knows.

In the 1960s and early 1970s a considerable furor was aroused by the public expression of some ideas that would have been regarded as self-evident two generations earlier. Several prominent scientists, of whom the best known, Arthur Jensen and William Shockley, maintain that peoples' intelligence is largely determined by genetic inheritance. They point out that some races consistently score higher than others on I.Q. tests and that some score lower on tests of deductive reasoning, though without appearing to be correspondingly deficient in creative or intuitive thought. They say, in effect, that all branches of humanity are not equally gifted. Now our concern here is not whether Jensen and Shockley are objectively right or wrong. Suffice it to say that their views are *not innately unreasonable*. It has long been obvious that people, like plants, animals, and insects, are shaped by both heredity and environment. The crucial question is *how much by each*? Nobody knows the answer precisely.

The point of the whole matter is not what is scientifically provable but what is socially and politically palatable. Those whom life has not favored, for whatever reason, like to believe that their troubles are due to adverse social, political, or economic conditions. They tend to reject the suggestion that the cause is deficiencies in their own intelligence or character. In this they are currently supported by a majority of the intellectually prominent and vocal people in the United States. All of them together have heaped much scorn on both the persons and ideas of Shockley, Jensen, and their followers. Yet if Jensen and Shockley had been contemporaries of Rudyard Kipling at the turn of the twentieth century, they would have been almost universally acclaimed as eminently "sound" men and their ideas accepted as close to axiomatic, for at *that time* both biological and social Darwinism were at the pinnacle of intellectual fashion.

Popular Attitudes—History is affected a good deal, too, by changes in what ought more properly to be called attitudes than ideas. Centuries ago toleration was almost universally regarded as a shameful thing. One tolerated sin or error because he lacked the moral stamina to defend or impose the truth. The actions of inquisitors pursuing heretics and of Reformation Christian denominations persecuting each other were well understood by persecutors and victims alike. Rare was the person who spoke out for the toleration of opponents' views. Now, toleration has by no means become universal in the twentieth century. The pogroms, concentration camps, massacres, race hatred, and ideological animosities of our age are notorious. "Hate" groups like the Ku Klux Klan in the United States and neofascist parties in many countries are well known. Nonetheless, in modern liberal democratic societies there is considerable willingness to allow a person to hold whatever political, religious, economic, or social ideas he chooses so long as he does not interfere with the exercise of these same privileges by others. A tolerant spirit is widely regarded as evidence of an enlightened, humane character—the mark of a civilized man.

The practical implications of this change of popular sentiment are enormous. In a society where toleration is held to be a virtue, minority groups and minority views of whatever sort have a much better chance to thrive than in a society where nonconformity is answered by repression. Unquestionably, in the great majority of cases the whole society benefits thereby: human happiness is increased, serious thought is stimulated, and a lively diversity prevails over dull conformity. Unhappily, the *consequences* of toleration are not always equally pleasant. It is an ominous fact that injudicious toleration can be the prelude to suicide. Each of the major Western totalitarian movements of the twentieth century, Italian fascism, German nazism, and Russian communism, could have been crushed had the governments they overthrew taken ordinary police measures against them, resolutely and in time. Once in power, these totalitarian movements, particularly nazism and communism, specifically disavowed toleration and persecuted their opponents without mercy, even to the extent of slaughtering them by the millions. This grim development has faced modern democratic states with an exceedingly perplexing practical question: just how much toleration ought to be, or can be, extended to totalitarian movements that avowedly intend to use such generosity to grow strong enough to destroy their gentler opponents?

Repression of Ideas—A much-debated aspect of this question is whether or not ideas can be destroyed by force. It was long an article of faith among believers in democratic government that this could not be done, but many events, past and present, raise doubts. It seems reasonably clear that force can sometimes destroy an idea if it is applied with sufficient ruthlessness. Half measures are inadequate, for their chief effect is to attract attention to what the persecutors wish to destroy, to make martyrs, and thus ultimately to stimulate the growth of the unwanted idea. The occasionally savage but always sporadic persecution of the early Christians by Roman emperors is conceded by all historians to have stimulated rather than discouraged the growth of Christianity. The same was true of the efforts of irate southerners to prevent the spread of abolitionist ideas before the Civil War. Southern postmasters might burn abolitionist literature unopened and southern congressmen might try to prevent the presentation of abolitionist petitions in the House of Representatives, but the main effect was to arouse additional sympathy for the abolitionist cause in the North. Similar efforts by the New England Puritans to repress unwelcome Quaker ideas in the seventeenth century were equally unsuccessful.

When the repression has been more serious, success has been greater. Antebellum southern slaveholders tried to prevent blacks from becoming educated lest they thereby acquire unsettling ideas. They also forbade negroes to hold meetings without a white person present. Both measures were fairly effective. Unrest among slaves was common in the Old South, but rebellions were few and easily crushed. The most famous revolt, that of Nat Turner, cost perhaps 150 lives. Only a handful perished in John Brown's raid on Harper's Ferry, Virginia (now West Virginia).

Regimes elsewhere in the world have been much more thorough. The German nobles massacred something like one hundred thousand people when suppressing the Peasants' War of 1525. The rulers of Hungary salughtered a comparable number of rebellious peasants in their country in the same decade. The "enlightened" Czarina Catherine II executed tens of thousands of her subjects in suppressing the repeated uprisings of Russian peasants in the eighteenth century. In the nineteenth and twentieth centuries the Turks have dealt with their dissident minority peoples by periodic mass slaughter, most notably of the Bulgars in 1876 and the Armenians in 1915.

The Albigensian heresy of the thirteenth century was destroyed so completely by an alliance of the Inquisition, various French civil authorities, and British and French mercenary troops that we now have only a general idea of even the *doctrines* of the Albigensians. The torture chambers and murder factories of Nazi Germany silenced all public opposition to the Hitlerite regime and exterminated most of its serious domestic opponents. The concentration camps, secret police, and mental hospitals of Communist Russia and China stifle all overt opposition in those states. It is even likely that the accompanying governmental censorship and propaganda monopoly exercised by these merciless despotisms in time makes genuine a good deal of what was once purely formal support by their subjects.

Yet repression is never totally effective, and repression without any restraint whatever is never even attempted. Most people have sufficient humanitarian feeling, enough humility about the unlikeliness of their own infallibility, or sufficient sheer indifference that they shrink from total repression. Sixteenth-century Catholics and Protestants were guilty of savage mutual persecution, but each side preferred to convert an adversary rather than take his life. Few kings ever attempted to execute any appreciable number of their subjects merely for the crime of professing republican sympathies. Modern totalitarian states approach the ultimate in soulless inhumanity more nearly than any past regimes, but even the Nazis frequently preferred to work their victims to death over long periods rather than exterminate them outright. The Communists often try to reeducate ("brainwash") ideological opponents instead of massacring them.

Ideals as a Facade—It is commonly knowledge that men and governments are prone to discover noble motives when explaining to the public why they propose to do something, when the real reasons are quite different and less attractice. (In fact, who is so saintly that he has not himself done this on occasion?) Neither persons nor governments, however, are ever completely cynical, nor, for the most part, do they wish to be. Even if governments usually pursue policies for such earthy reasons as money, power, prestige, or national vanity, they have to present those policies to their peoples in the shape of ideals. It is a tribute to the power that ideas exercise over men that public support cannot be secured otherwise. This is particularly obvious in the case of wars. How many Americans would willingly go to war and risk death if they were told that it was necessary to save the British Empire, or to enable J. P. Morgan and Company to make $500 million, or to enrich the munitions manufacturers of half-a-dozen nations?[6] But if the war is

---

6. These were not, of course, the real reasons for American entry into World War I. They are mentioned here because it was often alleged for many years afterward that they were the decisive factors.

represented as an effort to make the world safe for democracy, or a war to make it possible to put an end to wars altogether, or a struggle to preserve "the American way of life" from destruction at the hands of Nazi Germany, international communism, or some other menace, public reaction is far different.

It used to be said, at least on the lower educational levels, that the American Civil War was fought over slavery. It was a useful corrective to this oversimplified view when books came increasingly to depict the war as a clash between the urban, industrial civilization and culture of the North and the rural, agrarian civilization of the South—and as a struggle over states' rights. Even granting these interpretations, however, who can suppose that a war would ever have been fought over such issues *alone*? It was the slavery question, fanned into flame by the abolitionists and *Uncle Tom's Cabin*, that caught men's minds, heated their imaginations, and outraged their moral sense.

People Can Be Imprisoned by Ideas—Ironically, governments sometimes become the prisoners of the ideals they hold before their peoples. In the First World War, Allied propaganda insisted that Germany was a vicious aggressor nation. She had started the war and her virtuous opponents were now fighting to make such action forever impossible in the future. Most of the Allied leaders knew that this was largely untrue, but their peoples came to believe it thoroughly. The result was that at Versailles in 1919 Allied statesmen were pressured powerfully by public opinion to impose on defeated Germany a peace treaty more severe than some of them believed to be either just or wise. After having systematically inflamed the emotions of their peoples during the conflict in order to secure maximum support for the war effort they discovered that these emotions could not be abruptly turned off once the war was over. In World War II it was the *leaders themselves* who fell victims. After mounting an extensive propaganda effort to convince the American public that all the Germans were Nazis and the Japanese semi-savages and that the only possible policy to adopt toward them was to demand their unconditional surrender, President Roosevelt made no attempt either to encourage anti-Hitler elements in Germany or to respond to Japanese peace feelers. President Truman hesitated long before accepting *one single condition*, retention of the emperor, as the price of an otherwise complete Japanese capitulation. Of course it is possible *eventually* to persuade people to abandon or modify wartime hatreds. This was shown by gradual Allied reconciliation with both Japan and Germany some years after 1945 in the face of the Communist menace. Still, it was not easy.

This complication was rarer in the statecraft of the past. Centuries ago wars were usually the business of kings and governments rather

than peoples. They were fought by professional armies or hired mercenaries, and it was not necessary to arouse the public at all. As a result,
making peace and changing allies was much easier than now.

Idealism in Government—The previous examples may have seemed
to assume that governments are quite "hardheaded and practical," as
current jargon has it, while their subjects are idealistic. This is not fair
to governments, for politicians and statesmen are moved by ideals just
as surely as their people, if not always in the same way or to the same
degree. When a politician orates about the necessity of defending
liberty against some menace or other he may well be thinking primarily
about some electoral advantage for himself or some financial gain for
his friends, but in all likelihood he is just as interested as his listeners in
defending liberty. If politicians did not stand in some measure for ideals
that most people desire they would not be elected. Even in totalitarian
states dictators cannot entirely ignore popular wishes and ideals. And
no man, merely because he runs for a public office or is elected to one,
thereby ceases to care for the ideals he has professed. The reverse is
nearer the truth. The politician is often nominated or elected *because*
he is known or believed to be a strong supporter of some popular ideal.
What reasonable man can suppose that William Jennings Bryan did not
believe the doctrine of free silver in 1896 when his matchless oratory
turned it into a magical invocation to millions, stampeded the Democratic national convention of that year, and won for him his party's
presidential nomination? Who can say that ideals meant little to the
men who embarked upon the Crusades against the Turks, or to those
who have fought in the innumerable nationlist rebellions and wars of
independence of the nineteenth and twentieth centuries?

The day-to-day activities of all governments are a blend of devotion
to ideals and more or less cynical concern for power, prestige, money,
and electoral advantage. Even our Founding Fathers acknowledged the
inevitable imperfections of public officials by separating the branches
of government so they could check and balance each other.

The platforms of political parties tacitly recognize the existence of
factions and special interests and the need to placate them. Invariably,
they are composed of a sufficient varity of "planks" to ensure that any
potential supporter will find something attractive. In addition, each
sizable group of loyal supporters is promised certain concessions or
pieces of legislation should the common effort result in victory. After
victory, big campaign contributors and exceptionally effective party
workers have a way of becoming ambassadors or turning up in well-paid
jobs in the federal bureaucracy. Yet American governments who use
their power thus have not forgotten the ideals they professed when out
of office. Domestically, they have enacted minimum wage laws, estab-

lished the Social Security system, passed much civil rights legislation, tinkered endlessly with welfare and agricultural schemes, devised programs to give disadvantaged children a better start in life, supported many different types of educational research, set antipollution standards, and considered innumerable schemes to insure people against financially disastrous illnesses. Not all such legislation has achieved the results desired. Some of it has failed entirely. Some of it is incompatible with or nullified by other legislation. But, overall, only the blindest of partisans would deny that what has underlain it has been a genuine desire to make personal freedom and equality of opportunity more accessible to everyone, to protect less talented or less fortunate persons against the harsher features of existence, and to guarantee to most of our people a chance to make a living in a respectable way.

In foreign affairs Republican and Democratic administrations alike have gone to war in both Korea and Vietnam. Of course they have sought to further U.S. national interests, but also to help allies to defend themselves against foreign invaders. Whether those interventions were wise, and whether they were implemented properly, have been, of course, hotly controverted questions. But again, only the most doctrinaire of partisans would deny that concern to help friends defend their independence was an importance factor in our government's intervention. A careful examination of the words and deeds of governments in other parts of the world would indicate a similar mixture of genuine devotion to perceived and advertised ideals with hunger for office and its spoils.

*Prestige of Old Ideas—*The course of history is influenced by the reverence men have for old, frequently obsolete ideas. Conservatives the world over commonly try to justify anything by demonstrating that it is derived from previous ideas, institutions, or usages. This process has been defined by a cynic as "the superstition that a thing is good because it is old, as distinguished from the opposite superstition that a thing is good because it is new." Americans are a curious people in that we cherish both "superstitions." An enterprising American innkeeper once labored mightily to exploit this national propensity when he advertised that his restaurant served "New, Improved Old Southern Fried Chicken."

In totalitarian countries ideas can be imposed to some degree by force, but a more common practice in free lands is to try to muster public support for some proposal by claiming that it resembles a generally praised concept from the nation's historic past. The proposal is said to be in accord with the ideas of the Founding Fathers, to be truly Christian, to represent the frontier spirit, or to typify southern chivalry.

*Ideas Are Often Changed—*Oftentimes a man's ideas are altered radically by his disciples and by succeeding generations. The process is simple. A man develops a certain idea on a particular subject or a new explanation of some important happening. He expresses it with exceptional clarity and verve. Soon it filters down to the population at large in a simplified, dogmatic form and becomes a cliché. This process is inevitable because a large sector of mankind is always too busy, indifferent, lazy, or mentally slow to take the trouble to try to understand anything complex. Thus our man's idea soon becomes a parrot cry on the lips of millions, uttered without thought on numberless occasions, applicable and inapplicable. Who has not heard ad nauseum, "It takes all kinds to make the world," "No more Munich agreements," "You can't buy the friendship of foreign countries," "Such-and-such political party is for the little man," and so on? Once such phrases had a specific meaning. Sometimes there is still some truth left in them. After a time, though, they seldom have any specific or useful application to new situations. They become the banal battle cries of partisans who wish to spare themselves the painful chore of trying to think seriously about unfamiliar problems. George Washington's famous admonition to his countrymen to avoid entangling alliances had a specific and sensible meaning in his own day (to avoid permanent ties with European nations), but the twentieth century world of nuclear weapons, intercontinental ballistic missiles, supersonic aircraft, and global ideological rivalry presents a totally different situation. Were Washington alive today it is safe to say that he would be far less enamored of his own axiom than are many of those who have heedlessly invoked it.

Frequently the devotees of an idea or system are considerably more zealous than its creator. One can sometimes discuss the shortcomings of an idea with the man who developed it, but seldom with one of his more fervent disciples. Many people dearly crave some ideal to believe in, some scheme or system to serve. When they get one they do not want to question it. How else does one explain the zeal of numerous advocates of Townsend plans and single tax proposals, or of the followers of innumerable political and religious visionaries in all ages?

Many *persons* would have different reputations in written history if they were able to insist upon a certain meaning being given to their words and if they were able to control what later generations have chosen to regard as the true significance of their careers. John C. Calhoun is remembered chiefly as the advocate of state sovereignty and the inventor of the theory of "nullification," yet for most of his life he was an ardent nationalist. Even his doctrine of nullification was devised in an effort to get around the secessionist crisis of the early 1830s and to save the Union, if in a manner which would also protect sectional rights.

The name of Theodore Roosevelt invariably invokes images of

oratorical bellicosity and "big sticks." Virtually forgotten is the fact that the same man won the Nobel Peace Prize for his efforts in 1904–5 to end the Russo-Japanese War and to secure the convocation of the Algeciras Conference. The conferees eventually devised a peaceful way out of a European diplomatic impasse which could have easily brought on a major war. Ex-Rough Rider though he was, Roosevelt feared the outbreak of a general European war. He did his best to postpone that evil day because he was convinced that the United States, due to its increased power and status in the world, would not be able to remain neutral.

For decades after 1932 Herbert Hoover was widely berated as the man who had either caused the Great Depression or failed to do anything about it. Collections of shacks built from boxes, slabs of sheeting, and discarded construction materials were referred to derisively as "Hoovervilles." All but forgotten were the international humanitarian labors which had gained for Hoover the fame that had made it possible for him to become president. Forgotten, too, was the fact that Hoover donated his entire salary as president to philanthropy.

John Dewey could do nothing about the absurd lengths to which some of his intemperate disciples pushed his educational ideas in various of the "progressive" schools of the 1930s and 1940s.

Alexander Hamilton wanted the United States to have a strong central government. Could he be restored to life now, he would surely be amazed to observe what has been done with the doctrine of "implied powers" and the "general welfare" clause in the Constitution. In the name of promoting the well-being of the masses, both of these clauses have been stretched to justify the steady expansion of powers, claims, and jurisdiction of the federal government.

Reaction against Ideas—Ideas frequently exert a strong influence by the reactions they provoke. In the early nineteenth century a number of Englishmen, inspired by Adam Smith and collectively termed the Manchester School, formulated a series of economic principles in an effort to discredit the mercantile system of economic thought prevalent in the eighteenth century. The keystone of the new system was laissez-faire, namely, a belief in the existence of an invisible law whereby the economic well-being of the whole society and of every person in it is, in the long run, best served by allowing all questions pertaining to trade, business, capital, and labor to be resolved without government interference. This view was regarded as veritable holy writ by most of the European and American middle class throughout the nineteenth century even though it demonstrably kept industrial laborers in a position markedly inferior to that of their employers. Yet laissez-faire policies were modified only slowly, in part because middle class people had struggled for generations to free themselves from the multifarious regulations and burdensome taxes that had been such marked features of the old mercantile system. Once freed from this web of bureaucratic restraint, their descendants could not imagine any possible good accruing from a return to the principle of state interference in commerce and industry.

By the middle of the twentieth century a widespread reaction against many features of laissez-faire was obvious, even in its strongest bastion, the United States. It was not merely that the American government, like most other governments, long since had come to interfere actively with the "natural" operations of economic processes. Equally evident were drastic changes in popular ideas and expectations. Everywhere now one heard less about duties, obligations, responsibility, and work—more about rights, privileges, equality, security, and "advantages"; less about "production"—more about the interests of "consumers"; less about the necessity of profits if business was to survive—more about the iniquity of excessive or "windfall" profits. Fundamental changes in the attitudes of the business community and their advertising flacks were equally evident. Now one heard less about the reliability of a product—more about its style; less about its durability—more about how much it contributed to the youthfulness and vigor of whoever bought it. Virtually nothing was said about the desirability of saving one's money, but invocations were incessant to seize one's "handy credit card" and dash off to purchase the latest model.

It is common knowledge among professional politicians that great numbers of people do not vote *for* candidates or ideas but *against* them. For a generation after the Civil War many people in the northern states refused to vote Democratic because they regarded the Democrats as "the party of treason." In most of the South, for a much longer period, no Republican had a chance of election because it had been the Republicans who had waged war against the white South and imposed Reconstruction upon it. The fact that the Republicans abandoned Reconstruction in 1876 as part of a "deal" to secure the election of Hayes over Tilden as president in the disputed election of that year had no influence on southern voting habits. Neither did the consideration that afterward the principles of the Republican party were usually closer to prevailing southern ideas than were the principles of the Democratic party. What American has not known (by now elderly) Democrats whose political conversation automatically begins with a denunciation of Herbert Hoover? How many others must there be who will vote Republican to the day of their death because they despise Franklin D. Roosevelt and the New Deal or because they have convinced themselves that only Democrat presidents get us into wars? An amusing example, known to one of the authors in the 1950s, was that of an old lady who refused to vote for any Democratic presidential candidate because only Republican presidents had been assassinated!

Ideas as Myths—If enough people are moved by an idea, be the idea itself reasonable or nonsensical, it acquires real historical importance. What people *think* is true is often more important in its influence on the course of events than what *is* true. It is clear enough now that persons of different religions can be loyal to the same political state, but for centuries after the Reformation vast numbers of people in all Western countries thought this impossible. As late as 1928 Al Smith's Catholicism was an important factor (among others) in his loss of the presidential race of that year. Millions must have voted either for or against John Kennedy in 1960 for religious reasons. In this case, Kennedy was elected despite his religion. In office, his ostentatious regard for the separation of political and ecclesiastical matters must have reassured many, for religion was hardly mentioned when his younger brother Robert became a candidate in 1968, nor is it publicly accorded any importance when the possible presidential candidacy of Edward Kennedy is discussed.

While ideas that are out of date often continue to exert an influence on many people, once an idea is generally *recognized* as being out of date it becomes an object of derision and ceases to have any influence. A good example is the idea of "the White Man's Burden." At the turn of the twentieth century Theodore Roosevelt, Albert Beveridge, and others were listened to with respect when they urged white men to assume the burden of raising up the colored races to civilized standards. By our time, however, white people are less assured than they used to be of their "natural superiority" to colored peoples. Most of them have ceased to believe that imperialism is either just or profitable. Hence if some present-day public figure seriously proposed that Europeans reconquer Asia and Africa in order to civilize the natives of those continents he would get a cold reception. Some would regard him with amused tolerance as a relic of a departed age; others would denounce him as a heartless rascal or neo-Nazi. There is hardly a surer way, now, to discredit a proposal of any sort than to claim or imply that it is "imperialistic."

Yet old ideas have a way of changing clothes and sneaking in the back door. The basic conception behind the Peace Corps—to employ the idealism, superior knowledge, and skills of "advanced" peoples to aid those less fortunate or "less developed"—is hard to distinguish from "the White Man's Burden" of Kipling's conception. In practice, of course, political and economic imperialism does not follow Peace Corpsmen in the way it followed Western religious and secular missionaries in the late nineteenth century, but the underlying ideal is not different.

Rival Ideas–Quite often strongly and sincerely held ideas clash. Sometimes one overcomes the other; sometimes they are compromised. The Declaration of Independence (written by a Virginia slaveholder) says that all men are created "equal" and that "they are endowed by their creator with certain unalienable rights ... life, liberty, and the pursuit of happiness." Doubtless those who signed the Declaration believed these words. Certainly such diverse men as John Adams and Thomas Jefferson did. At the same time, they recognized reality—that the slave system was an unfortunate legacy of colonial times. They appreciated its economic utility in the South and the unlikelihood of its early disappearance there. Moreover, many agreed with Jefferson that unpalatable though slavery might be in principle, simly to turn loose hundreds of thousands of illiterate, untrained blacks was not a supportable alternative. And looming over all was the *supreme* ideal: to establish the United States of America, an event of inestimable importance for all mankind.

By the time of the Philadelphia Convention of 1787 the practical question was: how could a "more perfect union" be created without the southern states, even with their slaves? The impasse was evaded by one of those "practical" compromises that long afterward appeared base and unworthy to idealists who never had to wrestle with the original problem. In this case it was a tacit agreement that the slaves were "not yet prepared to be free." They were, in effect, acknowledged to be something more than mere property but something less than full-fledged men. For example, henceforth, not *all* of them, not *none* of them, but *three-fifths* of them would be counted when computing the total voting strength of the slave states.

When the first American state constitutions were drawn up after the Revolution the "equality" promised in the Declaration of Independence assumed other strange visages unconnected with Negro slavery. The upper houses of state legislatures were so constituted that they could be filled only with prosperous landowning citizens rather than ordinary people. Indirect systems of election were commonplace. Property qualifications for voting were established in every state. In some states higher property qualifications existed for holding office than for merely voting. Such restrictions lasted a long time, in North Carolina until 1865, for example. Clearly the "natural rights of man" did not necessarily include the right to hold office or even the right to vote.

Throughout history, conflicts between liberty and equality have been endless. In our age totalitarian states (especially the Communist ones), in the name of "equality," limit liberty to an extent unknown in the most absolutist monarchies of the past. Even in our own country the two principles exist in a state of uneasy and shifting balance. If liberty is the most precious of all human "rights" then everyone should have the right to send his children to any school he chooses or is willing to pay for. But if "equality" is to become a reality for many "disadvantaged" children then somebody's "liberty" must give way to allow mixing of the "disadvantaged" with the rest of the population. If individual ability, individual qualification, and the right of an employer to hire whom he chooses are to be the dominant operative principles in determining who gets which jobs, then insistence upon "quotas" of "minorities" in various occupational categories cannot be countenanced. But if equality of opportunity is to be assured, and undesirable social prejudices overcome, then such people need special consideration for a time. The inordinate attention devoted to such issues by national, state, and local governments, not to speak of innumerable private organizations, and the widespread acrimony aroused by virtually any proposal from any quarter for dealing with them, testifies to the near impossibility of simultaneously realizing two ideals, each worthy in itself, both cherished in the abstract, but by their natures not entirely reconcilable.

Similarly, in twentieth-century America and Western Europe there has been a protracted struggle between the laissez-faire economic principles of the nineteenth century and the doctrines of socialism. The result has been a draw: victory for neither one, but an amalgamation of the two. Private ownership and management have persisted from the laissez-faire system but subject to governmental taxation, competition, regulation—even harassment.

Race relations in twentieth-century America have displayed a similar pattern. For decades most black people strove to be more like whites. By the middle of the century a great many whites were coming to accept this as either desirable or, at any rate, inevitable. Abruptly, sizable numbers of younger blacks and "militants" became convinced that it was either necessary or desirable to cultivate distinctively black qualities and charactertistics. Soon there was a proliferation of "Afro" haircuts, neo-African clothing, black studies programs, and other indications of a desire for separate black "identity." At the time of this writing (1975) the two opposing tendencies are still much in evidence. Whether they will remain in uneasy coexistence, or one will eventually overcome the other, remains to be seen.

A celebrated clash of irreconcilable ideas occured in 1914. At that time the international socialist movement had long claimed that the true divisions in society were those of class, between capitalist and laborer. Laborers in one country were said to have nothing in common with capitalists of their own nationality but everything important in common with laborers of other countries. Wars arose, it was said, because rival gangs of capitalists competed for markets. The outcome meant nothing to workers anywhere. In case of war the workers of every country should refuse to bear arms against their fellows elsewhere, for only the capitalists benefited. When the First World War began, however, all the belligerent governments called upon their male subjects to do their patriotic duty and defend their homeland. Socialists were placed in a dilemma. Which should they heed: their socialist principles or their natural patriotic feelings? In a few instances principles were victorious. Lenin and a few Bolshevik followers in Russia condemned the war. In Germany Rosa Luxemburg, Karl Liebknecht, and a handful of like-minded Social Democrats voted against war credits. In England Ramsay MacDonald and a few others went to prison rather than support the war. In the United States such socialists as Eugene Debs and Victor Berger opposed American entry into the war. With most socialists, however, nationalist feelings proved stronger. German socialists went to the front to fight for Germany, French socialists to fight for France, and English socialists to fight for England. Though many German Social Democrats began to have second thoughts by 1916–17 as prospects for a German victory dimmed, and most Russians of all political persuasions were thoroughly weary of war by 1917, as a global generalization socialist internationalism was put in cold storage for the duration.

A similar dilemma has beset the non Communist Left ever since. Most persons of this ideological orientation believe all wars to be bad, at least when the matter is considered abstractly. However, in cases of *particular* wars against military juntas, "rightest" dictators, and "reactionary" governments, they want so badly to see the distasteful regimes overthrown that they often put aside their pacifist principles. The world is then treated to such anomalies as spokesmen for the Spanish Republic of the 1930s remarking that "our best machine gunners are pacifists from the English universities" or more recent newspaper accounts informing readers that "students for nonviolence picked up rocks to throw at the troops." With certain religious groups, such as the Seventh Day Adventists, conflict between pacifism enjoined by religious principles and deeply felt patriotic feelings is compromised in a fashion that reflects much credit on the people concerned. In wars they serve in the medical corps, duty which can be quite as hard and dangerous and can require quite as much personal bravery as actual combat but which does not invole taking the lives of others.

Dilution of Ideals–Ideals do not always win. Any struggle for an ideal almost always involves quite different ideals, not to speak of "practical" considerations as well. In pursuit of the latter the original ideal is frequently forgotten. Someone once observed, wryly, that "happy are the people whose history is short." If so, we Americans are lucky. Our history is less complex than that of Europe. Thus European history sometimes provides better illustrations of certain historical phenomena than does the record of our national past. Such is the case here.

The Thirty Years War was an extraordinarily complicated, destructive, and ultimately indecisive struggle that raged intermittently over most of central Europe for a generation (1618–48). It combined clashing ideals, both national and international, personal and national ambitions, and sheer greed for plunder. In its early stages the war was basically a contest of principles: that is to say, it was more about Catholicism versus Protestantism than about anything else. By the 1630s this was no longer the case. Soon after the war began most of the Catholic states in Germany rallied to the support of the Catholic Holy Roman Emperor, Ferdinand II. However, the sweeping victories of the famous imperial mercenary, Wallenstein, frightened the Catholic states nearly as much as it did Wallenstein's Protestant opponents. They feared that once all the Protestants were defeated the haughty and ambitious Wallenstein might well turn on them and simply absorb them into his employer's Hapsburg Empire. Accordingly, in 1630 the members of the Catholic League put pressure on Ferdinand to dismiss Wallenstein—a clear case of local and dynastic interests taking precedence over religious ideals.

Similar developments took place on the Protestant side. First, Lutheran Denmark entered the war on the side of the German Protestant states. Danish motives were varied. Only one of them was religious. The Danes were beaten, but then Lutheran Sweden sent an army commanded by one of the great warriors of the age, King Gustav Adolf. The German Protestant states were nearly as frightened of their new Swedish allies as of their Catholic enemies, and for much the same reason that the Catholic states feared Wallenstein. Accordingly, they cooperated most reluctantly with the Swedes. On one occasion Gustav secured the alliance of Brandenburg, one of the Protestant states he had come to Germany to "defend," only by threatening its capital with his artillery. The Danes, for centuries the enemies of the Swedes, had difficulty hiding their hope that Gustav would be driven out of Germany by the imperial armies, religion or not. Meanwhile Richelieu, a cardinal in the Catholic church and the virtual ruler of Catholic France, was subsidizing the Lutheran Swedes to fight the Catholic emperor. His motives had nothing to do with religion. The Hapsburgs and the rulers of France had been rivals for over 150 years; and he wished to prevent the Hapsburgs from conquering all central Europe. Richelieu tried to save appearances by having Gustav promise not to molest Catholics in lands conquered by the Swedes, a pledge which the king largely ignored. The last stage of the war in the west was mostly a dynastic conflict between Spain and France, *both* Catholic states; and in Germany this stage consisted mainly of protracted marauding expeditions by the Swedes and various mercenaries.

Altogether, one would have to say that the Thirty Years War was fought fundamentally for an ideal—religion—in the sense that had it not been for the religious issue the war probably would not have occurred. Nonetheless, the ideal became so obscured and compromised by national fears and rivalries, by the personal ambitions of some of the participants, by the threat that a sweeping Swedish victory would pose for the German states, and by the even worse threat that a sweeping Hapsburg victory would pose for the whole continent, that in the latter stages of the war religion was virtually forgotten.

A much simpler, but somewhat similar, illustration from our own history is the course of the American Revolutionary War. That conflict began in the form of colonial resistance to various policies of the British government. It was accompanied by much oratory and writing about "liberty," capped by a Declaration of Independence (1776). Before many years had passed, however, we had acquired monarchical France as an ally. The primary French interest was not acquisition of independence for the British colonies but reversal of the verdict of the Seven Years War (1756–63) in which France had lost her own overseas empire. Soon monarchical Spain had become an unofficial ally, towed along in the van of France. Then the Dutch became involved: embroiled in a quarrel with the British. The issue? Dutch desire to profit from trade in war materials, an activity the British were so determined to prevent that they launched an unprovoked naval assault on the Dutch island of Saint Eustatius. This squabble at once aroused the interest of the Russians. They, too, had long resented British interference with neutral shipping. Now they, too, began to consider the possibility of war against beleaguered England. By the early 1780s what had begun as a rebellion of outraged colonials who said they were defending their usurped rights as free Englishmen was threatening to become a worldwide conflict in which European colonial and economic rivalries would be the main issues.

Thus ideals and principles possess great power to shape history, but they are constantly being altered, thwarted, or diluted by contrary ideals and by the activities of men and governments whose eyes are mainly on the acquisition of power and money.

7: How Organizations Influence History

The Nature and Proclivities of Organizations—We have seen that the influence of individuals in history is often specific and obvious; the influence of ideas is equally clear, if less specific. History is also made by institutions. Indeed, written history is largely concerned not with pure ideas, not with personal biography, but with the doings of such collectivities as governments, churches, armies, and organized occupational and economic groups. Each claims to stand for some great cause or to perform some indispensable service. To a considerable extent this is true, but each is also swayed by immediate material interests. Often these are at variance with the idealistic pretensions.

Institutions and organizations are formed for many reasons. Some, such as armies and government bureaus, exist in every civilized society because without them no society could be effectively administered or defended. Some institutions arise because social forces (ideas, beliefs, attitudes) tend to find institutional expression. Others arise because it is usually difficult for one individual to achieve much without joining an existing organization or founding a new one to express and promote his ideas. Whatever its origin, an organization seeks to increase its numbers and activities, to extend its power and influence, and to perpetuate itself. The officials of a long-established institution like a church or a national army commonly regard themselves as heirs to a legacy and trustees for those who will succeed them. Consequently, they strive to protect and defend their institutions and usually to aggrandize them as well. This attitude has been exemplified many times in European history when secular governments have confiscated church lands. Churchmen have invariably denounced such seizures, in part because they consider that they do not themselves own the property in question. It belongs to their church as an entity. They are only entrusted with its care and thus are obligated to defend it, quite apart from whether a particular confiscation might be just or unjust in itself. People who belong to an organization or are employed by it thereby involve their lives, careers, and ambitions in its fate. Predictably, most of them do their best to add to its power and authority either for the sake of doing this alone, because they think they can thereby better perform their own tasks, or for both reasons. Only a rare person will uncomplainingly subordinate his personal or organizational interest if it conflicts with a greater public interest. Clear evidence of this is found in the hordes of lobbyists who harass every legislative body in the world to promote sectional, class, and economic interests.

Governments–Governments have always exercised enormous influence in human affairs. It has been a common characteristic of governments in all times and places to try to control their subjects more effectively, to grow, to expand, and to try to dominate neighboring governments or peoples. Modern governments have at their disposal all the products of the Industrial Revolution and can thus pursue these natural tendencies more effectively than in the past. They register their subjects (citizens) at birth, fingerprint them, issue them identification cards, teach them to be national patriots, induct them into armies, release them at their (the government's) pleasure, and tax them all their lives at rates and under conditions of the government's own choosing. All this influences history so heavily and so obviously that written history used to be chiefly the history of governments and their activities. It is still the core of any general history.

Legislative Bodies–Governments themselves are, of course, only the sum of their branches: courts, bureaus, departments, commissions and, above all in democratic countries, legislatures. In American history the importance of legislatures was evident even in colonial times. Colonial legislative bodies were usually dominated by local "prominent" people: merchants, large landowners, industrial and mercantile interests from the "Tidewater," or eastern districts of the colonies. Understandably, they tried to defend and promote the interests of their clients. Quite as understandably, this led to struggles with frontiersmen from the inland sectors of the colonies for control of the legislatures. Occasionally, the rivalry was so intense that it resulted in armed conflict, as in Bacon's rebellion in seventeenth-century Virginia. More often, the colonial legislatures became embroiled in quarrels with the original proprietors of several of the English colonies, not to speak of additional battles with such colonial governors as John Winthrop, Philip Carteret, Peter Stuyvesant, and Edmund Andros. In these struggles the legislatures enjoyed enough success that they came to see themselves as having acquired numerous rights which even king and Parliament in London might not lawfully take from them. This state of mind contributed much to the coming of the American Revolution.

Throughout the nineteenth century Congress struggled with the president and the Supreme Court, not only over particular national policies but over the extent of their respective jurisdictions. Every U.S. history textbook describes the efforts of Congress to compel President Jackson to use federal money to build roads and canals.

These efforts were largely futile. After the Civil War Congress was much more successful—in a sense. It overrode the wishes and vetoes of Andrew Johnson, imposed its own version of Reconstruction on the defeated South, impeached the president, and came within one vote of removing him from office. If the main eventual result of this congressional "victory" was to intensify sectional animosities for a century, it was at least a congressional "success" in wresting power from the presidency. Other American presidents have had little success in bringing their policies to fruition because one or both houses of Congress happened to be controlled by the opposing party. In our own time, by contrast, laments are widespread and loud inside Congress and out, that the proper balance in our government has been destroyed by executive usurpation of congressional authority, a practice which allegedly began in 1968, 1964, 1960, or 1932, depending upon who happens to be lamenting.

Courts—American history has been shaped quite as much by the courts as by Congress. Unquestionably, John Marshall had as much to do with molding the character of our national government as any president—vastly more than most of them. In the years when he was chief justice of the Supreme Court (1800–1834), Marshall, in a series of historic decisions, established beyond challenge such principles as the right of the Supreme Court to determine the constitutionality of congressional legislation; the inviolability of contracts even when opposed by state governments; and the supremacy of federal courts over state courts, of the federal government over state governments, and of the Supreme Court over state governments. Collectively, these decisions, followed thereafter throughout the federal courts, established the federal government as not merely a government *of* the states but as a government *over* the states.

Several presidents have quarreled bitterly with the Supreme Court. Some have been victorious; some not. During Jackson's administration the Supreme Court ruled that the laws of the state of Georgia were of no effect within Cherokee Indian territory. To this, "King Andrew" allegedly replied, "John Marshall has made his decision; now let him enforce it." In actuality, nobody attempted to enforce it, and soon it was a dead letter. A century later Franklin Roosevelt denounced the "nine old men" who were, in his view, sabotaging American recovery from the Great Depression by finding much New Deal legislation unconstitutional. He threatened to increase their number to fifteen, presumably younger and more liberal men. Soon the Court changed its tack and began to pay more attention to the election returns.

Heeding the election returns has been a recurring characteristic of the Supreme Court. Though few presidents have been able to withstand or ignore its decisions, as Jackson and Roosevelt did, the Court has generally avoided clashes with other branches of the government by moving with public opinion. Many decisions by earlier courts have been reversed by later ones, oftentimes by a five-to-four vote in either or both cases. The oft-heard remark that the Constitution "is whatever the Supreme Court says it is" is an exaggeration, but one that encloses a kernel of truth. In the 1950s and 1960s, when Earl Warren was chief justice, a majority of the Court members declared openly that if the president and Congress failed to deal with pressing social issues it was the proper role of the Court to take the lead and do their duty for them. This stance provoked cries of outrage from "strict construction-ists" and many a disgruntled remark about "the nine sociologists." Nonetheless the Court handed down a whole series of decisions relating to race relations, education, police procedures, capital punishment, and "minority" rights that have markedly changed our national approach to several extremely knotty and controversial public issues.

If a particular president happens to dislike the general tenor of Supreme Court decisions his chief recourse, most of the time, is simply to wait for justices to retire or die and then to appoint in their places men whose judicial opinions are more to his liking. Occasionally he gets a chance to move rapidly, as President Grant did in the Legal Tender case of 1871. In the preceding year, in the case of *Hepburn* v. *Griswold*, the Supreme Court had decided by a vote of four-to-three that green-back dollars were not legal tender for debts contracted before the greenbacks themselves had been issued. This was a decision that alarmed "sound money" men. Congress then authorized the appoint-ment of two additional Supreme Court justices to make a total of nine. On the very day Grant made the appointments the Hepburn decision was reconsidered. The two new appointees voted with the old minority to affirm five-to-four that greenbacks were indeed legal tender for all debts. Two generations later Franklin Roosevelt was able to hasten a change of heart in the heretofore recalcitrant Supreme Court by appointing to it such "judicial pragmatists" as William O. Douglas, Hugo Black, and Felix Frankfurter. Richard Nixon (1968–74) openly sought "strict constructionists" of a conservative philosophical bent when deaths and retirements afforded him the opportunity to appoint four justices to the Supreme Court. He hoped thereby to reverse the generally liberal character of the Court's decisions in the preceding decades.

In such endeavors presidents have often been fooled. When Roose-velt appointed Frankfurter, conservatives were appalled. Frankfurter was little better than a communist, they said. Some of the more imaginative critics added that he was surrounded by a coterie of "little hot dogs who wag their tails madly at the word 'Moscow.' " Alas, for melodrama! Within a few years Frankfurter proved to be much more conservative than either friends or foes had supposed. Twenty years after his appointment it was generally conceded that he was one of the ablest and most impartial men to have sat on the Court in this century. Dwight Eisenhower (1952–60) appointed Earl Warren chief justice, thinking he was getting a judicial moderate. Instead, Warren proved to be a "socially-minded" liberal. Eisenhower is alleged to have grumbled to friends that it was the worst appointment he ever made. In 1975 the nine members of the Court ruled unanimously that Richard Nixon had illegally impounded funds appropriated by Congress, even though four of the nine justices had been appointed by Nixon. Should we be surprised at such independence of judgment? Not if we reflect that the men occupy the highest judicial office in the land, may serve until death or retirement, and will never have to run for elective office.

Bureaucracies–In all organized societies the bulk of the day-to-day business of ruling is carried on by regular government departments, bureaus, and commissions whose membership is permanent, professional, and largely unaffected by political changes in top governmental circles. In the last two centuries France has experienced a dozen different political regimes, most of them violently hostile to principles cherished by some of the others. Yet, whether France was governed by Louis XVI, Robespierre, the Directory, Napoleon I, Napoleon III, or any of a variety of republican regimes, her bureaucracy remained little affected by these surface oscillations. French civil servants grew steadily more numerous and powerful. Today they rule France in much the same fashion as did their ancestors in the eighteenth century. The situation is not much different in our own country. In the early 1970s a prominent American senator was once asked whether the United States was ruled by the president or Congress. He replied, "Neither. We are all ruled by permanent government bureaus."

The reason for this condition is not difficult to find. Any government that steadily assumes more functions and responsibilities, as all modern governments do, needs more and more civil servants to carry out its plans and orders. There is always a great deal that bureaucrats can do unobtrusively to promote or speed up whatever they approve and impede what they dislike. Professional civil servants in, let us say, the U.S. State Department, stay at their posts year after year for decades while the secretaries of state—Acheson, Dulles, Rusk, Rogers, or Kissinger—are changed every few years or even months. While it is the secretaries who are much in the public eye, they have to depend heavily on the advice of the permanent bureaucrats in all cases, and entirely in many. Thus government can be likened to an iceberg:

nine-tenths lies beneath the surface, escapes close public scrutiny, and is much the same at all times.

Specific examples can be drawn from the history of many countries. The German Weimar Republic, 1919–33, was weakened considerably by the fact that the permanent judiciary and civil service were predominantly monarchist in political sentiment and thus out of sympathy with the fundamental purposes of the Republic. Many scholars have pointed out that the bureaucracies of czarist and Communist Russia rule in much the same fashion, even to the maintenance of involuntary labor camps. The chief differences are that the Bolsheviks keep far more people in more such camps, run them with greater efficiency, and treat the inmates more savagely. For years the English Labour party complained that the permanent officials in the foreign office were nearly all Conservative in politics and outlook. This, they said, made it impossible for a Labour government ever to effect meaningful changes in the spirit of British foreign policy. In the United States Republicans have often made a similar complaint: that Democrats, who believe in "big government," expand the federal bureaucracy, "freeze in" new and largely "liberal" appointees by putting them under Civil Service, and thus make it both easy for the bureaucrats silently to undermine Republican administrations and impossible for Republicans to do anything about it.

Whether the complaints of British Labourites and American Republicans are justified or mostly imaginary is beside the point here. What is beyond question is that once bureaus are created it becomes extremely difficult to get rid of them. In the United States many were created during the depression of the 1930s to deal with problems peculiar to that decade. In some cases, their tasks have long since been fulfilled or have been changed markedly. Nonetheless, their members strive to preserve their jobs by finding new things to do and by devising new arguments to convince Congress of their importance and consequent need for appropriations.

The mere upkeep of an extensive government bureaucracy is a heavy financial burden. In 1974 the whole American bureaucracy—federal, state and local—totaled 14.5 million people. One sixth of all employed civilians were on the public payroll. The federal bureaucrats alone had increased their numbers every year for a generation, received fourteen across-the-board pay increases since 1962, and now cost the taxpayers $42 billion per year in salaries and benefits. Many of their jobs are obscure and technical, and they are protected by civil service laws from being fired for anything less than the most serious transgressions. Specific pressures on Congress are usually to expand some bureau and increase its appropriations rather than the reverse. Thus neither the cost of the federal bureaucracy nor the question of whether any given bureau really attains the objectives for which it exists ever seems to have much effect on the bureau's numbers, much less its continuance.

Government agencies to deal with poverty and welfare have proliferated on the federal, state, and local levels ever since the 1930s; all the problems connected with poverty and welfare have multiplied apace. Wags used to say that the Bureau of Indian Affairs employed more people than there were Indians. Whether true or not, there is little indication that "Indian affairs" are apt to decline, much less disappear, in the years to come. Whether the policies of the Department of Agriculture have had much to do with either farm surpluses or scarcities has long been debated. What is incontestable is that the department itself has grown steadily for decades. The Office of Chief of Naval Operations in 1974 employed sixty-five admirals, double the number it had during World War II. More than sixty federal departments and bureaus do police, investigative, and intelligence work of various kinds.

It is little wonder that presidents and ordinary citizens alike have generally despaired of really controlling the federal bureaucracy. John Kennedy once complained that combating bureaucratic obstruction was like "wrestling a featherbed." A generation earlier Franklin Roosevelt simply created more agencies if the old ones failed to function effectively—hardly a promising solution to the problem.

Several serious attempts have been made to reduce the numbers and improve the efficiency of federal officialdom, most notably by the Hoover Commissions after World War II and during the presidency of Richard Nixon (1968–74), but results have been modest. Altogether there seems little likelihood of a diminution in either the number or cost of our civil servants in the foreseeable future.[1]

Individual bureaucrats, because of their professional associations or access to important information, can often do much to embarrass governments, even to affect government policy. On at least three different occasions since 1960 they have created notable furors in the United States. In 1962 Otto Otepka, deputy director of the Office of Security in the State Department, refused security clearance to another State Department official, William Wieland. In 1963 Otepka was suspended from his duties by Secretary of State Dean Rusk for unauthorized disclosure of confidential loyalty files to a Senate committee. He was then demoted and his salary reduced drastically. A specially con-

---

1. For an extended description and analysis of this whole question, see *U. S. News and World Report*, November 4, 1974, pp. 21–22, 38–48.

vened loyalty board then cleared Wieland and restored him to full status. In 1968 came a change of administration. The Democratic President Lyndon Johnson was replaced by the Republican Richard Nixon. Otepka was soon appointed to a well-paid position on the Subversive Activities Control Board. The whole episode got much space in the newspapers. A few years later, a civilian government accountant, Gordon W. Rule, testified (December 1971) before Congress that billions of dollars had been wasted on cost overruns in contracts for the acquisition of weapons, an indiscretion which gravely embarrassed the whole U.S. Defense Department, produced several congressional investigations, and cost Rule his job. Soon after, Daniel Ellsberg, a Rand Corporation functionary, stole top secret government documents (the famous Pentagon Papers) that dealt with American participation in the unpopular Vietnam War. Within a short time they were printed by the *New York Times* and the *Washington Post*, two newspapers which opposed the war. Pressure on the Nixon adminstration to withdraw from the war was markedly increased thereby.

Political Organizations–Public life is influenced by *organizations devoted to politics* nearly as much as it is by branches and departments of governments. Well-organized and handsomely financed lobbyists deluge legislators with "facts," cajole them, promise them, and hint at financial or other favors that can be dispensed or, conversely, threaten them with retribution at the next election. All this is done in an effort to persuade them to vote in accord with the desires of a certain group, institution, or interest. The outcome of elections in democratic countries like the United States is as often due to political organization as to the innate worth and attractiveness of a party's platform. All professional politicians know this, speak openly of it among themselves, and consistently act on it. To the ordinary professional politician "issues" are largely a nuisance. The important business is to get the party's nominees elected, for that means power for the party and jobs for the party faithful. To win one must have attractive candidates, to be sure, and it usually helps to appeal to sectarian rancors and emotions, but one also needs lots of money—for campaign propaganda, speakers, radio and television advertising, door-to-door political canvassers, and cars to take the aged, infirm, or lackadaisical supporters to the polls on election day. The party that does the most and best in these respects frequently wins the election regardless of the comparative merits of the candidates or the party platforms.[2]

The foregoing paragraph is not designed to turn readers into cynics

---

2. This does not mean, of course, that professional politicians are entirely devoid of ideals. See Chapter 6.

but to remind them of some elementary facts. In democracies governments are chosen by voters. The voters select among candidates who represent parties avowedly devoted to certain ideological, economic, or other interests. The efficiency with which these parties are organized and financed is thus an extremely important *practical question,* for no politician, no matter how noble his character or sound his program, can accomplish much unless he is elected to office. Throughout most of the nineteenth century in the United States party loyalty was assured and the party faithful rewarded by a general distribution of offices after victory (the Spoils system). This was dealt a crippling, but not mortal, blow by the Pendleton Act of 1883, which began the establishment of a nonpolitical civil service. Subsequent legislation prohibited contributions to political parties by federal and state officials. Parties then had to look elsewhere for the money necessary to support their organizations, campaigns, and candidates. They began to get it from "special interests": for example, business corporations and professional groups, soon followed by labor unions. Meantime, the cost of campaigning mounted steadily as the number of voters increased and competition to get out the vote grew more intense. Then came the age of radio, then television, then the seeming necessity of employing professional advertising men in order to realize the full potential of these new media. This meant that so much money was needed that *fund-raising itself* was turned over to professional specialists—who were *themselves* still another expense.

By the latter part of the twentieth century a situation has developed that is fraught with anomalies, widely regarded as intolerable, and yet allows no easy escape. What originally appeared as a reform measure in politics, the Civil Service system, is now seen to have contributed a good deal to a condition whereby several hundred million dollars is spent on national and local elections in a presidential campaign year. Among those who denounce this state of affairs most energetically are representatives of the mass media. Yet where do most of the millions go? To the radio, television, and newspaper industries in the form of political advertising. What to do about it? Politicians who get less money than their rivals, and intellectuals who are out of sympathy with those parties and politicians who get the most, want elections to be financed by the federal government or by deductible contributions made by taxpayers.

Most taxpayers have shown little enthusiasm for either proposal. They appear to think that, in one way or another, parties and politicians get enough public money now, and that if they were given more it would not replace what is now secured from "special interests" but merely be added to it. An additional consideration is that incumbents enjoy immense natural advantages over challengers in elections. The incumbents are almost always better known. Frequently they can travel extensively at government expense and mail free of charge much thinly disguised campaign material on the pretext of "informing their constituents." They can hold press conferences and pose as disinterested statesmen serving the public good while their opponents cannot help but look more like mere politicians in search of an office. Incumbents usually find it easier to raise large sums for campaigns than do challengers. Yet if some total amount is set as a limit in a campaign this may well prevent a challenger from purchasing the exposure he needs so sorely if he is to have a chance to unseat the incumbent.

If there is a ready way out of this morass it is unknown to the authors. What is clear is that those parties that are best organized and have access to the most money have a decided advantage in otherwise entirely fair elections, and that this condition is difficult to reconcile with the principles of democracy.

Churches–For over a thousand years the character and destiny of the Western world was shaped even more profoundly by churches than by civil governments. How pallid and empty would be the history of Europe from the fifth to the fifteenth centuries if church history was left out of it. The church possessed a whole hierarchical organization of pope, cardinals, archbishops, bishops, canons, abbots, and priests. It was the concern of these churchmen to lead the whole society toward eternal salvation. The organization they served was regarded as the fountainhead of the moral and ethical ideals that were supposed to guide the whole society. The church possessed vast wealth, chiefly in the form of huge tracts of land, in every Christian country. It had its own administrative, legal, and tax system. All these cut across national boundaries. Its hold on the minds of people is impossible to determine precisely but it was surely immense. It was the church, not the state, whose agencies and ministrations touched the ordinary person most regularly and frequently.

The church claimed that the things of Heaven took precedence over the things of this world. In practice, this meant not only that Christian principles but also the possessions and privileges of the institutional church took precedence over the powers, interests, and ambitions of secular institutions. Real or apparent conflicts between men's allegiance to their civil and ecclesiastical superiors were incessant. Battles between kings and churchmen over the boundaries of their jurisdictions went on for centuries. In general, medieval kings conceived the ideal church-state relationship to be one in which they were supported by a "loyal" church whose major dignitaries within their own dominions were appointed and controlled by themselves. Most churchmen saw it as an arrangement whereby "loyal" kings supported their principles and granted them numerous immunities and privileges, but otherwise let them alone. No theme pervades medieval history more strongly than the struggle of these two institutions, state and church, for domination.

Of course the Western world now contains hundreds of millions of persons who are not even formally affiliated with churches, a situation inconceivable in the Middle Ages. Nevertheless, the influence of churches has by no means vanished. In colonial America whatever church was established in a particular colony exerted a profound influence over the whole life of that colony. The churches in the New England colonies, in particular, bequeathed to our nation its so-called puritan legacy: a collection of qualities which have profoundly affected the formation of our national character, mostly for the better. Because America has always had many churches rather than one, and because none of these has been "established" since we became a nation, it is more realistic to speak of the influence of "religion" in American life than to refer to individual denominations. Even so, it was primarily such Protestant denominations as Presbyterians, Congregationalists, and Methodists, supplemented by some Unitarians, that pushed early nineteenth-century reform movements. Later, some of the same groups, plus the Baptists, formed the backbone of the prohibition movement that struggled for decades before finally securing passage of the Eighteenth Amendment to the Constitution in 1920. Liberal Protestant churches and organizations, seconded in recent years by similar elements in the Catholic church, have done much to promote the "social gospel" by working for a variety of economic, social, and educational reforms. And secularized though the Western world might be in most of its public manifestations, every one of us knows many people whose outlook and conduct are formed to a far greater degree by the doctrines of their churches than by any secular institution or influence.

Armies—The needs, deeds, even the makeup of armies exert a variety of influences on any society that possesses military forces on a permanent basis. A sharp social cleavage between aristocrats and commoners has existed in all European countries until very recent times. There were many reasons for this, not the least of them being the persistence with which armies and navies drew officers from the nobility and ordinary troops from the ranks of the common people. Armies heavily influence a society economically too. To recruit, train, clothe, feed, pay, supply, transport, and pension hosts of soldiers costs vast sums of money, not to speak of the tremendous cost in modern times of weapons' research and development. The money has to be raised by governments. Whether they get it by borrowing or by levying additional taxes on their subjects, the whole society is affected in innumerable ways, obvious and subtle.

Historically, Americans have been a remarkably fortunate people. Throughout most of our history, real or potential enemies have been far away—across the oceans. Blessed with "free security," it was not until World War II that we ever had to spend much for military purposes. We have never been saddled with such crushing burdens as that borne by Prussia in the 1750s, when 90 percent of her budget was devoted to military expenditures; or by France in the 1780s when two thirds of the budget was spent directly or indirectly on the armed forces (a factor which helped bring on the French Revolution). But we have, in most of the years since 1941, spent anywhere from $20 to $90 billion a year to maintain our national defenses. Some have contended that if these vast sums could be spent on the production of consumer goods or diverted to other peaceful purposes American life would be transformed. Others have insisted that it is the military expenditures themselves which keep the economy going: that if all American industrial production was channeled into civilian goods the market would soon be saturated and the country plunged into a paralyzing depression. Be that as it may, costly military expenditures are a necessity in an age of global insecurity, and the defense establishment that they support has an influence upon contemporary American life that can hardly be overrated. Many individual companies and some entire industries are heavily dependent on defense contracts. High ranking military officers retire and then sometimes appear soon after as high ranking executives in these industries. Here they negotiate with former military and governmental associates for billion-dollar defense contracts which can mean prosperity or bankruptcy for their companies.

This situation has produced considerable uneasiness about the existence of a "military-industrial complex" and what it portends for the future. Several million less-renowned Americans are permanently employed in our defense system, whether as "chairborne" strategists in the Pentagon, ordinary men and women in the field forces, or civilian workers in defense industries. Many of the best scientific brains in the country are regularly employed in military research. For a generation after 1946 much of the younger male population was required to perform military service, a situation which produced profound, even menacing, social and political discontent during the unpopular Vietnam War. The effort to alleviate some of that unrest by adopting an all-volunteer army at once raised further problems. Professional troops are expensive, difficult to maintain in adequate numbers, and, as much past history has shown, apt to become dangerously separated, in psychology and ideals, from the society that employs them. Thus even if our armed forces never fire a shot in anger for the next century, their mere existence will continue to exert a heavy influence on our national life in a dozen ways, obvious and subtle.

Through the centuries current modes of military organization have strongly influenced the character of society as a whole. The preeminent position of the feudal nobility in medieval Europe was due in the first instance to their own military traditions and to the supremacy of cavalry in contemporary wars. The nobles were the only persons wealthy enough to own horses and armor. The decline in the importance of the aristocracy in the late Middle Ages was accelerated by changes in the composition and weapons of armies. The widespread use of mercenary troops and the introduction of such weapons as pikes, longbows, and handguns that could be used effectively by foot troops of common birth against armored feudal cavalry all diminished the importance of the aristocracy in war and therefore their importance in society as a whole.

The German historian-sociologist Werner Sombart claimed that the rise of mass armies in the seventeenth and eighteenth centuries gave great stimulus to the Industrial Revolution. Mass armies need hundreds of thousands of guns, swords, canteens, uniforms, bandoleers, and other equipment—all exactly alike. According to Sombart, these demands acted as a powerful stimulus to develop machine mass production. He believed, further, that the discipline imposed on armies is similar to that required for efficient factory production and that the latter was consciously modeled on the former.[3]

Armies and their needs sometimes clearly dominate a state and its policies. In the late Roman Empire the twin threats of barbarian invasion from without and civil war from within were so constant and the consequent needs of the army so obvious and heavy that the Emperor Diocletian (284–305 A.D.) deliberately reorganized the whole Roman government and economic system to take account of it.

The conglomeration of scattered and poor north German states (collectively called Prussia) could never have survived and grown into a great nation had not Prussia's seventeenth- and eighteenth-century rulers carefully built up an army of exceptional size, strength, and efficiency. A native Prussian writer near the end of the eighteenth century remarked that Prussia was not a state that *kept* an army but an army that used Prussia as a recruiting ground. The Prussian military

---

3. Sombart's thesis has not gone unquestioned. For a sharp dissent see John U. Nef, *War and Human Progress* (sometimes published under the title *Western Civilization since the Renaissance* (New York: Harper and Row, Torchbook ed., 1963).

tradition, thus established, strongly influenced the whole subsequent history of Germany. Down to 1945 military interests and considerations were consistently given precedence over civilian. Between 1871 and 1918 the Imperial German Army was virtually an independent political force. Its commanders were responsible not to the German parliament or even to the nation but to the emperor personally. The general staff maintained its own informal diplomatic service apart from the regular diplomatic corps. It was very nearly a state within a state. It was not coincidental that in World War I the leaders of the army, Hindenburg and Ludendorff, assumed the direction of political affairs too. From 1916 to November 1918 they ruled Germany as co-dictators in all but name.

Ever since the revolutions of 1917 the rulers of the Soviet Union have placed the needs of heavy industry and the armed forces above the production of consumer goods. This, combined with ill-concealed Russian designs on the territory of neighbors and Russian hostility toward the non-Communist world has, in turn, been the chief reason for the development of the immense American military establishment which has influenced *our* society in so many ways.

Occupational Organizations–The eighteenth-century philosopher Condorcet thought the source of many of the world's ills lay in the propensity of occupational and professional groups to abuse their power. Organizations, he said, are originally founded to perform some useful service for the whole community. As time passes, however, their members try to establish monopolies over whole fields of knowledge or human activity. They become essentially esoteric societies, devoted increasingly to exploiting their advantageous position for their own benefit rather than serving any true public need.

Condorcet exaggerated, of course, as indignant people usually do, but the medieval guilds certainly deserved his indictment. The guilds were originally organized to insure a decent livelihood for the persons engaged in a certain craft or trade, to maintain standards of workmanship, and to insure a fair selling price to the public. They eventually became closed corporations whose members sought to exploit the public for their own profit. The masters of a guild restricted the number of apprentices to be trained and insisted upon working practices that had the general effect of insuring that there would always be more work available than trained guild members to perform it. This allowed the guildsmen to dictate the conditions under which they worked. Not surprisingly, as soon as they grew strong enough both absolute monarchies and revolutionary regimes either manipulated the guilds to serve state interests, drastically reduced their powers, or simply abolished them.

Many powerful contemporary organizations display a mentality distressingly reminiscent of that of the old and unlamented guilds. Great business corporations are enormously influential throughout the non-Communist world. They "develop" the world's natural resources; manufacture myriad products, both needed and unneeded; employ millions of people; spend billions of dollars on research to improve old products and devise new ones; spend further billions maintaining a whole new industry (advertising) which busies itself persuading all and sundry that life is hardly worth living unless one buys myriads of industrial products whether or not he can afford to; and provide jobs that make it possible for hundreds of millions of people to live who could not have subsisted in an agricultural society. Much (not all) of this is good, any reasonable person would say. But, as usual, there is a darker side. Gigantic, multinational corporations have frequently been accused of influencing the outcome of elections or, in the case of the International Telephone and Telegraph Company in Chile in 1973–74, charged with having conspired to overturn an "unfriendly" political regime. Many others talk much about the virtues of free enterprise but connive to establish monopolies over whole industries, fix prices of their wares at artificially high levels, pollute the land, water, and atmosphere with their wastes, and resist every effort at restraint in the public interest.

The conduct of modern labor unions bears an uncomfortable resemblance to that of the corporations. Unions themselves are usually founded by idealistic men who are laborers or craftsmen. In their early years union demands are commonly for higher wages, better working conditions, recognition by employers, and other objectives directly connected with the work and living standard of the members. Most such demands are thought by fair-minded people—at least afterward—to have been largely justified. With the passage of time, however, many unions come to be led by men who do no manual labor, and in some cases who have never done it, but who are professional "labor experts." These persons often strive for "better contracts" every year, mostly to keep their own jobs and get raises for themselves. Their followers, meantime, come to insist upon being paid on a variety of occasions when they do no work, to employ six men on a job that two men could do easily, or to refuse to use efficient methods if this would mean a reduction in the number of union men on a job. Some go so far as to employ threats or actual violence to prevent nonunion men from working, and to indulge in an array of other abuses with which any knowledgeable person is all too familiar. Not coincidentally, the totalitarian governments of the twentieth century have usually dealt with labor unions in much the same way that earlier governments treated the guilds: by subjecting them to stringent state control or abolishing them entirely.

Things are not much different with certain occupations where a great deal of formal education is required in order to perform one's professional tasks, and where the members often determine the conditions for admission to the profession—sometimes to the point of actually controlling the facilities for training prospective new members. Now of course the services performed by the "learned professions" are both extremely important and universally known. Where would any modern society be without the teachers who, at every level, educate everyone in it? What would we know about how we are governed (or misgoverned), or what goes on every day all over the world, were it not for the journalistic profession? How disorderly, indeed hopelessly tangled, life would be without lawyers and judges to define and apply the law in innumerable public and private instances every day? To appreciate what life would be like without a competent medical profession it is necessary only to do a little reading in the social history of ages past when doctors were few, ignorant, and unskilled.

Yet all these groups and the professional organizations that represent them are not notably more self-critical than the corporations and the labor unions. Journalists frequently show a massive unconcern for the practical effects of what they print. They appear to think that they have a natural right to know everything that goes on anywhere, anytime, and to publicize it at their pleasure. They attach inordinate importance to beating out other newspapermen—an issue of small concern to the remaining 99.5 percent of the population. Any criticism of journalism is at once met with a barrage of charges that the critic is a totalitarian at heart, does not understand "the role of a free press in a free society," or wishes to interfere with "the people's right to know." Teachers' associations talk much about improving education but their demands, to people outside the profession, sound much like the usual demands of other organized occupational groups: less work, more money, and more privileges. The habit of the legal profession to treat trials as contests, battles of wits between high-priced champions of contending parties, instead of efforts to get at the truth of some matter, and the common sight of a known criminal escaping just punishment because a lawyer was able to get him off on some technical point, does not enhance the ordinary person's respect for either the law or those who practice it. The tendency of the medical profession to close ranks against the world when one of their number is accused of some extraordinary incompetence and to charge fees which other people think too high indicates the widespread incidence of the same "guild mentality" in an otherwise highly respected profession.

Other Organizations—Modern societies are also heavily influenced by organizations less well known than most of the foregoing. Perhaps the "mass media" should not be called an "organization." Its numerous members, however, do belong to a profession and they exert enormous influence over all of us. One reason is simple and unavoidable. We have seen that a historian cannot possibly include all his source material in his "history," but must select what he deems most representative and important. Similarly, ever newspaperman, every TV or radio newscaster, must *select* from innumerable potential news items those he thinks most important or interesting. These, then, become "the news." Those items omitted remain largely unknown. In this way "the news" as we think of it is, to a great degree, "made" for us by those in the communications business. There is little point in complaining about this for there is no escaping it. It is merely that we should not forget that the condition exists, that there is no such thing as truly objective or impartial "news."

In the United States private foundations exert much quiet influence over many sectors of our national life, perhaps most notably in the field of education. Because they possess a great deal of money, they are free to contribute to the support of this cause, withhold from that one, give to an institution they regard with favor, deny to another institution or organization that employs someone whose ideas are disliked, and to finance research or exploratory projects in areas that interest those who control the foundations.

Secret societies, even mere social clubs, sometimes influence history considerably. In innumerable cases careers or interests have been forwarded or retarded because such-and-such a person was a member of a certain college fraternity, belonged to the Elks, or did not belong to the Knights of Columbus. The influence exerted by the Freemasons has long been legendary—doubtless some of it imaginary as well. In eighteenth-century Europe Freemasons were closely associated with a deistic outlook in religion which contrasted sharply with loyalty to established churches. Many Freemasons were also admirers of the world view of the Enlightenment. These unsensational facts have caused a few impetuous historians to credit (or blame) them for causing the French Revolution. In the United States the influence of Freemasons in government at every level was sufficiently evident to generate much anti-Masonic sentiment in the 1800s. It even led to the formation of a political party by that name, which endured for about a decade. Much better know is the real and malign influence of the Ku Klux Klan. In the southern states after the Civil War the Klan was long used to "keep down" the Negroes. It existed in much of the rest of the country too, and as late as the 1920s Klan support or opposition still determined the outcome of many state and local elections.

Institutions Inspire People—Institutions and organizations exert a strong influence on individuals too. Many a man supports an institution as zealously as an ideal, sometimes because he sees the ideal incarnated in the institution. The "company man" type is well known in any business organization. The modern labor movement, for all its frailties noted previously, owes much of its success to the efforts of dedicated men who spent their lives struggling to improve the lot of their fellow workers. Every government agency has its quota of "tireless public servants" who are such in reality as well as in name. Every school system has a number of teachers who *are* selfless and devoted, who genuinely give their lives to the education of the young. Social reform organizations of all sorts—antislavery societies, temperance groups, charitable organizations, civic reform movements—always owe much to individuals who are inspired by their purposes and serve them loyally for years. Every army contains some professional officers who are zealous patriots, who risk popularity and sometimes even their careers by their constant prodding efforts to keep their country's defenses strong. One such person was Col. William Mitchell, one of the early prophets of air power. Mitchell was so intemperate in his advocacy of greater U.S. efforts in this sphere that he was eventually court-martialed and suspended from duty from the army in 1925–26, only to be subsequently vindicated by events and belatedly honored for his prescience and courage. A generation later, during the Korean War, in a case where the issues were less clear-cut, Gen. Douglas MacArthur chose to end his long and illustrious career rather than accept what he regarded as politically mistaken directives.

Sometimes men are put to a particularly hard test: they have strong loyalties to two different institutions or entities and are forced to choose between them. Robert E. Lee, a man of high personal character and one who disapproved of slavery, was devoted to both the United States and to his native state of Virginia. He could have had command of the Northern army in the Civil War but eventually decided that his loyalty to Virginia was more compelling and accepted the less promising Confederate command instead. Caught in the same dilemma, Gen. George H. Thomas, another Virginian, chose the Union Army. Ironically, he was never fully trusted by those whom he decided to serve.

The Prestige of Age—An institution, like a person that has grown old, often enjoys a measure of prestige and influence for that reason alone. How often do businesses stress that they were "founded in 1844!" How many insurance companies have New England colonial names that suggest sound, reliable, conservative values and business practices! How many are the schools and other public corporations that emphasize that they were established 200 or 500 years ago! How many advertised foods either have "Grandma" in their titles or pictures of "Grandma" on their wrappers in an effort to convey an image of wholesomeness and quality! How many American political speeches have contained fulsome references to the Founding Fathers! How many times has the Constitution been called upon to justify some practice or point of view, even though the meaning of the Constitution is being changed constantly by new judicial interpretations! Ironically, how often has the American Revolution been invoked to justify some present or desired revolution, either at home or in some other part of the world—as though revolution could *itself* be some sort of an institution!

In the realm of party oratory it is hard to imagine a Republican speech without at least one invocation of the name of Abraham Lincoln, though a resurrected "Honest Abe" would surely be amazed at some of the principles (not to speak of the practices) of the modern Republican party. In the same vein, the Democrats still raise funds through Jackson Day dinners, though Old Hickory would likely be as surprised as Lincoln at what has happened to the party to which he once belonged. Political parties even deliberately appropriate names that have a favorable link with the past. When it was organized in the 1850s the modern Republican party chose that name in order to suggest connections with the ideals of Thomas Jefferson and his "republican" followers. Somewhat earlier, in 1836, those opposed to what they regarded as the autocratic tendencies of "King Andrew" Jackson styled themselves Whigs, after the British Whigs who had supposedly drawn the claws of royal despotism in seventeenth-century England and thereby shown themselves to be fearless champions of liberty.

Even geographic names reflect respect for age, sometimes to a comic degree. Pittsburgh was once called "the Birmingham of the United States," after the English industrial metropolis, only to see Birmingham, Alabama, subsequently referred to as "the Pittsburgh of the South."

American devotion to anything suggesting youth or newness is, of course, legendary. Occasionally, exceptionally imaginative people are able to combine the prestige of both youth and age. Thus the Kennedy administration was dubbed "the New Frontier"; "new," as befitted the youth of most of its prominent figures, but at the same time "frontier," to remind us of the old and honored frontier spirit that bespoke so much American greatness.

Altogether, the ordinary course of events is undoubtedly influenced more by the routine activities of institutions than it is by the deeds of exceptional individuals or the force of ideas. The student should keep in mind, however, that distinctions of this sort are artificial. It is people who compose institutions, and the institutions themselves are often called into being in an effort to turn an idea into a reality.

8: Economic and Technological Factors in History

Economic Historians—Any discussion of the economic interpretation of history should begin with some observations about those who believe in it and promote it. By far the most famous of these was Karl Marx. Marx held that the mode of production in economic life is always the most important factor in shaping every aspect of existence. At any stage in history those who control the means of production are thereby in a position to dominate society as a whole. If the means of production change or fall into new hands all other aspects of life change rapidly too. History is chiefy the record of the efforts of the masses to make a living. This has produced constant class conflict between the "haves" and the "have nots," those who control the means of production and those who are forced to depend on them. Noneconomic factors, Marx thought, were of only secondary importance at most.

Some "economic interpreters" are genuine Marxists; some are only "fourth-rate Marxists":[1] that is, people who have become accustomed to thinking in Marxist categories without fully realizing it and who would repudiate with indignation any suggestion that they are Marxists at all. Finally, there have long been many historians, not socialists of any kind, who nonetheless, have been strongly convinced of the overwhelming importance of economic influences on history. Many American historians are of this sort.

History, as it appears in most textbooks and is absorbed by scores of millions of students, has been colored heavily by the "economic interpreters." In England, many of the major early works on the Industrial Revolution were done by socialists. This is neither surprising nor disreputable. Socialists, from the nature of their philosophical convictions, tend to be drawn to the field of economic history. Moreover, there is no reason to regard them, as a group, as being less fair or less truthful than people of other political or social views. Nonetheless, socialists dislike capitalism and can hardly be expected to minimize anything that would discredit it. Consequently, they tended to stress the *social cost* of the early industrial age more than its *economic gains*.

---

1. For a good brief discussion of this distinction see J. H. Hexter, *Reappraisals in History*, (New York: Harper and Row, Torchbook ed., 1961).

They painted the sufferings and degradation of early nineteenth-century industrial laborers in darker colors than the facts warranted. Most of all, they declared or implied that industrialism had *caused* the poverty, squalor, and suffering when in fact these lamentable conditions have existed throughout all history and are still extremely common in most of the world at this writing (1975).

In our own country Charles A. Beard created a sensation in 1913 with the publication of *Economic Interpretation of the Constitution of the United States*. In it Beard analyzed the personal circumstances and financial interests of the members of the U.S. Constitutional Convention. He maintained that economic factors had been uppermost in the minds of those who had framed our Constitution and then worked for its ratification. A follower of Beard, Merrill Jensen, has attributed much of the dissatisfaction with the government established under the Articles of Confederation not to the innate deficiencies of that political system but to the consideration that the 1780s was a decade of economic depression. Those who framed our national Constitution at the end of that decade, he thought, wanted mostly to serve their own interests. The whole Beard-Jensen thesis has been much disputed by other scholars, but there is no doubt that it has had great influence on the way much American history has been written in the twentieth century.

Similar examples abound. Louis M. Hacker contended that the War of 1812 developed much more from the desire of frontiersmen to secure western lands than from its ostensible causes: popular indignation at British interference with American shipping or concern about the Indian problem. In his *Age of Jackson* Arthur M. Schlesinger, Jr., maintained that the election of President Andrew Jackson was due primarily to a coalition of land-hungry westerners and eastern workingmen who were mutually hostile to what they regarded as "monopolies": for example, eastern banks, shippers, and manufacturers. Schlesinger's thesis, like Beard's, provoked much scholary controversy. Perhaps its most telling critic has been Bray Hammond. He has shown conclusively that the struggle was not so much between "common people" and "capitalists" as between a coalition of westerners and new or emerging capitalists on the one hand, and older, established eastern interests on the other. The former group supported Jackson because they wanted to end the National Bank's restriction on easy credit, a policy which Hammond regards as gravely mistaken. Currently (1975), the "Schlesinger thesis" is accepted only in a much-diluted form.

While Frederick Jackson Turner is not usually thought of as an economic determinist, his famous "frontier thesis" began with the assumption that virtually free land was the factor which consistently enticed men westward. There the conditions of life did much to produce that "typical American" whom most of us in our hearts admire: the proverbial blunt, plainspoken, uncomplicated man who prizes his personal liberty, looks after himself, and thinks himself as good as any man.

As noted earlier, the Muckrakers contended that U.S. history had been influenced heavily, and for the worse, by late nineteenth-century financiers and industrialists. Like the English socialists writing on the early Industrial Revolution, the Muckrakers emphasized the socially undesirable aspects of increased industrial production rather than the undoubted benefits to all American society that resulted from it.

An accurate assessment of economic factors as shapers of history is complicated further by the consideration that many people get their most vivid impressions of the past not from history at all but from literature. Upton Sinclair's *The Jungle* was a pure polemic, a searing indictment of the filth and fraud that permeated the meat-packing industry about 1900. Unquestionably it had more influence on the way Americans have thought about this subject than any number of far more learned and balanced historical monographs on the problems and practices of meat packers.

Though strict proof is impossible, it is extremely likely that the personal experiences of certain influential American historians have colored our view of the past. For many years one of the most influential of scholarly works in American history with a strong antibusiness bias was Vernon L. Parrington's *Main Currents of American Thought.* Parrington was not trained as a historian. He began his professional career as a professor of English at the University of Oklahoma. In 1908 the president of that institution was replaced by a political supporter of Governor C. N. Haskell. Haskell, a close personal friend of John D. Rockefeller, was later accused of improper association with the Standard Oil Company. Meanwhile his protégé, the new university president, fired several members of his faculty, among them Parrington, allegedly for harboring "subversive ideas." Parrington always remembered the incident with resentment. He wrote his book following his dismissal.

A decade later Charles A. Beard had a somewhat similar experience at Columbia University. In 1917 he resigned from the faculty there because he believed that conservative trustees from the business world wanted to purge the faculty of "liberals" like himself on the ground that they were un-American. Beard's "economic" interpretation of the framing and adoption of the U.S. Constitution has already been noted. Later in his career he wrote that U.S. entry into World War I had been due mainly to the desire of American bankers and manufacturers to protect their loans and markets in the Allied nations.

As the whole foregoing discussion indicates, economic interpreters of history have sometimes been polemicists quite as much as historians. Moreover, any reader who has persevered this far in the present book will be aware that there are sound reasons for objecting to *any* single interpretation of history, be it economic or some other. Additional objections to a strictly economic interpretation will be presented later in this chapter. But what has been proved thereby? That history is *not* influenced by economic factors? Of course not. Karl Marx was guilty of exaggeration. So were his intemperate or uncritical followers. And like the rest of us, non-Marxist economic historians have their biases. Yet we are still indebted to all of them for *drawing attention* to economic factors as shapers of history, the importance of which had been long overlooked or undervalued.

Class Rivalries–Class conflicts with some economic basis have always been common in history. Because they have been much sharper in other parts of the world than in the United States, the best examples are drawn from the history of other nations and times. In medieval Europe serfs and feudal nobles stood at opposite poles in the economic order. Serfs performed the physical labor required to maintain the whole society and nobles were the primary beneficiaries. The social cleavage between the two groups was a reflection of the economic difference. That the serfs were by no means always content with their lowly lot is evident from the frequency of peasant rebellions, especially in the later Middle Ages. One of the basic causes of the French Revolution (1789–99) was the gaping gulf in French society between the privileged classes, nobles and clergy who controlled much of the nation's wealth but were exempt from most taxes, and the bourgeoisie and peasants who did most of the work that supported the country but who also were taxed heavily and were disdained as a lower social order. In the nineteenth and twentieth centuries antagonism between the capitalist and laboring classes in most European countries has been constant and frequently sharp. Moreover, it has been made a good deal sharper by the very Marxist ideas which stress the condition, not to speak of Marxist political propaganda and conspiratorial activity.

Class rivalry based on opposing economic interests has existed in our own country too. On the most basic level, the poor have never loved the rich anywhere, anytime. More specifically, the antipathy of southern and midwestern farmers to eastern banks, railroads, and "Wall Street" has been legendary. Steady rivalry between capital and labor is expressed every year by scores of strikes and lesser disturbances. Even so, our class divisions and hostilities have been pallid beside those of Europe. In the late nineteenth century anarchists were common in Italy, Germany, France, and Switzerland. In Spain they constituted a mass political movement. In the United States anarchists were few and obscure. In America Marxism has appealed mostly to discontented intellectuals. It has never had a mass following among workingmen. Such extremist labor groups as the Molly Maguires and the Industrial Workers of the World never commanded mass support and were short lived. The American socialist leaders Eugene Debs and Norman Thomas never despaired of the democratic process as a vehicle for furthering the welfare of common people. Each of them ran for president several times. Samuel Gompers, long president of the AF of L, said frankly that he wanted to see businessmen make profits, for then they could afford to pay good wages. Much nearer our own time, the extremists of the 1960s never acquired a sizable following. Most Americans viewed them with a mixture of wonder, shame, and disgust.

The Economic Basis of National Power—At all times and places in history the economic resources of given areas and the economic beliefs and practices of peoples have had much to do with the power or weakness, prosperity or poverty, growth or stagnation, of nations and empires.

Research into the economic history of ancient Rome has indicated clearly the extent to which unsolved economic problems contributed to the downfall of antiquity's mightiest empire. Roman industry was not sufficiently developed to enable cities to be self-supporting. Instead, Roman cities were parasitic, constantly drawing in wealth from the countryside. For centuries after the Carthaginian Wars (third and second centuries B.C.) small, independent farmers were driven off the land due to their inability to compete with huge plantations owned by aristocrats and worked by hordes of slaves taken in Rome's victorious wars. The formerly independent farmers gravitated to the empire's cities. A few were able to find employment in handicraft industries, but most became part of the ever growing, worthless urban mobs who had to be fed and kept amused to prevent them from becoming politically dangerous. The expense to the government was crushing, and the situation grew steadily worse with each passing generation. The currency was inflated and taxes were raised until the taxpayers grew apathetic or fled the land, but the problem was never solved. More fundamental still, Rome lived for centuries by conquering new lands and systematically looting them of stored wealth and slaves. Eventually there was nothing left to conquer and the empire was forced to subsist on its own resources and to bear the cost of administering and defending the conquered territories as well. The burden was crushing and Rome eventually collapsed beneath it.

If Rome had insufficient economic resources and did not use those productively, the same cannot be said of the national monarchies of early modern Europe. By the seventeenth century they were industriously seeking ways to increase state power by economic manipulation. The system they created was called mercantilism. Mercantilist statesmen believed that the total amount of trade in the world was fixed. Each was convinced that his own country should increase its share of this total and that this could be done only by taking some of the trade of its rivals. This belief, and the policies that followed inevitably from it, soon complicated the foreign relations of mercantilist states. The trade rivalry that ensued was the most important cause of several wars involving France, England, and the Netherlands in the last half of the seventeenth century.

According to another mercantilist doctrine colonies existed for the benefit of the mother country: to supply her with cheap raw materials and to provide a market for her manufacturers. This doctrine was equally productive of trouble. The English effort to make it a reality was one of the major causes of the American Revolution. The Navigation Acts of 1660, 1663, 1673, and 1696, and the Molasses Act of 1733, were all designed, in various ways, to serve the interest of Britain. Naturally, these measures were resented in the colonies, but the resentment was limited because all the British governments from 1721 to 1763 were dominated by either Robert Walpole or the duke of Newcastle. Both men believed in a policy of "salutary neglect" toward colonial trade. In this atmosphere smuggling was rampant and evasion of the Navigation Acts easy.

Then in 1764 came an abrupt change. Parliament passed the Sugar Act. This was followed by unmistakable indications from London that serious efforts were going to be made to enforce not only this new act but all the old Navigation Acts as well. Overnight colonial smugglers were threatened with ruin. In the same year Parliament prohibited the use of paper money as legal tender in the colonies. This was news of the bleakest sort, for many colonials had long been heavily in debt either to private persons or to public agencies in England. Now they were being told, in effect, that they might not print the paper currency that was sorely needed in their businesses and that helped ease the payment of their debts. (The paper money was easily inflated.) Great bitterness was aroused by these plain clashes of economic interest between Britain and her colonial subjects. It was all capped by the Tea Act of 1773, another law of the same stripe. Two years later the Revolution began.

In our time if a statesman said his policy was "mercantilist" he would be viewed with wonder. Nevertheless, outdated though the *name* may be, all sorts of mercantilist assumptions and practices are as much in evidence now as in the heyday of the Navigation Acts. Not only dictatorships but democratic governments like our own still try to regulate the prices of such products as wheat and oil by international agreements, by export and import taxes, and by domestic "price controls." The U.S. government subsidizes our merchant marine. The governments of many democratic countries subsidize companies engaged in civil aviation production and other defense industries just as statesmen in seventeenth-century Europe used to subsidize industries they deemed essential to the preservation of national strength. Old mercantilists were convinced that the total amount of the world's trade was limited and that, therefore, a nation had to jealously guard its own share. Neomercantilists observe that the world's natural resources are limited and conclude that each nation had better guard whatever it has. Nineteenth-century believers in free enterprise scorned the way earlier mercantilists hoarded gold and silver and manipulated the currency. Latter-day mercantilists torture currencies outrageously and not only hoard precious metals but juggle their prices in the bargain. Old mercantilists thought wealth in money the best guarantee of victory in war. Though this precept was laughed at for two centuries by squadrons of economists and historians all over the Western world, a cardinal feature of American foreign policy since 1945 has been to pump billions of dollars into dozens of countries from Western Europe to South Korea, from Vietnam to Latin America, in order to strengthen both their will and their means to resist domestic and foreign communism. The objective throughout, whether in seventeenth-century Europe or twentieth-century America, has been to manipulate economic resources and policies in order to strengthen the nation and further its policies. Clearly, slogans and paper justifications for state policies have changed a lot in 300 years; realities much less.

Economic Motivation behind National Policies—The importance of economic factors is not confined to providing a basis for national power. The material needs and desires of people have much to do with shaping the *policies* of any nation no matter how sound or unsound its economic underpinning. The influence of such factors on the development of the Americas has been obvious virtually from the day Columbus set foot on San Salvador in 1492. The early explorers and settlers of the New World came seeking many things: fame, adventure, religious freedom, and the conversion of the Indians to Christianity. But above all they coveted economic things: spices, gold, silver, and precious stones. Their descendants soon pursued other, less flashy but just as real, economic objectives: naval stores and other raw materials, free land, and, at length, merely a generalized chance for a more prosperous life.

For centuries the land was plentiful, but there was never enough cheap labor to exploit it to the fullest in tropical and semitropical regions where the heat was intense and diseases were both numerous and lethal. The solution was to introduce Negro slavery. The racial and social consequences have bedevilled our country every since. Farther north, rivalry over the valuable fur trade was an important ingredient in the Anglo-French wars of colonial times which ended in the ultimate defeat of France in 1763 and her virtual exclusion from continental North America thereafter.

From the earliest colonial times few themes are so pervasive in American history as land speculation and westward expansion. Urban centers wanted the hinterlands settled so that a profitable trade might develop. Southern planters always needed more land since first tobacco and then cotton wore out land rapidly. Frontiersmen, "squatters," discontented city dwellers, and millions of immigrants of a dozen nationalities, pushed ever westward. They occupied land, clamored for cheaper (or free) land, and squabbled incessantly with the various eastern interests that, for one reason or another, wanted to restrict access to the public domain. Within innumerable local regions the machinations of town promoters and real estate developers had much to do with determining the character of local history.

Economic Experiences–The mere economic *experiences* of peoples and nations, quite apart from their needs and desires, have often greatly influenced subsequent events. American faith in "free enterprise" derived considerable impetus in the early nineteenth century from the misjudgments of a number of state governments. They borrowed heavily abroad to finance the building of roads and canals. Unfortunately, many of the projects were not soundly conceived. Then came the depression of 1837. State after state defaulted on its debts. The conviction grew rapidly that henceforth state and national governments should leave such recondite matters to the presumed superior business judgment of private individuals.

In our own century the celebrated stock market crash of 1929 and the subsequent global depression shook the world so heavily and in so many ways that the reverberations have never entirely died away. In the short run the depression produced unemployment and economic hardship of unprecedented dimensions, plus the social discontent inevitable in such a case. In the United States there was a peaceful political upheaval: everywhere Republicans were turned out of office and the Democrat, Franklin Roosevelt, was elected president. A vast array of recovery, reconstruction, and social welfare projects followed, all of which permanently increased the role of the federal government in the nation's everyday affairs. Abroad, war reparations and Allied war debt payments were suspended, never to be resumed. This development further intensified the growing American conviction that all Europeans were shifty rascals who weasled out of just debts.

Preoccupied with their own hellishly complex economic problems and apprehensive about the very survival of democracy, the people and governments of France, Great Britain, and the United States paid far too little attention to what was portended by the rise of the Nazi dictator Adlof Hitler. Imbued with isolationist folly, pacifist dreams, and resentment of "ungrateful" Europeans, feverishly preoccupied with overcoming the slump in our own country, we reduced our military expenditures and then raised up higher and higher tariffs against foreign products. The latter policy alienated Japan, a nation that lived by her export trade. It was followed by American opposition to the Japanese effort to conquer China and, eventually, by an embargo on the shipment of war materials to Japan. The Japanese attack on Pearl Harbor came soon after.

Domestically, the harrowing memories of the Great Depression still benumb our souls. Election returns since 1934 indicate clearly that a majority of politicians and public alike will run any risk, take refuge in any illusion, embrace any temporary panacea, if it can be represented as necessary to head off a recurrence of the debacle of the 1930s. Whenever the country experiences, however slightly, an economic downturn the political party in power hastens to assure everyone that it is only the most insignificant of "recessions," really only a "rolling readjustment," certainly not the early stages of a "depression," against which the government has taken and is taking every possible precaution. The party out of power at once expresses grave fears that the habitual bungling of those in power will indeed produce the dreaded "depression." Much of the public, meanwhile, promptly takes fright and demands federal intervention into ordinary economic processes in order to forestall possible catastrophe. So often has this scenario been played out that it sometimes seems that we fear depression more than war. Be that as it may, there is no doubt that the public fears not just depressions but mere "recessions" more than inflation. Although inflation is a far graver threat to the nation in the long run, most people think primarily of what affects their own lives at the moment and thus clamor for the expenditure of money and the invention of programs which they hope will ward off any potential economic slump. Whatever the state of the federal budget, whatever their private beliefs, politicians of both parties comply with alacrity rather than face the wrath of the voters in the next election. Meanwhile inflation accelerates and the national debt soars astronomically.[2]

---

2. A highly placed American public official, Leon Henderson, once observed that "A little inflation is like a little pregnancy—it keeps on growing." Subsequent experience has borne him out with a vengeance.

The Economic Basis of Ideals—Not only the policies of nations but the very ideals of mankind often derive significantly from economic conditions. All the great revolutionary ideologies of modern times have some economic basis. One of the keynotes of nineteenth-century liberalism was the demand for freedom from government (mercantilistic) interference in private economic affairs. Socialism and communism grew directly out of conditions dramatized by the Industrial Revolution. It was not that industrialism *created* the long hours, low wages, wretched working conditions, and noisome slums of infamous legend. All these had long existed in all societies that possessed either cities or handicraft industries. Indeed, by dramatically increasing the amount of wealth in existence, industrialism for the first time made it possible to attack such social ills with some prospect of success. But, as is so often the case in human affairs, facts were not the issue. What people *thought* was true was more important than the truth itself. The outpouring of wealth from the factories was evident to everyone in the early nineteenth century. For the first time in history millions of people became convinced that it was now possible for most, perhaps even all, people to enjoy a better standard of life. Yet the long hours, poverty, and squalor remained. "Why?," asked humanitarians, intellectuals, and workingmen alike. "Because the greedy capitalists are robbing us," was a very general response. Thus in every Western country where industrialism began, the continuance of social blight was quickly followed by the emergence of some brand of socialism as a proposed remedy.

It was little different with fascism. Though both the Italian dictator Mussolini and the German dictator Hitler poured out torrents of militarist, nationalist, and racist bombast, both gained much public support by their promises to solve the economic problems of their respective countries. Both kept the promises to a degree, Hitler in particular bringing Germany out of the depression of the 1930s and restoring full employment by embarking on an enormous arms building program.

Revolutionary movements in any part of the world since 1945 usually try to gain mass support by calling loudly for land reform, the expropriation of foreign companies, a general elevation of living standards, or some other obvious economic objective.

On both sides of the Atlantic the modern welfare state is the direct result of mass demands for a higher material standard of life and a greater degree of economic security for everyone. Unemployment insurance, accident insurance, old age pensions, medical insurance, and social security exist in some form in nearly all Western countries. They are only the particular manifestations of this general desire, which stems from ages of poverty and economic insecurity.

Technology as a Molder of History—It would be easy to contend that a discussion of technological advances does not belong in the same chapter with a consideration of economic forces as movers of history. Technology, after all, has close affinities with science, and both are products primarily of man's imagination, curiosity, ingenuity, and intelligence. Still, technological advance invariably produces economic repercussions. Particularly since the Industrial Revolution, technological change has been tied closely to improvements in modes of production, to the manufacture of mountains of material goods, and to the multiplication of wealth. Thus the economic *consequences* of technological change are of such magnitude that it seems reasonable to treat the two phenomena together as shapers of history.

1. *War*—The nature and results of warfare have always been severely limited by prevalent modes of military organization and available weapons. As we have seen, when mounted knights dominated war they dominated medieval society. When weapons were invented that allowed common foot soldiers to defeat armored knights the aristocracy declined in every sphere of life. When European national economies became sufficiently thriving and well organized that kings could hire, train, and supply armies of one hundred thousand to three hundred thousand men, nations like the Netherlands and Sweden, whose small populations allowed them to raise forces of only thirty thousand to fifty thousand men, sank permanently to the rank of second- and third-rate powers.

The famous conquest of Mexico by Cortez was possible primarily because of divisions among the Aztec and other Indian tribes plus a dreadful smallpox epidemic that destroyed the Indians in droves. Nonetheless, it also owed a good deal to two Spanish weapons unknown to the Indians: horses and firearms. The victory of the North in the American Civil War was likewise due to several factors. One of them was simply that 92 percent of the nation's manufacturing was in the North; another, that the North had a much superior railway system.

As noted earlier, the horrible casualties of World War I led to twenty years of emotional revulsion against war. This produced, in democratic nations, the ruinous "appeasement" of the 1930s that almost allowed the Fascist dictators to win World War II without having to fight it. Those World War I casualties were caused by the invention of barbed wire, machine guns, shrapnel, rapid-firing artillery, gas, submarines, and other devices: in brief, to the wedding of modern industrial technology to war. In both World Wars, but especially in the second, the flood of products of every sort that poured out of American factories, laboratories, and shipyards was crucial for the ultimate triumph of Allied arms.

Equally crucial to the war effort was the superiority of Allied scientific expertise. One has only to ask himself where we would all be now if Nazi Germany had been the first to develop atomic bombs? Or, where would we be if the English had not developed microwave radar, which broke the German submarine menace and made it possible for U.S. and British supplies to get to Russia and thus keep the USSR in the war. Ironically, many of the scientists most responsible for Allied supremacy in atomic and other fields of research were men driven out of Europe by Nazi persecution of the Jews. It has been said, with but small exaggeration, that from the German point of view the loss of Albert Einstein (who fled the Third Reich) was as grave a defeat as the loss of Stalingrad.

Since World War II the absolute necessity for modern armies to keep abreast of the latest scientific and technological developments has been so obvious that the world's major governments annually pour tens of billions of dollars into every type of military research. For the same reason they have been equally avid to establish and maintain the highest level of scientific and technological education. Centuries ago, when the weapons were swords, lances, and quarterstaffs, to fall behind in the "arms race" meant little. When the arms have become nuclear bombs, supersonic aircraft, and exceedingly complex electronic equipment, to fall behind may be but a brief prelude to national extinction. Indeed, in our age man has for the first time in history devised a practical means of eliminating himself as a species. (Interestingly, at almost exactly the same time, in the long span of history, man has also finally learned how to escape from our planet and, possibly, one day to migrate to and populate other parts of the universe.)

2. *The Industrial Revolution*—The growth of the industrial factory system of production in the last 200 years, and particularly in the last 100, has probably changed Western man's manner of life more than any other event in history. The Industrial Revolution itself was not possible until certain technological problems were solved. Machine mass production required fine machine tools and interchangeable parts. The tools could not be made without metals of superior quality and the invention in the seventeenth century, of various instruments that made it possible to weigh and measure more precisely than before. Interchangeable parts awaited the genius of Eli Whitney—far more renowned for his invention of the cotton gin. Only when these technological advances had taken place could the vast factories and sprawling industrial cities follow.

The Industrial Revolution solved innumerable problems that had vexed humanity for millennia. It also brought a congeries of problems unknown before and aggravated many that had long existed. The population of the world has nearly quadrupled since 1800, a growth physically impossible in an agricultural society. The jobs provided by industry allowed hundreds of millions of people to secure the means of subsistence where before they would have had no livelihood. At the same time, packing vast numbers into huge cities has raised problems of heating, lighting, transportation, feeding, garbage disposal, entertainment, law enforcement, and social intercourse that never before existed on a comparable scale. It has compelled governments to play an ever expanding role in the everyday lives of all of us. The automobile, moving pictures, radio, and television have provided entirely new modes of entertainment for most of the population of the Western world. The automobile has already raised pressing questions about the use and proper allocation of such natural resources as oil. Radio, and especially television, have given us occasion to ponder the long-range effects upon our whole civilization of a constant bombardment of words and pictures of certain types. Will the banality of endless soap operas, quiz programs, and "family" shows inexorably lower our whole cultural level? Will the pervasiveness of savagery and violence gradually debase and barbarize us? Will the domination of news programs by a few networks, most of whose "newscasters" and "commentators" share a common political and social outlook gradually destroy the objectivity of news coverage? If this should happen, what would be its effect on our national political life? Does television exposure already doom political candidates who happen to be unattractive physically or lacking in "charisma"? We do not know. All we can say for certain is that the omnipresence of radio and television in modern life has given thoughtful people plenty to think about.

3. *American Experience*—Perhaps the readiest way to appreciate the influence of technology on history is to trace its course briefly through our own national past. The very discovery of America followed soon after the invention of the compass and astrolabe had markedly reduced guesswork in navigation, and the development of the caravel had made it possible to sail more effectively against the wind. These advances added greatly to the willingness of mariners to undertake longer voyages into uncharted oceans. The Indians were subdued, basically, by the white man's diseases, firearms, and alcohol. But their ultimate defeat also owed much to their increasing dependence on the white man's technology. Once Indians got used to European, and then American, clothing, foods, weapons, and utensils (not to speak of vices), they lost much of their old self-reliance and were more easily conquered.

Advances in transportation were crucial for the development of interior America. Early in the nineteenth century steamships traveled on the major rivers, notably the Ohio and Mississippi, transporting both new settlers to new frontiers and the products of old settlers to market. West of the Alleghenies these rivers overcame the north-south transport problem, as the railways were eventually to solve the east-west problem. Steamboats were soon followed by canals and then by railroads. The latter were an especially potent influence on the development of America. Even before the Civil War they had made our society mobile for the first time. They also linked together scattered big cities, and tied the northeast to the northwest politically. After the war they made it possible for U.S. soldiers to pursue, and thus subdue, the plains Indians far more rapidly than would otherwise have been the case. They were also directly involved in the rapid destruction of the great buffalo herds of the western plains. Buffalo were killed by the millions—for meat to feed the labor gangs who built the railroads and for sport by the numerous hunters who could be transported easily by rail to the buffalo country.

Meanwhile, Eli Whitney had invented the cotton gin, a momentous event in our national history. When seeds had to be picked by hand the only kind of cotton that could be produced economically was the long-fibered variety which could be grown only in a few choice places in the South. The gin, however, cleaned *any* kind of cotton, and with incredible rapidity. At once it became profitable to raise short staple cotton, which could be grown all over the South, even in the uplands. A bare recitation of statistics indicates the economic revolution that followed. In 1791 the United States produced 2 million pounds of cotton. Then the cotton gin was invented in 1793. By 1801 we produced 49 million pounds of cotton: in 1811 80 million pounds. In the years immediately preceding the Civil War we produced seven-eighths of the world's cotton, and cotton constituted more than half the value of all American exports. The noneconomic results were equally profound. Slavery, which nearly everyone in 1790 had expected to die out gradually, abruptly got a new lease on life for the planting, growing, and harvesting of cotton was ideally suited for a slave system. It was a simple process, yet one that kept people busy most of the year. Between 1820 and 1860 the number of slaves in the Southern states nearly tripled from 1.5 million to 4 million, and their average price did triple. Needless to add, increased race mixture increased racial tension and prejudice apace, bequeathing to our nation passions and social problems that have never subsided.

Farther west the Great Plains could not be opened to agriculture until the invention of barbed wire to contain animals and the expansion of the railroads to haul farm produce to market. Moreover, because of the light soil and scanty rainfall farming there could not be carried on successfully until the development of a variety of mowers, reapers, threshers, and other machines, powered first by horses, then by gasoline motors, which allowed a few men to harvest thousands of acres of grain.

Before the industrial age the majority of mankind were farmers, and agricultural yields were so low and precarious that the specter of famine was seldom absent. By 1890, a century after Malthus's prediction of disaster from overpopulation, U.S. farmers were producing more food than their countrymen could eat. In much of the twentieth century the combination of agricultural machinery, selective stockbreeding, and extensive use of manufactured fertilizers produced such a glut of farm products that U.S. governments burned food, dumped it into the sea, gave it away to foreign countries, appropriated billions to store it, and paid farmers more billions to take land out of cultivation. Meanwhile, doctors regularly admonished a rapidly growing population that most of us were too fat.

Yet, once again, if technology and science overcome problems, they also create problems. The startling advances in medical research in the nineteenth and twentieth centuries transformed our whole age. The germ concept of disease, vast improvements in sanitation, the development of vaccination and immunization, notable gains in our understanding of nutrition, remarkable improvements in surgical techniques, and such "breakthroughs" as the wartime development of penicillin, conquered most of the world's worst plagues, cut child-birth losses dramatically and, in conjunction with the jobs provided by the Industrial Revolution, made possible a population growth hitherto unknown in history. We hear much less now about "food surplus" problems in the United States or anywhere else and much more about the return of the ancient specter of famine in many parts of the world. But, once more, the pendulum may sweep back. Recent achievements in medical research, particularly the development of contraceptive pills, now provide the means, if not yet the motivation, for humanity to control its numbers. What will be the pattern of the future? We do not know, but technology will surely have much to do with its formation.

Apart from questions of population, technological advances have repeatedly transformed many features of our lives since about 1800. Throughout history packing people into big cities was an invitation to epidemics and plagues. Modern industry changed all that. It provided bricks, concrete, and asphalt to cover the muddy streets and drain off the stagnant water that bred epidemics. It made iron pipes to supply pure water and efficiently drain off sewage. It built better water pumps to provide fire protection. Such a seemingly elementary invention as mass-produced nails enabled builders to construct far more and cheaper homes by the 1850s.

By the time space in cities had become a pressing problem relatively cheap and abundant structural steel had been developed to make possible the erection of skyscrapers. Their utility, in turn, depended upon vastly improved elevators. In the same era Edison, Westinghouse, and others devised much improved systems of lighting which made it safe to stay out at night in cities and thereby opened up an abundant urban life after dark: a whole new world of restaurants, theatres, and sports arenas, which profoundly affected the recreational habits of millions. Transportation improvements wrought similar social revolutions. By the 1870s traffic jams of *horse drawn* vehicles threatened to paralyze such cities as New York and Chicago. Then came the electric street car and subway. The problem vanished, only to reappear in a couple of generations when gasoline-powered automobiles paralyzed the streets. This time the remedy was to build a marvelously complex and fabulously expensive array of urban tollways and freeways supplemented by an equally splendid and costly interstate highway system. Finally, the airplane has greatly increased our mobility and drawn all parts of the world more closely together.

Communications developments shook us quite as heavily. The telephone linked us all together in a way unimaginable before. A marvelous boon to the isolated and lonely, it also made us the most talkative people in the world and perhaps the poorest correspondents. Along with the typewriter, it wrought something of a sexist revolution. More than any other inventions, more than any laws, more than all the rhetoric of missionary feminists, the telephone and typewriter "liberated" millions of women by providing them respectable job opportunities outside the home. Cheap newspapers, radio, and television have of course multiplied many times the amount and variety of ideas and information that impinge upon us every day. All these communication and transportation advances, taken together, are more responsible than anything else for the steadily increasing sameness of ideas, habits, aspirations, products, buildings, foods, clothing, speech, and recreational tastes so often remarked about in the United States.

Perhaps the ultimate demonstration of the importance of economic and technological forces in history is this: it was economic advances and technological breakthroughs that made possible the urbanized society of the modern industrial West. It was the conditions of life in that industrialized society which directly gave rise to the great revolutionary ideologies of modern times. Of these, nazism and fascism caused World II, and communism now controls a third of the earth.

Technological Advances Follow Need—"Necessity is the mother of invention" is a venerable cliché. But like many clichés, it is not less true or less important for being trite. The fact is that inventions, which cause economic changes and, indirectly, many other changes as well, are themselves often the product of keenly felt economic desires or needs. Water mills and windmills were developed in those areas where they were most needed in medieval Europe. Water mills were first employed not in some such place as Norway, Switzerland, or Finland, but in southern France about the fifth century A.D. Here grain was grown and swift streams provided power. Here mills could be used to grind grain into flour, a task formerly performed by either slaves or horses. But slaves were now in short supply because the population of the disintegrating Roman Empire had declined in the preceding two centuries, and horses were needed either for additional plowing or for warfare. Windmills first appeared in northern France and in the Low Countries. They, too, were used to grind grain into flour, to power light, simple industrial machines and, in the Netherlands, to drain marshes and create badly needed arable land. In the nineteenth century, on the American Great Plains, an area lacking wood, coal, waterfalls, or electricity, windmills were widely used to pump water for livestock.

One of the main motives for English exploration and colonization of North America was a desire to exploit the timber resources of the new continent. By 1600 most of England's best forests had been cut down, partly for naval supplies and stores, partly to produce the charcoal then necessary for smelting iron. Timber for naval supplies could be secured from the lands around the Baltic, to be sure, but one's own colonies would be a safer and more dependable source.

The water frame, spinning jenny, and other devices that revolutionized textile manufacturing during the late eighteenth century were not the products of theoretical scientists. They were developed by "practical" textile mill owners and workers who were trying to find better and faster ways to make cloth. The obvious and pressing need for a better way to separate cotton fibers from cotton seeds eventually brought forth the cotton gin, which revolutionized the whole cotton industry and the social patterns of the U.S. southern states as well.

The smelting of iron was long impeded because charcoal was the only fuel that could heat the iron ore to a sufficiently high temperature, and charcoal could be secured only by cutting down forests and burning the wood. Then a way was discovered to smelt iron with coke, derived from coal. At once the coal mining industry was stimulated. However, many of the best coal veins ran deep underground. Deep mines tended to fill up with water. This unpleasant fact soon brought about efforts to devise better pumps to get rid of the water. The early steam engines resulted. Ironically, they were so inefficient mechanically that for a time they could be used *only* for pumping water out of coal mines since it was only in such mines that coal was sufficiently plentiful to run the machines!

Machines, of course, require regular lubrication. By the mid-nineteenth century machines had become so numerous in the United States that whale oil, the most common lubricant, was often in short supply. Substitutes were sought avidly. An excellent one, existing in seemingly unlimited quantities, was soon found—petroleum. A little more than a century later it is dawning on all of us that oil and other conventional fuels and lubricants do not exist in unlimited quantities after all. Consequently, more and more attention is now being devoted to the development of nuclear energy, solar energy, thermal energy from the earth's hot springs, and even that time-honored source, wind power.

Where no need is felt or no incentive exists to pursue technological progress such progress is extremely slow or absent. Water mills were known to the ancient Greeks and Romans but were seldom used because both societies were founded on slavery. Slaves have no incentive to devise better ways of doing things since such achievements gain them neither wealth nor fame nor freedom, but only some different task. Masters have no incentive either as long as slave labor is plentiful and cheap. Hence water mills in ancient times remained the playthings of a few speculators. The operation of the same principle could be discerned two thousand years later in the United States. The North, which did not have slavery, was more industrialized than the antebellum South, and its people were more inventive.

Likewise, if there seems no ready way to apply an invention or a revolutionary idea it is often stillborn. Leonardo da Vinci sketched plans for flying machines, submarines, and a variety of ingenious mechanical contrivances, but nothing came of them because sixteenth-century Europeans had neither a pressing need for such devices nor any ready way to manufacture them. In the late seventeenth century however, when further, and much desired, scientific advances were stymied by the need for more advanced mathematical techniques, it was more than coincidence that Leibniz and Isaac Newton should have developed calculus at the same time and in complete independence of each other. Similarly, in the late nineteenth century when the population was growing rapidly, wealth was increasing even faster, more and more hard surfaced roads were being laid down, and the internal combustion engine had been invented, it was hardly an accident that a whole array of primitive automobiles appeared. In fact, they issued forth from so many workshops scattered about the Western world that it is impossible to say who "invented" the automobile.

Weakness of the Economic Interpretation of History—The economic interpretation of history, like every other one-track interpretation, has limitations. To hold that history is determined entirely, or even mainly, by economic factors involves several assumptions of dubious validity. It assumes that people always know what their economic interests are; it assumes that human conduct is consistently motivated by rational considerations; it excludes free will; and it denies that men are moved significantly by nonmaterial factors. In brief, the economic interpretation of history, like other materialistic philosophies, proceeds more from a study of things than from a study of people.

To begin with, even supposing that people always act in accord with their economic interest the fact remains that they frequently do not know what it is. For generations American businessmen usually supported political candidates who opposed legislation designed to improve the wages and working conditions of labor. Yet the huge profits of American industry were due directly to the mass market in the United States for consumer goods of every variety. That mass market, in turn, existed because the high wages paid to American labor provided a mass purchasing power unique in history. Millions were able to buy goods that in other countries only a handful of the wealthy could afford. The manufacturer made a smaller profit per individual item but a larger profit overall because of the increased volume of sales. Despite this easily understood and widely recognized phenomenon some American businessmen still oppose any extension of its basic principle and many of their European counterparts continue to cling to a policy of high profits per article for a limited market.

As has been pointed out in Chapter 6, the voting habits of people are influenced by loves, hates, cliches, ignorance, and irrational devotion to half-truths, which have little to do with the economic interpretation of anything. If one insists upon viewing the world through the spectacles of economic interpretation few sights could be more bizarre than the two major American political parties.

For many decades after the Civil War the main supporters of the Republican party were eastern manufacturers and businessmen and midwestern farmers, two groups whose economic interests were largely opposed. The south, as a region, remained adamantly Democratic for a century. The reasons were not economic but psychological. It had been Republicans who had forced Reconstruction on the South. Republicans long seemed more friendly towards Negroes than did Democrats. Those Southern people who might have been pro-Republican, the Negroes themselves, were effectively kept out of political life. Since 1933 the Democratic party has consistently drawn heavy support from the labor movement, ethnic minorities, black people, and the highly educated, though the economic interests, not to speak of the values, tastes, habits, intellectual interests, and ultimate intentions of these groups differ to an almost comic degree. In the late twentieth century the Republican party contains many businessmen, many farmers, a growing number of working people who have grown prosperous, some eastern liberals, many southern conservatives who used to be Democrats, and a lot of people from every walk of life who are adamantly hostile to all things that suggest communism. The following of the Democrats is equally mixed: the majority of eastern and academic liberals, some southern conservatives, Negro and Chicano "minorities," a considerable though declining proportion of European "ethnics," some farmers, and nearly everyone who claims to speak for "youth." To explain it all in economic terms would far exceed the ingenuity of Karl Marx. Even Alice in Wonderland would be stumped.

Another key weakness of the economic interpretation of history is that in any specific situation economic considerations are almost always hopelessly jumbled with other factors. It is often alleged that the imperialism of the late nineteenth century was economically motivated. To some degree this is true. The United States and European countries wanted parts of Africa, Asia, and the Pacific Islands for the gold, diamonds, precious woods, rubber, tin, copra, and other products they contained. But they also wanted such territories as coaling stations for their ships, fields for missionary activity, and (in the case of France) sources of manpower to fill out their armies. Most important, they wanted the places to increase their national "prestige," very often merely to prevent some rival country from getting them.

As noted earlier (Chapter 5), judged from the standpoint of economic interest or, indeed, any *rational* consideration, the Spanish-American War was needless. President McKinley knew perfectly well that we could have extorted from Spain any kind of settlement of the Cuban situation we wished without going to war for it. Moreover, most businessmen who, according to theories about economic determinism, ought to have favored a war to secure Cuba as an area for economic exploitation, showed no enthusiasm at all for such a conflict. The only entrepreneurs who pushed for and eventually got the war were some newspaper tycoons who prospered by creating and then exploiting "sensations." They were supported mostly by young Republicans who wanted a victorious war for no economic reason at all but merely to prove that America had "arrived" as a great power. The same people, for the same reasons, had for some years wanted overseas colonies and a big battle fleet. In the same years it would have been in our economic interest to have allowed the European powers to divide China among them and impose modern organization on it, for this would have been beneficial to our trade there. However, we disliked the *principle* involved. So we insisted that China should be "free," and enunciated the Open Door policy instead.

It is impossible to say whether imperialism "paid" in an economic sense. If one makes a narrow comparison between the money spent by various European and American governments on acquiring, pacifying, and governing such places as Morocco, Madagascar, or the Philippines and the money which the same *governments* ultimately extracted from the places, then imperialism did not "pay" at all. Quite the opposite. It was an expensive luxury. Oftentimes, however, while *governments* did not get back their investments, an array of private soldiers, administrators, traders, investors, and other entrepreneurs extracted many times as much wealth from certain colonial areas as their *governments* had spent in securing the places. The British exploitation of India is the classic case. In still other instances, such as the American acquisition of the Philippines, recent research indicates that the government got little return for its money and effort, and that private American traders probably would have done just as well dealing with an independent Philippine Islands as with those territories under U.S. control.

At any time since 1948 we have stood to lose heavily, in an economic sense, in the Middle East by our support of Israel, a policy bound to alienate the strategically placed, oil-rich Arab states. Why then have we supported Israel? Partly, as we have seen in Chapter 1, from a combination of sympathy and remorse derived from Jewish suffering in World War II; partly because of a desire to help a small, struggling state establish its independence; partly because of the influence of Jewish money and votes in U.S. elections; partly to counter Russian influence in the area. Altogether these sentimental, idealistic, and power-political considerations have produced, under both Democratic and Republican administrations, a consistent policy which is clearly opposed to American *economic* interests—but not to our other interests.

Even if one grants, for the sake of argument, the Marxist contention that history records mostly a struggle between classes for wealth it only poses a further question—why do men desire wealth? In part, of course, for the physical comforts and security it brings; but also for the prestige accruing to it and for the power it brings over other men. In the business world the amassing of profits and wealth has always been the barometer of success, the way one "keeps score." One of the rewards of "success" is that the person or class with wealth is always in an advantageous position to influence those who wield political authority, who lead the society intellectually, and who determine its ethical norms. The desire for power over others is one of the most deeply ingrained elements in the human character. Politics is always a mixture of many things: pursuit of ideals, a desire to serve, a scramble for money, but above all a contest for power. It makes no difference whether the locale is ancient Assyria, medieval Italy, twentieth-century America, or avowedly Marxist Russia.

Differences in Time—Finally, the importance of economic con-

siderations in history was smaller centuries ago than it is now because society used to be dominated by kings and aristocrats. Their
class ideals were not economic but military and chivalric. The European aristocracy lived primarily to pursue honor and glory. They
thought mostly in terms of prestige and power for themselves, their
families, and their social class—normally in that order. Commerce
they considered socially degrading. Merchants they scorned as inferior social types. The old European nobility as a class so little
understood the world of economics that many of its members lived
perpetually on the verge of bankruptcy. In America the planter
class of the Old South, while by no means identical in outlook or
practice, displayed many of the same traits as the European aristocracy.

For centuries European kings waged wars without a thought for
the lives or interests of their peoples. They lavished money on
wars, entertainments, and sumptuous courts, borrowed from anyone
who would lend, and frequently did not even keep budgets. Kings
like those of Prussia who enforced efficiency and spartan economy
upon every branch of their national administrations were extremely
rare. Prodigality was accounted a distinctive princely characteristic,
if not necessarily a virtue.

Rulers and dominant classes in the past were often swayed by
ideals which conflicted with their economic interests. The sixteenth-
and seventeenth-century kings of Spain drove out of their realm
their most prosperous and industrious subjects, the Moriscos and
Jews, because they did not wish to rule heretics and infidels. Louis
XIV of France similarly expelled the thrifty Huguenots(1685) because his absolutist temperament could not bear the thought of tol-
erating subjects who refused to share his religious views. Similar, if
less dramatic, examples abound in American history too. Such wealthy nineteenth-century merchants and industrialists as Gerritt Smith
and Lewis and Arthur Tappan risked their fortunes to support the
unpopular abolitionist cause. At the turn of the present century
American businessmen who would have benefited economically
from an influx of cheap foreign labor often supported proposals to
restrict immigration because they viewed the immigrants, by now
mostly from southern and eastern Europe, as people whose whole
social heritage, psychology, and religious orientation was incompatible with traditional American institutions and values—a view remarkably similar to the way sixteenth-century Spaniards regarded
the Moriscos and Jews.

Let us conclude by citing a couple of particularly vivid examples. In 1620 the Holy Roman Emperor Ferdinand II signed the

death warrants of hundreds of rebellious Bohemian nobles. With tears streaming down his cheeks, he exclaimed, "I would sacrifice my life if it would make all these unbelievers believe."[3] How does one explain such conduct in economic terms? And where does one find an economic explanation for the disastrous Italian campaign of 1494 undertaken by Charles VIII of France? The half-mad king thought of himself as a new Alexander destined to reconquer the Byzantine Empire from the Turks and to be crowned emperor of the "New Rome" in Constantinople.

Economic factors often strongly influence the course of history, but they no more control it exclusively than do great men or great ideas.

---

3. On another occasion the emperor declared that he "would rather rule a desert than a land of heretics." Though his mood was plainly less compassionate, it is no easier to discern an economic motivation than in the first instance.

9: Man and His Physical Environment

Geography and the Character of Civilization—No nation or people can be properly understood without some knowledge of its geography: its physical surroundings and means of support. Local climatic conditions and the changing seasons regulate the choice of a people's food and clothing. The weather and available raw materials normally determine the nature of buildings and building sites. It has even been contended that whether or not a civilization thrives and grows depends largely on climatic conditions. The most recent and dramatic exposition of this view is that of the twentieth-century philosopher of history, Arnold Toynbee. It is a matter of fact that most of the world's thriving civilizations have grown up in the temperate zones. This (and much more) Toynbee accounts for by his famous "challenge and response" theory. In brief, his argument is that those peoples achieve, thrive, and advance who live in conditions sufficiently difficult to challenge them to put forth their best efforts, but not so harsh as to require the expenditure of all their energies merely to keep alive. People in the tropics have produced few great civilizations because the conditions of life are too easy to require them to do their best. When building consists chiefy of piling palm leaves or jungle grass over wattles, when a few leaves or an animal skin suffices for clothing, when feeding oneself is mostly a matter of hunting, fishing, or picking fruit off trees, supplemented by the simplest type of agriculture, it is difficult to be persuaded of the utility of working eight or ten hours a day to produce surpluses for export.

At the opposite pole Eskimos and Laplanders have produced little because their physical environment is so harsh that all their energies are exhausted by the effort to secure food, clothing, and shelter.

The peoples of the temperate zones, by contrast, have to work just hard enough to gain a livelihood that they acquire the habit and psychology of work and thrift. Yet they do not work so hard that all their higher creative impulses are stifled by ceaseless and exhausting struggle with the elements. The habits of working regularly and saving that are thus acquired in the temperate zones carry over into all human activities after the needs of mere existence are satisfied. The result has been the development of the world's great civilizations. To this whole theory the objection is sometimes raised that the civilizations of ancient Egypt and the Near East grew up in subtropical areas, but there is reason to believe that these places were considerably cooler in ancient times.

Before the modern industrial age the influence of geography and climate upon a people's mode of life was easily observable, indeed could hardly be overestimated. All nomadic societies tended to be much alike in their institutions and social habits. All of them developed in similar areas: desert, semidesert, and treeless plains. Most of the population were herdsmen who lived off the products of their animals. If mineral deposits existed in a given locality mining usually became the chief occupation of most of the people there. If fish were plentiful most of the people became fishermen. On fertile plains most became farmers. Such a people as the Dutch, living at the mouth of a great river system on the sea along an important trade route, were readily drawn to commerce. The Vikings, who inhabited the rocky, forbidding shores of medieval Norway, had to depend on the sea for a livelihood. Eventually they became intrepid explorers and pirates who harried the coasts of Europe for generations before settling inland in the tenth and eleventh centuries.

The New England colonies in North America were likewise founded along a rocky coast in a harsh climate. The poor and stony soil made agriculture difficult and unremunerative, but the forests provided an abundance of timber and naval stores and the sea myriads of fish. Soon the New Englanders became famous sailors, and the region became the center of the American whaling, fishing, and shipbuilding industries. Farther south, a milder climate and an abundance of rich soil made agriculture easier and more profitable; hence the predominance of farmers over fishermen and sailors in the middle and southern British colonies. In the southern colonies the soil was best along the seacoast and the lower courses of the numerous rivers, the so-called Tidewater. Here the readiest road to prosperity lay in the cultivation of tobacco, cotton, rice, or indigo, depending on the time and locale. Tobacco and cotton, however, wear out the soil, so it soon became necessary to farm hundreds or even thousands of acres in order to allow much of the land, at any given time, to lie fallow and regain its fertility. Moreover, as production increased, the price of tobacco and cotton tended to fall, a condition which the landowner usually tried to combat by farming still more acres to produce larger crops. Thus grew up the plantation system in the South.

The topography of the South had much to do with subsequent American history. The early colonial plantations lay in lowlands, only a few feet above sea level. Because the tides pushed far up the rivers it was possible for planters to build their own wharves or to use the wharves of their neighbors. From these they could ship their cotton and tobacco directly to England rather than sell it to colonial middlemen. Consequently, an urban mercantile class like that of New England or New York never developed in the colonial South save only in Charleston, South Carolina. With no mercantile class worth mentioning, with its planters, their families, retainers, and slaves tending to live in a central cluster of buildings on the plantation near their wharves, the South retained a predominantly rural mode of life far longer than the northern or middle colonies.

The planters were prone to overestimate the value of their crops and thus to order in return more English finished goods than they could pay for. Inevitably, they fell into debt—but into debt to English firms and banks rather than to those of fellow colonials. The difference was crucial. It meant that the age-old resentment of debtor for creditor was directed toward England and Englishmen, not toward fellow colonials. It contributed considerably to the coming of the American Revolution.

Geography has usually had a great deal to do with where the earth has been settled and how the settlements developed afterward. Among the earliest civilizations were those of Egypt and Mesopotamia. Both were in fertile river valleys where floods left rich soil on the land each year and where irrigation canals were easy to dig. In the New World our civilization became predominantly European rather than Asiatic for reasons that are partly geographic, partly not. Apart from geography, Europeans have always been inquisitive, restless, and adventurous while the great civilizations of eastern Asia have been more placid and static, less interested in other peoples, and thus less desirous of seeking trade routes or making contacts with other cultures. Nonetheless, geography played an important part too. In the days of small sailing ships it was incomparably easier to maintain contacts with Europe 3,000 miles across the Atlantic from the *settled eastern coast* of North America than with Asia 6,000–7,000 miles across the Pacific from the *largely unsettled western* coast. (Of course Asia and America are much closer together in the far north, but the crucial consideration was contact between *civilizations*, not merely the geographical proximity of east Siberian Eskimos to Alaskan Eskimos.)

Geography had much to do with the ultimate English rather than French predominance in North America north of the Rio Grande. So far as we know, it was the merest accident that Jacques Cartier happened to sail up the Saint Lawrence (1635), the only river in eastern North America which leads easily and directly to a water route far into the interior of the continent. Thus the French were far ahead of the English as explorers and traders in the Great Lakes region and even into the Mississippi Valley. While this situation was highly advantageous for the French fur trade it was not so for the extension of French national power. It dispersed French settlers and French influence widely and very thinly. The English colonies were more compact. British colonists found the Appalachian Mountains to be sufficiently difficult to surmount that they tended to establish smaller but more thickly settled enclaves along the Atlantic coast. In the ultimate struggle for supremacy in the eighteenth century the scattered French traders and villagers proved no match for the more numerous and concentrated English settlers to their south.

The geography of our own Atlantic coast has had much to do, ultimately, with the form of government assumed by the independent United States. Unlike the west coast, our east coast has numerous bays, inlets, and landlocked harbors, many of them deep. This afforded British entrepreneurs and colonists an opportunity and an incentive to establish many *different* colonies rather than just one large, homogenous colony. The different colonies, founded by different kinds of people for different reasons remained separated from each other geographically in their formative years and developed independently of each other. Consequently, when they all broke with Great Britain they were by no means identical in outlook, interests, or desires. There was no possibility that they might form a consolidated republic. Only with difficulty did they compromise their individuality sufficiently to form a federal union of thirteen allegedly sovereign states. The cry of "state's rights" resounded for decades afterwards, had much to do with the coming of the Civil War, and has not vanished even in our own time.

In medieval Europe towns usually grew up in geographically "logical" places: at fords in rivers, at the confluence of rivers, at river mouths, at crossroads, or in easily fortified places. This also proved to be true in the New World, even *predictably* true.

The story of such prediction begins with an early nineteenth-century German geographer and visionary, Alexander von Humboldt. Humboldt wrote a multivolume study of the universe entitled, appropriately, *Cosmos*. In it he argued that the patterns of development in all societies are determined by nature. He thought the peoples of the world had always been in constant movement along an isothermal zone where yearly temperatures were most favorable for the growth of civilizations. Cities, he believed, would necessarily arise at intervals of not less than 100 miles in this favored zone.

Two American writers, William Gilpin and Jessup W. Scott, became inspired by the esoteric theories of Humboldt and the practical possibility of getting rich by land speculation. Gilpin envisioned the territory of the present United States as a vast bowl in the heart of the "isothermal axis." He predicted that the Mississippi Valley would one day become "the amphitheatre of the world," rich in climate, people, agriculture, and great cities. Exotic vocabulary aside, his estimate was basically sound.

More interesting and also fairly accurate were some of the particular projections of Gilpin and Scott. They were sure Saint Louis was destined to be a metropolis, for it was located at the confluence of the Missouri and Mississippi rivers, on a site composed partly of low ground which would allow docks to be built easily and high ground which would afford protection from floods. They rated (correctly) the prospects of Cairo, Illinois, much below those of Saint Louis, for even though Cairo lies at the confluence of the Mississippi and the Ohio, it is entirely on low ground and thus susceptible to floods. They predicted that Chicago, located at the southern end of Lake Michigan, would become a great city, though for a time Scott thought it might be surpassed by Toledo, an error of degree but hardly a basic misjudgment. Gilpin picked Independence, Missouri, to become the gateway to the Great Plains because it is located where the Kansas River runs into the Missouri. On this he was only marginally wrong, and then only because the first railroad bridge across the Missouri happened to be built not at Independence but at Kansas City, a few miles away.[1] Both men were convinced that San Francisco, situated on the best natural harbor along thousands of miles of Pacific coast, was destined to become the great city of the west.

---

1. It might interest the reader to know that Scott and Gilpin backed their judgment with their pocketbooks. Gilpin invested in land in Kansas City and Scott in Toledo. Each turned a good profit though neither became rich.

The major ports and cities on the Atlantic seaboard had developed earlier, but in equally likely places. Philadelphia enjoyed a central location among all the British colonies. It was situated near the mouth of the Delaware River, adjacent to deep water but protected from the open sea. Boston lay inside a deep and sheltered bay. New York had the best natural harbor of all: deep, protected, and located at the mouth of the Hudson River which was navigable for 150 miles inland. In 1800 for example, it would have been hard to find a town more clearly destined by geography to become one of the world's great port cities whenever its hinterland should be developed. New York City's development was forwarded dramatically by the building of the Erie Canal in the 1820s, for this linked the Hudson River to the whole Great Lakes region hundreds of miles inland.

Geography and War—Military history makes little sense unless one has some knowledge of geography. Military operations have always depended on the location of mountains, passes, rivers, swamps, plains, forests, natural "strong points" capable of being fortified, and lands rich enough to provide forage for horses. In the French and Indian War (1756–63) most of the serious fighting took place at or near geographically crucial places. One such was Fort Duquesne which dominated the eastern entrance to the Ohio Valley. Others were Fort Oswego on the south shore of Lake Ontario, Fort William Henry at the lower end of Lake George, and Fort Ticonderoga on Lake Champlain, all of which lay athwart the most convenient land and inland water approaches to Canada. Still others were Louisbourg on Cape Breton Island and, above all, Quebec on the lower Saint Lawrence. Together, they dominated the sea route into the interior of Canada. English control of the sea, seconded by the genius of James Wolfe, eventually proved decisive at Louisbourg and Quebec respectively, and in the war as a whole.

In the American Revolutionary War twenty years later British control of the sea was extremely convenient in many ways, not least of which was that it enabled the British to pull troops out of tight spots periodically. Nonetheless, it never sufficed to overcome the many advantages which nature had bestowed on the colonials. To gain their independence they had only to hold on and avoid a crushing defeat in the field. For the English, by contrast, victory required the conquest of a dozen thinly populated territories, having neither a political nor commercial "nerve center," scattered along 2,000 miles of coastline, their interiors a trackless wilderness, in climates ranging from sub-tropical to near-Arctic, and the whole lot 3,000 miles across the ocean. Small wonder that when these natural advantages were augmented by French aid, foreign military experts, the pertinacity of the colonials, and the leadership of George Washington, it was the British who eventually tired first.

In the Civil War (1861–65), as in the French and Indian War, most of the battles were fought around places which geography had given strategic importance. Overall, the Appalachian Mountains divided the war into two separate theatres. In the eastern theatre the fact that the capitals of North and South, Washington and Richmond, were only 110 miles apart insured that a disproportionate share of the fighting in the war would be in their vicinity. Bull Run, Spottsylvania, Cold Harbor, Chancellorsville, the Wilderness, Manassas, Antietam, Gettysburg, and the Peninsular Campaign were all fought in the same general area. Several of the battles, including much the most important, Gettysburg, were not deliberately planned but began largely by accident when troops on both sides lost their bearings in the heavily wooded hills of southern Pennsylvania, central Maryland, and northern Virginia. They simply stumbled onto each other and began to fight. The presence of the Shenandoah Valley just beyond the first range of the Appalachians enhanced the attractiveness of the area for military operations because the valley ran north and south, had a plentiful food supply, and was easy to traverse. Thus it was frequently used either as an invasion route or for diversionary maneuvers.

In the western theatre, repeated northern efforts to gain control of the Mississippi River eventually succeeded in 1863. This split the Confederacy in two and virtually forced out of the war its far western portion across the Mississippi. Earlier Union successes at Shiloh and Corinth had opened the Tennessee and Cumberland river systems to allow eventual northern penetration of the deep South.

Overall, the Union victory owed much to the superiority of northern industry, and to the railroads and naval strength derived from it. The Union naval blockade, which starved the South of needed war materials and gradually undermined Confederate civilian morale, was applied by ships built in the navy yards of northern ports and manned by sailors from Philadelphia, New York, and New England, who had long done the nation's fishing and carried most of its commerce. The factory system in America had begun in the textile mills of New England—run by water power derived from the falls in the short, swift rivers of the northeast. These were soon followed by factories of many kinds. They were powered by coal. They processed iron and other mineral resources, all of which lay either in the North or in the West (which the North could control). Thus did the Confederacy succumb not only to the superior numbers of the North but also to the wealth and goegraphical advantages nature had bestowed on her antagonist.

Geography and National Power—Geography and the chance disposition of natural resources have had much to do with forming the characteristics of nations and shaping national policies. The ancient Greeks were notoriously quarrelsome and unable to achieve political unity. One reason derived from nothing more complicated than the terrain of Greece. The country is a series of steep mountain ranges separated by narrow valleys. This configuration broke up the population into small enclaves and made communication between them difficult.

In more recent times isolationist sentiment among great powers has been strongest in nineteenth-century Japan, nineteenth- and twentieth-century England, and the United States. The United States and Japan are far removed geographically from that home of major wars, continental Europe. England is separated from it by the English Channel, and she used to be protected, in addition, by the world's strongest navy. The only European countries that were able to remain neutral in World War I were those on the periphery of the continent: Scandinavia and the Netherlands in the north and Spain in the southwest. In World War II the situation was similar: out-of-the-way Spain, Portugal, Ireland, and Sweden alone managed to escape participation.[2]

The relationship of geography and natural resources to national power is even more obvious. In the nineteenth century an important reason why the nations of northwestern Europe outstripped the Mediterranean states in the race for wealth, power, and colonies was because iron, coal, and other raw materials essential for industrial development are found in greater quantity and variety in northern than in southern Europe. In our own time the United States and the USSR are commonly spoken of as superpowers. Five minutes' examination of a globe will indicate many of the reasons why. To start with, they are huge land masses of several million square miles. By contrast, most of the nations of the world, including all the most advanced states of western and central Europe, are

2. Switzerland is a special case. Its mountainous terrain, which confers great advantages on the defensive in war, combined with its lack of mineral wealth, have caused most soldiers to regard the conquest of Switzerland as not worth the effort. Moreover, it is convenient for all participants in wars to have some neutral state nearby where they may maintain secret political contacts. Switzerland is admirably situated for this purpose. Thus the Swiss were able to escape participation in both World Wars.

no bigger than American states. The only nations in the world even comparable to the United States and the USSR in territorial extent are: Canada, most of which lies in the frozen Arctic; Brazil, half of which consists of the world's largest jungle in the Amazon Valley; China, well over half of which is either barren desert or the world's highest plateau in Tibet and adjoining regions; Australia, mostly a desert; and India, much of which is desert. The United States, by contrast, lies entirely within the temperate zone (save for Alaska), contains a wealth of iron, coal, oil, and minerals, still possesses extensive forests of high quality woods, has the world's largest area of rich farmland in the Midwest, has abundant fisheries off both coasts, enjoys plentiful rainfall over about two-thirds of the country, and has many good harbors. All these natural blessings made it possible for tens of millions of immigrants to flock to our shores and find a livelihood. They, in turn, provided a constantly expanding market for the products of our industry which fed on the natural resources. Meanwhile, the abundance of land spared us serious social discontent by draining off dissatisfied people to lands as yet unclaimed and undeveloped. Small wonder that our population skyrocketed from 4 million in 1790 to 210 million by the 1970s, while at the same time we attained the world's highest level of mass consumption of material goods.

The bases of Russian national power are equally obvious. Though much of the USSR lies in the Arctic the whole state is so huge that even the portion lying in a temperate climate is larger than all but a handful of the nations of the world. The Ukraine is, after the American Midwest, the world's second largest expanse of fertile farmland. Russian forests are the world's most extensive, and the USSR, like the United States, has an abundance of iron, coal, oil, natural gas, and minerals, plus a population of 250 million to develop all the wealth. Clearly, gigantic states like the United States and the USSR were bound to become great powers whenever they got efficient, or even merely ruthless, governments dedicated to national development. Undoubtedly other of the world's larger and richer nations will be similarly developed in the future. Prime candidates are surely Brazil and Argentina, whenever they are able to attain and maintain political stability.

Exaggeration of Geographical Influences—Like every other factor which influences history the importance of geography can be overrated. One must never forget that though people may be strongly influenced by their environment they are not its helpless slaves. A certain geographical as well as political logic lay behind our proclamation of the Monroe Doctrine in 1823. Interference in the affairs of the New World by the great powers of Europe could never be easy because they were thousands of miles away. Still, if we meant to enforce the Monroe Doctrine we should have begun at once to build a big navy. Instead, we were content to rely on the British navy to enforce it for us—though in international affairs there is never any assurance that a state which happens to be friendly today will necessarily remain so in the future. After 1890 we at last began to build up our own navy, only to allow our merchant marine, which contributes much to overall naval strength, to decline. The reason? It is cheaper to transport goods in ships flying the flags of such nations as Panama and Liberia. Geographical logic may incline but it does not compel.

Opportunities Missed—The blessings bestowed by nature are of no importance if they are not recognized and used. The fertile lands of the Argentina pampas and the American Midwest lay just where they do now for thousands of years before Columbus set foot in the New World, but the Indians never used them for anything but hunting. The oil of Oklahoma, Texas, and the Middle East lay undisturbed for millennia because neither American Indians nor Arabs knew anything about oil or its uses, much less possessed the means of extracting it. California was just as rich in natural resources when ruled by Spaniards and Mexicans as it has proved to be since, but it remained an undeveloped pastoral state until Americans acquired it. North Carolina had as much water power as the New England states but a textile industry never developed there before the abolition of slavery and the importation of outside capital. History has always depended quite as much on the imagination and willpower of individuals, even on sheer caprice, as on geographical advantage, the location of natural wealth, or, indeed, any rational consideration.

Changing Times—Finally, the importance of geography as a determinant in human activity has declined as man's control over nature has increased. Before the industrial age sizable cities could grow up only on the seacoast or along rivers, for large numbers of people require a plentiful supply of water for drinking, cooking, and other household purposes, and a cheap, easy mode of transportation. Before the advent of railroads the settlement of the New World usually proceeded up river valleys. With the coming of railroads, however, it became possible for many people to be transported rapidly and supplied easily without reference to river systems or coastal harbors. Then came the automobile and an extensive system of hard-surfaced, all-weather roads, followed soon after by the airplane. By now it is possible for us to ignore, even defy, many of the former inexorable limitations imposed by geography. The phenomenal "development" of Florida in recent decades was *stimulated* mostly by the propaganda of land promoters, but it became *possible* only when railroads and highways were built. Miami is the only major American city founded in the twentieth century. Other real estate promoters and "developers" have similarly persuaded millions of Americans to buy land and settle in the deserts of California, Arizona, New Mexico, and other western states. In many such places life for any significant number of people was physically impossible until scientists and engineers filled scores of western streams with dams to provide water to drink and to irrigate farmland, electricity to light the homes and cities of the new immigrants, and power to run all the gadgets that seemingly make their lives worthwhile.

Occasionally the limitations of a geographical interpretation of history can be glaringly obvious. About 1870 it had become clear that eventually there would be a great port city somewhere on Puget Sound, the best natural harbor on the Pacific coast north of San Francisco. Seattle, then merely an overgrown sawmill town, was well situated on the sound but no better so than a number of other villages. Town leaders realized that if Seattle was to grow and prosper mere location was not enough. The town needed a railroad. It was assumed that the need would be filled when the Northern Pacific was completed. Surely Seattle would be its western terminus. In 1873, however, the directors of the Northern Pacific announced that they would end their line in Tacoma, a tiny settlement twenty-five miles south of Seattle. The decision had little to do with railroading, much to do with land speculation. The Northern Pacific had quietly bought up most of the land in and around Tacoma and hoped to make a killing. Seattle fought back by building its own railways. One went over the Cascade Mountains to Walla Walla, another north to join the Canadian Pacific. By 1893 the directors of the Northern Pacific felt compelled to buy these lines to stifle competition. It then made Seattle its terminus after all. But Seattle got in the last blow, in the same year acquiring a second transcontinental railroad, the Great Northern. Thus, ultimately, Seattle *did* become the premier metropolis on Puget Sound, and Tacoma did not, but the outcome had more to do with civic action than geography.

10: Conclusion

Cicero once said, "I shall always consider the best guesser the best prophet." What he did not say was that the best guesser is usually the person who is best informed, the person who has studied most carefully all aspects of a given situation. It is always tempting to try to interpret the past in terms of a single cause, for the human psyche always yearns for clarity, order, system. Now one cause of a certain event may be, and frequently is, more important than any of several others; but human affairs are seldom simple. Complex phenomena invariably derive from several sources. He who sees in the past the operation of a single overriding element inevitably distorts the past.[1] This, in turn, leads him to misunderstand the present—hardly a recommendation for estimating the future.

As the reader of this book is aware, the same events or circumstances have been used frequently to illustrate several different points. The Civil War has been cited to explain how (1) the interpretations of history change and (2) the importance of ideals like abolitionism and a desire to preserve the Union as shapers of history. That war also illustrated how the times sometimes makes the man (General Grant), and how such technological developments as the invention of the cotton gin, the building of railroads, and the expansion of industry have had enormous historical repercussions. Finally, it showed how heavily warfare is influenced by geography. The New Deal of Franklin D. Roosevelt has been invoked to demonstrate the importance of ideas in history, the constant interplay of change and stability, the significance of the individual man, and how such organizations and institutions as the presidency, Congress, the Supreme Court, and the federal bureaucracy shape the destinies of our nation. The administration of Jefferson illustrated the role of chance in history (the Louisiana Purchase) and the problem of interpretation of sources (the Burr "conspiracy"). The New England Puritans have been cited for their contribution to the formation of

---

1. A cynic once defined history written in this fashion as "the reduction of the complex truth to the simple lie."

the American national character; but it has also been noted that
that character owes much to geography, the frontier, immigration,
national ideals, and democratic institutions. Various features of the
history of warfare have been discussed to exemplify the importance
of men, ideas, organizations, geography, and the level of technological development in the conduct of military operations and,
therefore, indirectly as determinants in history. Lastly, in all historical situations there is another factor, not easily analyzed but invariably present: the craving of human beings for domination over
others. Whatever the reason, be it personal ambition, the desire to
achieve an ideal society, or some other, in the final analysis men
desire to direct, control—rule.

It is all ultimately reducible to what has been called the only
true law of history, the law of multiple causation.

11: Doing a Term Paper

*Why Write a Paper at All?—*In most history courses of the survey type a research paper is required. Many students regard this as the most onerous part of the course, a particularly fiendish tyranny practiced upon them, and for no discernible reason, by their teachers. They appear to think that, somehow or other, the paper is done for the benefit of the teacher. Actually, there are a number of excellent reasons why term papers are required in survey courses.

1. A person goes to college, presumably, to become educated. Nobody can call himself truly educated unless he can write clearly and correctly. One learns to write respectably in the same way he learns to do anything else—by practice.

2. A part of history is learning facts about the past. Another part is learning how historians discover those facts, think about them, interpret them, and mold them into history books. It is for this reason that the student is required to take notes in a special way, prepare his bibliography cards in a certain manner, and observe specified rules of form when doing his paper. No paper of 1,000–2,000 words can involve more than a tiny fraction of the research that goes into the writing of an entire book, but a paper of even this short length, if prepared carefully from six to a dozen sources, will give the beginning student some experience in the problems of assembling historical data and practice in the correct and systematic expression of his ideas.

3. If one does a good paper on a certain topic he acquires a knowledge of at least one small area of history that is much fuller and more detailed than the type of knowledge derived from survey courses generally.

4. Many college courses, in a variety of fields, require term papers. For the beginner in history, to do a serious research paper, following all the rules of form is good practice for what will come later.

Here, as elsewhere in the study of history, begin by taking a commonsense view of the matter. Suppose one's paper is to be a study of the battle of Saratoga. Start by reading all the material

that can be found on the event until all the facts and all the interpretations that have been placed on those facts are thoroughly understood. Then sit down and write a clear, direct account of the
matter that would be understood by a person of ordinary intelligence and information, citing the sources on which the paper is
based. The whole process has three steps: (1) collect the information, (2) think the problem through, and (3) write it out in your
own words in a manner in which you would like to read it if it
were written by someone else.

RULES FOR THE PREPARATION OF A TERM PAPER

1. *Selection of the Topic*—Normally essay topics are recommended by the instructor, though at times the student may be allowed to select his own. In the latter case be sure to secure the
advice and consent of the instructor. A good instructor will assign
term papers early in the semester. A good student will begin at
once to give serious thought to the selection of a topic. Failure to
do this often results in a hurried, last-minute choice, followed soon
after by an earnest request to be allowed to change the topic, all
culminating in a third-rate paper handed in late.

2. *Preliminary Readings*—Once the topic has been chosen the student should begin by acquainting himself with it in a general way.
Topics usually deal with relatively minute portions of history about
which a beginner normally does not have much knowledge. If the
student begins by reading an entire book on the matter he often
finds himself bewildered by a mass of details and unable to distinguish what is of basic importance from what is merely explanatory or peripheral. Hence it is a good idea to begin by reading
brief summaries of the matter in order to get its main features in
mind, and then to work gradually into the details.

A good practice is to begin by reading the pertinent section of
the textbook. Usually this will not be more than a few pages,
sometimes no more than a paragraph or even a couple of lines. The
next step should be to read a few encyclopedia articles about the
subject or biographical sketches of persons prominently associated
with it. This will increase the extent of one's general knowledge of
the matter. Among the better encyclopedias found in any college
library are *Encyclopaedia Britannica, Encyclopedia Americana, Dictionary of National Biography* (relates to the British Isles only), *Encyclopedia of the Social Sciences, Catholic Encyclopedia,* and *Dictionary of American History.* Use only the better encyclopedias.
There are many reference works which have short articles written

on the popular level. There is little in these books that is not treated better in the ones named above.

Once one has acquired a good "encyclopedia knowledge" of his subject he should then go to the card catalog and get books that deal with it. By now he should be able to understand a detailed, minute discussion of any aspect of the problem. At this point, too, he may well discover that his topic is too broad to be dealt with adequately in a short paper. If this seems to be the case he should discuss the matter with the instructor.

3. *Preparation of the Bibliography*—A bibliography should now be compiled. (A bibliography is a list of all the materials consulted in the preparation of the paper.) On cards or slips of paper, the student should indicate the books or articles dealing with his particular topic, *using a separate card for each title.* The reason for the last admonition is that in any research paper or book the bibliography is listed alphabetically. In some books and dissertations the bibliographical entries run into the hundreds. If the student puts down many titles haphazardly with several on any given sheet of paper, he will waste more time shuffling paper when the time came to append the bibliography to his finished work than it would have taken to put each item on a separate card in the first place. This would not be a problem in a short paper where only a few sources are used, but one of the purposes of the paper is to teach the student the *research method* and thus bibliographical entries should be put on separate cards—the best practice in serious, lengthy research.

Each bibliography card must contain (1) the name of the author, (2) the title of the book, with place of publication, publisher, and date of publication (in that order), and (3) a brief statement of the use which can be made of the book in the preparation of the essay. If the student follows these directions he will have all the information he needs to prepare the final bibliography for his paper when the paper itself is completed. If he does not do this he will have to go back to the library and get the books again in order to get the bibliographical information that must be included in the bibliography of the finished paper. By then someone else will probably have checked out the needed books.

In the case of materials taken from an encyclopedia the bibliography card should show (1) the name of the author, if the article is signed, (2) the title of the article, (3) the name of the encyclopedia, (4) the edition (most encyclopedias have gone through many editions), (5) the volume number, and (6) the pages on which the article appears.

In the case of magazines or newspapers the card should show the author, title of article, name of magazine or paper, date of publication, and pertinent pages.

In the case of a work where different authors have done different portions, the card should indicate (1) the author of the *chapter you used* (not the editor of the whole book or series), (2) the title of that chapter (in quotation marks), (3) the title of the book (underlined), and (4) place of publication, publisher, and date.

Typical bibliography card:

> Alexander, Charles C. *Nationalism in American Thought, 1930–1945.* (Chicago: Rand McNally and Co., 1969).
> Has a good chapter on the various intellectual patterns of isolationism in the 1930s, pp. 164–89.

A bibliography can be built up in several ways. There are usually book lists at the end of each major section of a textbook. Sometimes there are lists at the end of each chapter or at the end of the book. Encyclopedia articles will sometimes cite references in the main body of an article: nearly all will include a few at the end of the article. Many good leads can be obtained by glancing over the footnotes and extensive bibliographies which are invariably included in scholarly books. A book that deals with one's subject will probably list other useful works in its bibliographical section. Especially recommended for their bibliographies are the *Guide to Historical Literature,* the *Harvard Guide to American History,* the *New American Nation Series* (New York, 1954) and the *History of American Life* series (New York, 1921–45).

Last, and most important, consult the card catalog in the library. Here some resourcefulness must be displayed. Suppose the title of one's topic is "The Battle of Saratoga." Start by looking under "Saratoga." There may or may not be an entire book written about the subject. If there is not do not go away in despair (or elation), thinking that no material exists. Any history of the American Revolution will certainly contain material about the battle since it is considered a major turning point in the war. Who was the commander-in-chief of the Continental Army? Washington. Who were the victorious American generals at Saratoga? Horatio Gates and Benedict Arnold. Perhaps they wrote their memoirs? If not, surely somebody has written biographies of one or all of them. Then consider the British side. Any history of Great Britain in the eighteenth century in which the American Revolution is discussed would have something. Any biography of King George III, or his prime minister, Lord North, or his colonial secretary, Lord Germain, who planned the ill-fated British campaign, would be useful. Maybe some of them wrote memoirs too? How about General Burgoyne, who lost the battle, or General Howe, who failed to carry out his assigned role in the British strategic plan? Perhaps they wrote memoirs? Certainly they must have had biographers. Look for a history of the British army. There is an excellent, multivolume one by Sir John Fortescue. What other nation was especially interested in the outcome of Saratoga? France. The French reaction can be discovered and studied in any good diplomatic history of the period. One can nearly always find information about virtually anything in a library if he will but exercise a little ingenuity.

If the subject concerns something that has taken place in the last century or so there will almost certainly be magazine articles about it. To look for materials of this sort consult *Reader's Guide to Periodical Literature* or *Poole's Index to Periodical Literature.* For recent history the files of the *New York Times, Time, Newsweek, U.S. News and World Report,* and similar publications will nearly always have information. For specialized topics such as recent business history one could consult such papers as the *Wall Street Journal.*

A subject from almost any period in history will have had articles about it published at some time or other in learned journals. Among many of these the *American Historical Review,* the *Journal of American History* (formerly the *Mississippi Valley Historical Review*), the *William and Mary Quarterly,* the *Journal of Southern History, Current History, Pacific Historical Review, Catholic Historical Review,* and the *Journal of Negro History* are well known. Highly respected but too numerous to list are the state historical periodicals such as the *Indiana Magazine of History*. Scholarly periodicals are usually indexed.

4. *Note-Taking*—Notes should be taken regularly, as the source materials for the paper are read. The notes should include anything that might be of value in the preparation of the paper. Do not be alarmed if the stack of notes grows high. It is not uncommon to accumulate ten times as much material in notes as ever finds its way into the finished paper. It is much easier to throw away a note that was not needed than to go back to the library and try to find some bit of information or some quotation that was not taken down at the time but was needed afterward.

Students frequently wonder why they have to take notes at all. For short papers based on only a few sources, it would be easier to get four or five relevant books, read around in them, spread them all out on a table, thumb back and forth through them, take a sentence here and an idea there, paste them together with an occasional sentence of one's own, and eventually construct a paper of sorts. No serious research can be done this way, though, since any lengthy or detailed work requires the use of many different materials, often from several libraries. Nobody's memory is good enough to recall masses of details accurately for any length of time, and libraries will not normally let one keep books for long periods. Moreover, it would be hopeless to try to write a paper from thirty or forty sources in the manner described above. The only way serious research can be done is by taking notes as one goes along. It is the only way great quantities of information can be accurately reduced to usable dimensions. Remember, one of the purposes of doing a paper at all is to learn the *research method*. Hence, notes should be taken carefully for even the shortest papers. Notes may take one of several forms:

a) A summary in the student's own words of the contents of a paragraph, page, or chapter. This is by far the commonest type of note. The bulk of one's notes should always be of this type. If the source material deals with the subject of the paper only in a general way it may be possible to summarize several pages in a few sentences or a short paragraph. If the material is immediately pertinent to the subject the notes should be much fuller. *How* much fuller is a matter of judgment: but do not forget, one takes notes for his own use. Anything that might go into the final paper ought to be taken down.

b) A direct quotation of a passage which seems of special interest or importance. This ought to be done sparingly since it is not advisable to clutter a paper with many direct quotations. This will be explained later.

c) A simple statement (reminder) that something of interest is to be found at a certain point in a specific book or article. Notes of this type should be rare. If the material really is of interest it would normally be better to take notes on it when one reads it. Occasionally, however, one may own books relevant to the subject or may have easy access at any time to relevant materials. In these cases a note of the "reminder" type may save some needless notetaking of the regular sort.

A sample subject note on our hypothetical topic, "The Battle of Saratoga," ought to be something like the following. At the top of the note card there should be a brief statement of what aspect of the subject the note concerns: e.g, "Burgoyne's Battle Plans." Then should come the body of the note. At the end the source should *always* be indicated. It is not necessary to write the author, book title, and bibliographical information on every note card. Keep all of this information somewhere on *one card*. Use some sort of abbreviation or key to identify individual note cards derived from any one source. *Every* note card *without exception* must contain the *page number* or *numbers* in the source from which the material in the note is derived. The reason for this is that if footnotes are to be of much use to the reader they have to refer to a *specific page or two* in a source. (A reader is not helped if you tell him that a certain point may be verified if he will but read pp. 98–184 in one of your sources.) When taking notes the student has no way of knowing how and when he is going to cite sources when he writes his paper weeks later. Hence he should always keep track of the *exact page* from which every bit of his note material is drawn.

In all cases notes should be taken on small cards or small pieces of paper. Write only on one side of the card and put only one idea on each card. There are sound reasons for all these injunctions. Small cards are easier to handle than whole sheets of paper. If the student writes on both sides of a card and puts several ideas on a single card he may save some space but when he gets ready to write his paper he will spend far more time shuffling cards, turning them over and over, and crossing out parts of them as he uses bits of material here and there, than he would have had he used more cards to start with, written on only one side, and used a separate card for each different idea. It takes more cards but it saves time in the long run. Moreover, if ideas are kept separate and writing is only on one side it is easy to read through the note cards and arrange them in the order that will be followed when writing the essay.

5. *Preparation of the Topical Outline*–The student then should think over his topic as it appears in his subject notes and prepare a short topical outline (about half a page) indicating in the proper order the points he intends to bring out in his essay. If he finds that he does not have enough information on some aspects of the essay further research on that point should be done before the writing begins.

6. *Preliminary Approval*–Bibliography cards, subject notes, and topical outline should be ready for submission to the instructor no later than midsemester. If these are approved, the student may then begin to write his essay.

7. *Writing the Essay*—After the student has completed his research he should read through all his notes and preliminary outlines, think about the whole problem, arrange his notes in the order in which he expects to use them, and begin writing the essay. He should endeavor to tell the reader what he has found or concluded, as clearly, simply, and straightforwardly as he can. The following directions and advice should be heeded.

a) Make sure that the title of the essay accurately describes its contents. Do not entitle a paper "Andrew Jackson as President" and then write exclusively about his destruction of the Bank of the United States.

b) In a short essay avoid any but the briefest introduction. Get to the point quickly and do not digress. If the paper is eight to ten pages long the introduction and conclusion should not exceed half a page each.

c) The purpose of writing history is to tell the truth as nearly as possible. The first attribute of any historical essay is accuracy and reliability. If this can be combined with elegance of expression, engaging figures of speech, wit, irony, and the other ingredients of fine writing, so much the better, but accuracy must always take precedence over the fine phrase and the striking adjective if their use in any way distorts the truth.

d) The essay should reflect a calm, detached spirit. National, political, religious, or class convictions must never be allowed to destroy the objectivity of the essay. It is the historian's business to describe what happened, how it came to happen, and what resulted from the said happenings. It is not his business to champion Democrats against Republicans, Catholics against Protestants, or unions against management. Naturally, he will have personal convictions about these and similar matters, but they do not belong in writings that purport to be history.

e) Weigh the evidence. Do not be surprised if puzzles, conflicting accounts, or radically different interpretations of events are encountered in research. Sometimes accounts of events are changed markedly because new information becomes available that was unknown to earlier writers. Virtually any issue in the past which has provoked a controversy has been written about by special pleaders for every party to it. Their interpretations of events and even their accounts of *what happened* often vary widely. Finally, opinions will always differ about what *is* really significant in any given situation and what is the proper interpretation of it. Every professional historian has encountered innumerable problems of this sort.

When sources disagree it is sometimes possible to resolve the conflict, and sometimes not. If one is faced with such a conflict he should begin by reading as many other accounts of the events in question as he can find. If most writers incline to one view, and only one or a distinct minority hold out for something different, the majority is apt to be nearer the truth, though this is by no means *necessarily* the case. It is always possible that one man might be right and 100 wrong, though this is not normally so. Sometimes it is possible to find out that one party was in a better position to know the facts than another or that his experience and judgment were such that one would expect his interpretation to be reliable. Sometimes the writer's own common sense inclines him to one side or the other in such cases, though this is, of course, by no means an infallible guide.

If differences of interpretation can be clearly traced to the sectarian or party interest of one of the writers, then the views of the other should normally be preferred. If the interpretations reflect party interest on both sides, probably the truth lies somewhere in the middle. If each version seems to possess about the same degree of probability just let it go at that and suspend judgment. It is not possible to resolve every difference. To take sides when the facts do not warrant it, just to "come to a decision," may be creative writing but it is worthless as history. The best solution, in practice, is to include in the body of the paper what seems the most reasonable and likely version or interpretation of a controversial episode; then insert a footnote citing the sources for this version, the sources that disagree, and the reasons for their disagreement.

f) Be impersonal in a formal paper. Do not begin, "In this paper I am going to prove to you .... " Begin, "The purpose of this essay is to demonstrate .... " Do not write, "Now you see that the decline of the Knights of Labor was due to .... " Write rather, "From the foregoing it is clear that the decline was due to .... "

g) Always identify any unfamiliar persons, terms, titles, offices, and the like. Remember, it is your business to enlighten the reader, not to confuse him or make things difficult for him. Everyone has read exasperating books full of a bewildering assortment of persons and names, none of which are identified. Persons or designations of the first magnitude need not be specifically identified but all below it should be. Reference in the essay to George Washington, the British Parliament, or the papacy need not be accompanied by identifications. If names of this sort are unfamiliar to the reader he ought not to be reading the essay in the first place. However, references to Camille Morand, Rudolf von Kluttzhof, the Kickapoo tribe, or the "Wobblies" should always be followed by a description of the person or term since the reader cannot reasonably be expected to be as knowledgeable in these cases as about George Washington. The description need not be long. Merely mention that Camille Morand was governor of New Hampshire (1844–48), a general in the Confederate army, a French fur trader, or whatever the case might be.

h) Avoid excessive use of quotations. To be sure, a direct quotation does have its place. If a given situation is summed up briefly and succinctly, or with engaging wit, or in some particularly apt and forceful manner, it is better to put the quotation in your essay than to try to retell the matter yourself. This is very much the exception, however, unless the quotation is taken from a primary source (letters or speeches of participants in an event or documents from that period). Nine times out of ten it is preferable to use one's own words. Never use long quotations of half a page or more. Long quotations clot the flow of the narrative and are more apt to irritate the reader than to please him. Ask yourself: how many times have I encountered long quotations in a book and skipped over them in order to get on with the narrative?

When one begins to write it is wise not only to forswear long quotations but to avoid writing directly from one's own notes as well. The reason is that the sight of a certain description staring at one from a note card frequently induces paralysis of the imagination. One simply cannot think of another way to say a thing than the way it appears on the card. Since what is on the note card is apt to be a close paraphrase of the original source, if one transfers the phraseology of his note cards to the essay the essay will read as though it had been virtually copied. It is much better to read all one's notes for a given section of the paper, think about the matter, put the notes aside, and then write the account in one's own words. *Then* refer to the note cards again and correct inaccuracies or add any information of importance that was omitted. Writing directly from notes tends to ruin the literary quality of a paper too, for the finished product becomes a mixture of the styles of all its sources. It has a choppy, inconsistent quality, sounding here like one of the sources and there like another one. If the notes are read and then put aside, and the paper written without looking at them every minute, the whole paper will at least be in the writer's *own* style, for better or worse.

i) Anything that would normally be italicized in a printed book should be underlined: e.g., the names of ships (*Titanic*), newspapers (*New York Times*), magazines (*Harper's*), or the titles of books (*Moby Dick*). Magazine articles, titles of short essays, and nicknames ("Old Hickory") should be placed in quotation marks.

j) Be careful of errors in composition, misspelled words, faulty grammer, and incorrect punctuation. As a matter of pride, a person should always write as well as he is able. An essay that is sloppily written and full of grammatical blunders ought to be failed as readily as one with historical inaccuracies. In no case should one blame "a friend who did the typing." It is *your* paper and *your* responsibility. You cannot think much of it if you do not take the trouble to proofread the final copy.

Among the commoner literary faults are failure to capitalize consistently, dividing words at places other than the ends of syllables, and leaving one letter dangling at the end of a line. Also, spell out numbers of one or two digits, but use figures for others.

k) Avoid extensive reliance on antiquated secondary works. More recent books are sometimes based on information unknown to earlier authors and usually they are less prone to partisanship. Be sure to include in your research recently published secondary works on your subject.

l) Write well. Real literary excellence is to some degree a gift, but anyone can improve his writing in two ways: practice and reading good writing by others. The latter is an important reason why the habit of reading "quality" newspapers and magazines should be cultivated. Benjamin Franklin developed his literary style by reading and rephrasing Addison and Steele's *Tatler*. Present-day publications that would serve the same purpose are *Harper's, Atlantic Monthly, New York Times, The Guardian,* and *Saturday Review.* Aside from the value of the information found in these and similar publications, their literary quality is excellent. If a person of any intelligence reads good writing with some consistency eventually his own style will improve.

In addition to this general advice there are a number of specific ways one can improve his writing.

i) Try to write so clearly that no sane person could possibly misunderstand you. When you have finished writing the essay read it over slowly and carefully. If *you* have to read anything a second time to be sure of its meaning it is certain that the matter will be less clear still to someone else. Rewrite it.

ii) Write chiefly in short, direct sentences. A person of exceptional literary skill can employ many long, involved sentences and still convey his message clearly and attractively, but most people cannot. Any essay should contain some lengthy sentences of course, for otherwise it sounds abrupt and choppy, but clarity is usually best achieved if the majority are fairly short. Whenever sentences begin to run consistently to three or four lines look for ways to divide them and simplify the narrative.

iii) Write as economically as possible. Just to write at great length is not necessarily a virtue. If one understands a subject thoroughly one can condense it and still present it adequately. Much vagueness and verbosity is due not to immense learning but to lack of understanding. One should write at sufficient length to explain the subject thoroughly, but no more.

iv) Be sure that what is put on paper represents the thought that is in your mind. Remember, the reader cannot read your mind; he can only read what you put on paper. If you do not use words explicitly and precisely, he is bound to misunderstand you. A very common fault among students is to use as synonyms words that have only a *roughly similar* meaning. For example, "large," "many," "great," "important," and "impressive," have vaguely similar meanings but by no means can they be used interchangeably.

v) Eliminate clichés. Few things are more tedious than reading an essay full of tired, old figures of speech that one has encountered scores of times in the past. Use your imagination. Try to think of new ways to express familiar ideas. Do not forget the synonym dictionary, Roget's *Thesaurus*. It has rescued many a writer whose imagination was stranded on one word. Also, do not repeat a word soon after its first usage. Look for a synonym.

vi) Do not start sentences with conjunctions. Persons who write for a living become arbiters of literary fashion and break rules as they choose, but the beginner more often needs practice in observing long-standing usages rather than in breaking them.

vii) Be consistent with tenses. Write either in the present or the past tense throughout the paper. The past is ordinarily preferable since the events took place in the past. In any case, do not wander aimlessly from one to the other, saying in one place, "George McClellan *took* command of the army and *marched* south," and in another, "McClellan now *sees* that the Confederate forces *will be* too much for him."

viii) Do not be alarmed at the prospect of rewriting. Most experienced or professional writers rewrite many times to get just the right polish and the correct shade of meaning. Lord Macaulay, one of the great literary stylists of the nineteenth century, lamented that readers of a book had little idea how much trouble its composition had cost the author.

ix) Self-criticism. It is easy to see flaws in someone else's work but nobody is a good critic of his own. One can become a fair critic of one's own writing, however, if he will put it aside for a time and read it after it has "got cold." Try reading something that you have written several weeks or months or even years ago. It can be positively embarrassing! Errors and clumsy phrases of every sort strike the eye immediately. Not infrequently one mutters to himself in half-disbelief, "Did *I* do that?" The moral is that, whenever possible, prepare a written assignment well in advance of the due date. Lay it aside and do not look at it for several days or weeks, as time permits. Then, shortly before it is to be submitted, read it over. Normally one will find mistakes and infelicitous phrases that would have escaped his attention had he read the paper only immediately after it was written.

If the student heeds these injunctions, and particularly if he reads "quality" writing with some regularity, he will usually begin to see improvement in his own writing. Few experiences are more rewarding.

RULES FOR THE FORM OF THE ESSAY

1. *Margins*—The margin on all sides of the page should be approximately one inch, not less.

2. *Page Numbering*—Part 1 should be numbered in the center, at the bottom of the page. All other pages are numbered in the upper right hand corner. The bibliography page is numbered just like a page in the regular text of the paper. Use arabic numerals.

3. *Spacing*—Double-space the regular text of the paper throughout. Footnotes, bibliography items, and quotations of more than three lines are single spaced in a manner explained below.

4. *Punctuation and Capitalization*—Follow standard rules. In case of doubt consult your English handbook.

5. *Indentation*—Paragraphs must be indented uniformly. See Rule 6 for the indentation of quotations, which exceed three lines.

6. *Direct Quotations*—All quotations from books, articles, newspapers, or other persons must be enclosed in quotation marks and the source indicated in a footnote. If the quotation is more than three lines in length it should be boxed: e.g., indented five spaces on *both sides* and *single spaced*. This arrangement allows the quotation marks to be dropped since the fact that the material is a direct quotation is apparent from the indentation and single spacing alone.

7. *Footnotes*—The purpose of footnoting is to aid the reader. A footnote informs the reader from what source or sources certain information has been derived, it provides him with a guide if he wishes to read further on the subject, and it enables him to check the accuracy of the writer's assertions and interpretations. When to use footnotes is to some degree a matter of judgment, but the following principles ought to be kept in mind as a guide.

a) All direct quotations of any kind from any source *must* be footnoted. There are no exceptions. Direct quotations should be used sparingly, as explained earlier, but if they are used they must *always* consist of the *exact* words of the source. To use only the approximate words of the source and then enclose them in quotation marks lays one open to the charge of misquoting and distorting the meaning of the original.

b) When the work of a writer is paraphrased, that should be indicated in a footnote. (It is seldom a good practice to paraphrase, as it is not far removed from plagiarism. It is preferable to think about the facts and ideas found in a source and then to express them in one's own words.)

c) The source should be cited if the student introduces obscure or little known information. For instance, if he read parts of ten books for his paper and found a certain bit of pertinent information in only one of them this should ordinarily be footnoted.

d) Any technical or highly detailed information should be footnoted. Suppose the subject is a naval battle and one has occasion to relate that a certain ship had a crew of 350, was 488 feet long, carried seventy-seven guns of a certain caliber, had four-inch oak deck planking, and ninety sails of various sizes. Nobody carries information of this sort around in his head. The reader should be told whence the author has acquired it.

e) Whenever a motive, opinion, or state of mind is ascribed to someone mentioned in the paper the source should be cited. The reason is that these are matters about which absolute certitude is impossible. No one can read someone else's mind and divine his thoughts beyond the possibility of error.

f) If sources differ in their interpretation of events what seems the most likely version should be followed in the text. Then a footnote should be included indicating this fact and also informing the reader that other writers disagree in certain respects.

g) If one uses material from a primary source a footnote is necessary. (The difference between primary and secondary sources is explained below in the *Bibliography* section).

h) Footnotes should be employed occasionally to guide the reader to the principal sources of information used in preparing the paper.

i) Footnotes are frequently used for comments by the author that would not fit readily into the main text. They are sometimes employed to insert interesting information that is related to some point in the text but is not sufficiently important to be put into the text itself. They may also be used to refer the reader to other parts of the paper.

j) Footnotes should *not* be used when relating mere routine information about which there is no doubt or controversy and which is readily available in a score of places in the library. Do not footnote some statement like, "President Lincoln was assassinated while attending Ford's Theatre." Such information is available in any textbook.

k) How many footnotes to put on a page is a matter of judgment. Two, three, or four is perhaps a general average but the number depends mostly on the subject of the paper. If the paper is largely descriptive and the facts contained in it are not in dispute not many footnotes are needed. If the paper concerns a controversial subject or one about which there is little knowledge and much conjecture, footnotes should be more plentiful.

The following rules should be observed when footnoting.

1) Footnotes should be at the bottom of the same page as the material to which they refer in the text of the paper.

2) The number cited in the text of the paper comes *after* the material referred to, not before it.

3) Number the footnotes consecutively from the beginning to the end of the essay. Do not start with "one" again on each page.

4) Do not cite textbooks. The reason is that it is the nature of a textbook to cover a long period and a great variety of subjects rather sketchily. Necessarily, the author of a textbook has to discuss many subjects about which he has less than an expert's knowledge. Hence a textbook should not be cited to clinch an argument or prove a point.

5) After the last line of the regular double-spaced text of the paper, double-space again and type a solid line for about fifteen to twenty spaces from the left margin of the paper. Then double-space again and begin to put in the footnotes. Footnotes are all single spaced. There is no double space between separate footnotes. Each separate footnote is indented five spaces on its first line, in the same way that a new paragraph is indented.

The following are samples of the commoner types of footnotes, with directions for their proper punctuation.

A. The commonest type of footnote is the reference to a one volume book written by one author.

1. Bruce Catton, *A Stillness at Appomattox*, p. 73.

Note that the author's first name comes first. The footnote contains the name of the author, name of the book, small *p* to indicate the page, and the exact page or pages from which the information was obtained. If the information had come from pages 73 *and* 74 the citation would have been *pp.* 73–74.

B. A work by one man which runs to more than one volume is done as below. The only difference from the example above is that the small *p.* for the page is omitted when a volume number appears. The volume number itself is given in Roman numerals.

2. Henry Adams, *History of the United States, 1801–1817*, II, 423.

C. Some books are cooperative works in which different chapters or sections are written by different authors. Such a one is the *Cambridge Modern History*. In these cases cite first the author of the chapter or article *you used* (not the editor of the whole book or series), followed by the chapter title in quotation marks, the chapter number, the title of the whole work (underlined), volume, and page.

3. J. R. Moreton Macdonald, "The Terror," chap. XII, *The Cambridge Modern History*, VIII, 338–39.

D. If the author of a portion of a cooperative work cannot be identified, the footnote should begin with the chapter, article, or division title. This is quite common in the case of encyclopedia articles, some of which are signed with a full name, some with initials, and some not at all. If the name or initials are there, use them. If not, begin with the title of the article.

4. "Abolitionism," *Encyclopedia Britannica*, (11th ed.), I, 278.

Note that the samll *p* is not used in the case of encyclopedia or magazine articles.

E. A footnote referring to an article in a periodical contains the author's name, the title of the article in quotation marks, the title of the periodical, the volume number, date of publication, and page or pages.

5. Alice D. Nelson, "People of Color in Louisiana," *Journal of Negro History*, I (October, 1916): 123.

F. If the reference is to a collection of documents, cite the author of the pertinent document, the name of the document, the editor of the book, title of the book, and page or pages.

6. B. K. Walterhouse, "Famine Among the Algonquin Indians," in Homer T. Motherwell, ed., *Documents Illustrative of Eighteenth Century America*, pp. 55–57.

If the document is unsigned begin with its title.

G. A similar citation covers the case of one book quoted in another. Suppose you are reading Clark Wissler, *Indians of the United States*. In a footnote Wissler mentions a book by John Collier, *The Decline of the Miamis*, and includes a quotation from it. Part of this quotation you wish to put in your paper. You have not read Collier; only the footnote in Wissler referring to Collier. The citation is as follows:

7. John Collier, *The Decline of the Miamis*, p. 83, cited in Clark Wissler, *Indians of the United States*, p. 122.

H. References to newspapers give the title of the paper, date of issue, and page, if the place of publication is included in the title; otherwise the city is given in parenthesis after the title.

8. *Chicago Tribune*, July 14, 1937, 14.
9. *Our Sunday Visitor*, (Huntington, Indiana) May 3, 1955, p. 6.

Note that the titles of books, magazines, and newspapers are always underlined (they would be italicized in print). Titles of chapters or articles *in* books, magazines, or newspapers are, however, placed in quotation marks.

I. When a reference is made to a source already cited in a footnote immediately preceding it is often convenient to use a Latin abbreviation (ibid.) in place of repeating a lengthy book title or description of a magazine or encyclopedia article.

10. William Johnson, *History of Sweden*, p. 106.

11. Ibid., p. 130.

Note carefully: ibid. means that everything is the same as in the preceding footnote except perhaps the page.

BIBLIOGRAPHY

The bibliography is a list of all the books, articles, and other sources of information that have been of value in preparing the essay. It is not necessary to footnote a source in order to include that source in the bibliography. However, the source should have at least added to one's knowledge of the problem in order to be included. Textbooks should not be included in the bibliography since it is assumed that a student reads his textbook. If accurate and full information has been taken down on the note cards the bibliography can be prepared from them. The bibliography is always located at the end of the essay. The bibliography page is numbered.

In printed books or lengthy dissertations the bibliography is usually broken down into several categories. For a short research paper it is sufficient to divide it into primary and secondary sources. A primary source is normally any account or document contemporary with the events described and written by someone in a position to know the facts. A secondary source is a general history or other account *based* on primary sources or other secondary accounts, but not contemporary with the event described. There is one exception to this general distinction. For recent history (within the last century) an account is considered primary only if it was written by an actual participant in the events described or by one who was in a position to observe them at first hand. An account written by someone who lived at the same time but had no such first-hand knowledge would be regarded as secondary.

Each category, primary and secondary, should be arranged alphabetically, according to the author's *last name.* (Note the difference from footnote form, where the author's first name comes first.) If the name of the author is not known list the item alphabetically according to the first significant word in the title. Each bibliographical item should contain, in that order, author or editor, complete title, edition (if there has been more than one), place of publication and publisher (except for newspapers, magazines, and encyclopedias), and date of publication.

Following are samples of bibliographical entries. Note the form and punctuation. The item should be entered exactly like this.

Primary Material

Blaine, James G. *Twenty Years in Congress.* 2 vols. Norwich, Connecticut: Henry Holt and Co., 1884.

Chicago Tribune, July 14, 1937.

Note that if the item extends to more than one line the second and all succeeding lines are indented five spaces. (Just the opposite of paragraphs or footnote indentation.) The purpose of this is to enable the reader to glance quickly down the left side of the bibliography page and see the chief sources of information.

Note also the item from Blaine. As it appears here, the entry indicates that Blaine's work *totals* two volumes and that the writer has used the first volume. Had he used both volumes "Vol. I" would have been omitted and the entry would have ended with "1884." The inference would have been clear that both volumes had been used. The number of volumes in *the whole set* is always shown immediately after the title of a book, and the volume or volumes *you used* after the date of publication.

Secondary Material

"Abolitionism," *Encyclopedia Britannica*, (11th ed.), I, 275–87.

Adams, Henry. *History of the United States, 1801–1817.* 9 vols. New York: C. Scribner's Sons, 1917–1918.

Catton, Bruce. *A Stillness at Appomattox*. Garden City, New York: Doubleday and Co., 1953.

Nelson, Alice D. "People of Color in Louisiana" *Journal of Negro History*, I (1916), 120–35.

Note in examples one and four (above) that the page numbers for the *entire article* are included. In the case of books written by one person page numbers are never included. If the book is a cooperative work like the *Cambridge Modern History* include the page numbers for the particular chapter read: for example,

Macdonald, J. R. Moreton, "The Terror," Chap. XII, *The Cambridge Modern History*, VIII, 330–61.

Index